Crashes and Collapses

Crashes and Collapses

Crashes and Collapses

Thomas L. Bohan

Checkmark Books®
An imprint of Infobase Publishing

CRASHES AND COLLAPSES

Checkmark Books
An imprint of Infobase Publishing
132 West 31st Street
New York NY 10001

Library of Congress Cataloging-in-Publication Data

Bohan, Thomas L.
    Crashes and collapses / Thomas L. Bohan
       p. cm.—(Essentials of forensic science)
    Includes bibliographical references and index.
    ISBN-13: 978-0-8160-5513-5 (hc)   ISBN-13: 978-0-8160-7899-8 (pb)
    ISBN-10: 0-8160-5513-0 (hc)   ISBN-10: 0-8160-7899-8 (pb)
    1. Forensic engineering. I. Title.
    TA219.B64 2009
    363.25—dc22   2008014223

Checkmark Books are available at special discounts when purchased in bulk quantities for businesses, associations, institutions, or sales promotions. Please call our Special Sales Department in New York at (212) 967-8800 or (800) 322-8755.

You can find Facts On File on the World Wide Web at http://www.factsonfile.com

Text design by Erik Lindstrom
Illustrations by Accurate Art, Inc.
Photo research by Suzanne M. Tibor

Printed in the United States of America

MP ML 10 9 8 7 6 5 4 3 2 1

This book is printed on acid-free paper and contains 30 percent postconsumer recycled content.

I dedicate this book to my three
youngest grandchildren,
Evan, Malcolm, and Nina,
and to the memory of
Helena Lizanecz Bohan 1962–2003

.

CONTENTS

ACKNOWLEDGMENTS

I am pleased to acknowledge the help of my editor Frank K. Darmstadt in prying the completed version of this book from my reluctant fingers and especially his tirelessly good-natured support during the final year. I note my gratefulness for the continuing support of Joseph A. Keierleber, whose work with me over the years has provided the talent needed to reduce to visible images for court and press my forensic findings and arguments. Further in connection with images, I here record that one of the greatest pleasures that I had in working on this project was my work with Suzanne M. Tibor, as she discussed with me and then quickly located and acquired the photographs with which I wished to illustrate the text. Finally, I thank Professor Suzanne Bell for her prime role in involving me with Facts On File, Frank, and the project.

INTRODUCTION

Most forensic scientists, though they may not admit it, derive pleasure from their field's sudden TV-driven popularity. Men, women, and children across the country, drawn to the array of shows that have blossomed from the first *C.S.I.* program in 2000, have developed a great interest in, even love for, forensic science; teenage clerks at electronics stores pronounce it to be "cool." The downsides of this new world for forensic science and forensic scientists are the misconceptions sown by the same dramas, misconceptions that when they reach the level of "psychic detective" absurdities, threaten to drive some practitioners berserk. Rather than just being annoyed, an increasing number of forensic scientists are taking advantage of the opportunity given them by public fascination with their field and telling their own stories. Doing so, they can show a wide audience what they actually do and reveal the role that real science and not pseudoscience plays in their work. *Crashes and Collapses* includes a collection of stories based on real cases involving the forensic engineering sciences. It may surprise those whose view of forensic science has been formed by those television shows to learn that a large fraction, perhaps most, of forensic work involves the engineering sciences and that this has been the case since ancient times. This book is about some of that work and is aimed at introducing curious adults as well as middle- and high-school students to the world of forensic science in such a way that they will be better able to evaluate what they hear and see about forensic investigations and also about the broader world within which these investigations take place.

The engineering sciences include the physical sciences such as chemistry and physics, as well as all of the engineering fields. The engineering sciences dominate forensic investigations of events underlying civil disputes. The engineering sciences also play an important role in criminal investigations, especially when it appears that a crime may have been disguised as an accident. A distinguishing feature of the forensic engineering sciences is that when one of its specialists is called in on a case, it is often unclear exactly what he or she can contribute to the investigation. It is a common occurrence that the authorities who have called on them, while convinced that they can help, are at a loss as to what exactly they can do. This is especially true in the area of forensic engineering science known as accident reconstruction.

Most of the cases described in the book reflect investigations carried out by the author. However, none is presented in exactly the way it happened. Changes have been made to obscure identities and to better shape the narrative as a teaching device. (For example, the driver in the case describe in chapter 2 as a hit-and-run did not flee the scene.)

It has been said that until one can describe an event with numbers, one has not even begun to understand the event. It is certainly difficult to gain an understanding of forensic science, and impossible to practice it, without developing thought patterns that are directed toward quantitative descriptions. Unfortunately, the dominant attitude in modern America, conveyed to young people throughout their schooling and well instilled in them by adulthood, is that numbers and quantitative thought are somehow foreign to normal human interests and activity. Those who would take charge of society, which includes those who aspire to be forensic scientists, must resist this attitude and learn to develop quantitative habits of thought early in life. It is hoped that the manner in which *Crashes and Collapses* has been constructed will help in that development. This does not mean that it is filled with mathematics. Indeed, it contains essentially no calculations that cannot be followed and reproduced by anyone who is able to multiply and divide. What has been done is to repeatedly describe events quantitatively (with numbers) with the intention that the person reading these descriptions will follow along with a pen or pencil in hand so as to check the numbers. This is also the case with respect to the development of the important formulas in the book. The idea is that the person reading through those developments (sometimes called derivations) will check each step, confirming that they have been done correctly or discovering that they have not been. It is thought that careful reading accompanied by writing should be enough to make clear the meaning of all the equations, even for those who have not yet learned algebra. In order to make the book accessible even to very young students, vectors have been avoided. In those discussions where vectors are traditionally used to justify results, such as in deriving the forces that act on a person riding a merry-go-round, new non-vector approaches have been developed.

Throughout *Crashes and Collapses,* the term *science* will used to mean any specialized skill or systematic study. It may be used to describe the knowledge an automobile mechanic has about a differential gear to the same extent that it may be used to depict a physicist's understanding about Newton's laws. This broad use of the term is completely reasonable, given that the root of science is knowledge itself. A few words still exist in English that reflect this definition, including one having particular relevance to criminal law: *scienter (sigh-EN-ter).* To ask "Did the defendant have *scienter*?" is to ask whether the defendant had knowledge that the action with which he or she is charged was wrong. Did he or she intend to commit a wrongful act?

The term *forensic* as used here can be traced back more than two thousand years to the Roman forum, the center of public activity of the Roman republic. Activities that occurred at the forum were called "forensic," activities that included the resolution of disputes between Roman citizens, a resolution that involved debate, as is reflected to this day by debate teams adopting the word *forensics.* The word is now most popularly understood to refer to the investigation of crimes and accidents and the presentation of evidence at trials relating to those investigations. Related to this meaning, the division housing the criminally insane in many state hospitals is designated the forensic unit.

Here, the term *forensic* will refer to anything that can play a role in a court of law. Included will be such things as investigations of crimes and accidents and the techniques used to carry out those investigations. It follows from this and from the earlier description of the meaning assigned to the term *science,* that forensic science consists of the use of specialized skills or knowledge to investigate matters that may arise in a court of law.

Chapter 1 opens with a quick history of forensic engineering science, moving in one step from the work of Archimedes in the third century B.C.E. to that of Caltech's Richard Feynman in the late 20th century C.E. Because the success of forensic work is measured by its role in the legal process, chapter 1 next reviews the legal structure in the United States, including the rules by which trials are conducted and the difference between fact witnesses and expert witnesses.

Chapters 2 and 3 form a critical part of the book. In combination with chapters 4 and 5, they cover the investigation of motor vehicle crashes known as accident reconstruction. Forensic scientists doing accident reconstruction are from the engineering sciences and are known as "accident reconstructionists." Chapter 2 introduces Newton's laws of motion, which underlie accident reconstruction. Also key to accident reconstruction is knowledge of how vehicle operators recognize and react to danger. Chapter 2 therefore also explores how our eyes and brain interact so as to present us with images of the surrounding world. Chapter 3 segues into other aspects of accident reconstruction, including the deduction of the speed of a car that has flown through the air. The chapter also deals with objects within a car that record crash details, both the devices designed for that purpose such as the so-called black boxes and those, such as light filaments, that by their nature are unintended recorders of such details.

Chapter 4 is devoted to the critical-speed-scuff method for determining the speed of cars that have laid down cornering marks, the marks from side-slipping tires on cars following curved paths. This method merits separate treatment both because of its importance and because it seems incredible that it works at all. In addition, taking up the critical-speed-scuff method in some detail provides the opportunity to address "centrifugal" force and the confusion it causes.

Chapter 5 describes a criminal case where the perpetrator's attempt to make a crime appear to be an accident failed because of a lack of understanding of Newton's laws and other basic facts of physics.

Chapter 6 presents the facts and analysis of a subway train accident, a so-called man-under event. Building on problems arising from the manner in which information was provided to the investigator in this case, this chapter discusses obstacles that can confront forensic investigators when they have to work with information produced by others. The discussion leads naturally into the introduction of the idea of precision in measurement and how limits on precision must be recognized in reporting the measurements and inferences drawn from those measurements.

Chapter 7 is directed at the collision of a ship with an underwater ledge, a case in which buoyancy and Archimedes' principle were of major importance in understanding whether actions by the ship's owner worsened an already bad situation.

Chapter 8 describes the collapse of a large bucket crane that fatally slapped its operator against an airport tarmac. The chapter shows how a theory of the collapse was developed and tested. Since the collapse involved a hydraulic device, the inclusion of this case permits hydraulic systems in general to be described as part of the explanation of how this particular device failed.

Chapter 9 deals with the failure and subsequent collapse of scaffolding in a wind squall. It permits the introduction of the role of weather in accidents and the observation that one has to deal quantitatively with whatever mechanism one suggests has caused an event.

Chapter 10 throws the practice of forensic engineering science back to the reader, inquiring what should be done upon being presented with three different complex, high-profile questions that forensic science is called on to answer.

(Note: This book uses the most common scientific convention to indicate that quantities represented symbolically are to be multiplied together. This convention differs from the format used in middle school in that no multiplication symbols are used. Thus, M multiplied by A (or, equivalently, M times A) is represented as MA and not, for example, as M×A or as M·A. This book also expresses weights in the metric system (S.I.) in terms of newtons—the unit of force in that system—and not in kilograms.

1

History and
Guiding Principles of
Forensic Engineering Science

Investigations of crashes and collapses are done by forensic engineering scientists, a group whose interests are distributed across all the engineering fields as well as the allied sciences, such as physics and chemistry. After exploring the rise of that group through human history and identifying specific persons within it, this chapter concentrates on those skills and specialists engaged most directly in sorting out the causes of vehicle crashes and structural collapses.

ARCHIMEDES (287–212 B.C.E.): EINSTEIN AND EDISON IN ANCIENT GREECE

Throughout history, persons skilled in mathematics and technology have been called on to resolve disputes. Those who first responded to the call were, by modern definition, the first forensic scientists. Even before the existence of the Roman forum, which gave the word *forensic* to the world, even before the beginning of recorded history, they were active. Within historic times, the best-known forensic engineer is Archimedes [Ark a MEE days] (287–212 B.C.E.), born nearly 2,300 years ago in the city of Syracuse on the island of Sicily, then at the western edge of the Greek Empire. Archimedes was that rare type of genius who was good at experimental work as well as at coming up with new and important theories about how the world works. In that regard, he was the master inventor Thomas Edison (1847–1931) and the master theoretician Albert Einstein (1879–1955) rolled into one.

The forensic work that made Archimedes famous down to the present day among scientists and the public at large was a project supposedly commissioned by his king, King Hiero II of Sicily. The king wanted assurance that he had not been hoodwinked by the royal goldsmith, to whom he had entrusted a quantity of pure gold with which the goldsmith was to make the king a crown. King Hiero approached Archimedes shortly after receiving from the royal goldsmith a crown weighing the same as the gold given to the goldsmith. The king worried that the goldsmith, who was of necessity clever with metals, had taken some of the gold for himself and then added enough of another metal to make the weight work out. Archimedes' job was to determine whether that had happened. Nowadays, that could have been determined by all kinds of methods, but at the time of Archimedes, it was not even possible to weigh things precisely. That Archimedes solved the problem quickly was a tribute to his abilities as an engineer. That the story is still remembered is undoubtedly a tribute to the colorful reaction Archimedes was said to have had at his joy in figuring out the answer, as is the fact that the Greek word eureka is so widely understood and used by non-Greeks to mean "I have found it." At any event, the story is that the solution to the crown problem suddenly struck Archimedes while he was bathing and that this led him to leap up and run naked through the streets of Syracuse, shouting "Heureka!"

The link between the bathtub and the solution of the crown problem is Archimedes' law of buoyancy, one version of which can be stated as follows:

An object placed in water will weigh less than it weighs in air by exactly the weight of the water displaced by the object.

The water shoved aside to make room for the object as it is immersed is the "water displaced." For example, if an object sinks and is completely

The supposed site of Archimedes' inspiration of how to catch a thief for his king *(HIP/Art Resource, New York)*

covered by the water, the volume of water displaced will equal the solid volume of the object. According to the law of buoyancy, the weight of that sunken object will be less than its weight before immersion by an amount exactly equal to the weight of a quantity of water having the same volume as the object. For example, consider the unfortunate man whose outboard motor weighing 150 pounds (667 N) slips from the transom of his boat and sinks in 50 feet (15 m) of water. After he attaches a grappling hook to it and starts to lift it up with a cable with a fish scale in it, he can tell by looking at the fish scale what the volume of the motor is. A cubic foot of lake water weighs 62.5 pounds (278 N). If the fish scale in the recovery line reads 87.5 pounds (389 N), he will know that the volume of his motor is one cubic foot. Even more unfortunate in terms of the motor's future would be the circumstance that he was boating in ocean water when the mishap occurred. On the plus side, however, it would be slightly easier to lift the motor back up. Since a cubic foot of ocean water weighs 64 pounds (285 N), he would only have to exert 86 pounds (383 N) to pull the motor back to the surface. Being familiar with Archimedes, these thoughts might be going through his mind as he recovers his motor. (By looking up the weight of a cubic foot of water in the Great Salt Lake, the Dead Sea, and the Caspian Sea, apply the law of buoyancy to estimate the weight reduction of the same motor submerged in those three bodies of water.)

If an object floats, what can one conclude from the law of buoyancy? A floating object is partially immersed. The fact that it is floating means that it has stopped falling. It is weight that causes an object to fall, so one can conclude that its effective weight has been reduced to zero. From the Law of Buoyancy, one concludes that the volume of water that the floating object has displaced has a weight equal to the object's weight in air. Statements regarding the number of tons a ship displaces are really statements as to the ship's weight, with a nod to Archimedes' law of buoyancy.

The beauty of the law of buoyancy in terms of the crown problem was that the crown did not have to have any particular shape for the conclusions to be drawn. It could even have passages through which the water entered when the crown was lowered into the water. The law of buoyancy therefore permits an immediate measure of the volume of even the most irregular and holey of objects. Thus, if a crown weighing 18 pounds (80 N) in the air weighed only 17 pounds (76 N) after sinking to the bottom of Archimedes' bathtub, one knows that the volume of the crown is equal to the volume of water that weighs one pound (4.45 N). (The sidebar on Units Systems and Dimensions explains why nearly every numerical quantity stated in this book is followed by a companion number in parentheses.) A cubic inch of gold weighs 19.3 times as much as a cubic inch of water. This is the same as saying that the density of gold is 19.3 times the density of water. Since the 18-pound (80-N) crown in the above example had the same volume as a volume of water weighing one pound (4.45 N), one can conclude immediately that it was not pure gold. If a crown of this volume had been pure gold, it would have weighed 19.3 pounds (85.9 N). The conclusion is that there must have been some metal of lower density mixed in with the gold. The metal silver would have satisfied that condition. Also, silver is easily combined with gold and was much less valuable than gold in Archimedes' time (as it is today), thereby satisfying both of the dishonest goldsmith's requirements.

It is unknown whether Archimedes had precise information about the densities of different metals. Also unknown is the precision with which he could have weighed objects. It is possible, therefore, that he would have had to arrive at his answer in a more roundabout manner than that just described. The earliest-known written accounts of Archimedes and the crown date from a couple of hundred years after the event and are sparse on details. In part because of this, there are scholars who doubt the truth of the story itself. A necessary though not sufficient condition for the story to be correct is that Archimedes possessed the techniques and the tools necessary to apply his law of buoyancy to the solution of the problem. He did have them, and over the ages, engineers have described several ways in which he could have performed the task assigned him by King Hiero with the resources he was known to have had.

Second only to his joyful shout *Heureka!*, Archimedes is best remembered for saying "Give me a lever long enough, a fulcrum on which to place it, and a place to stand, and I can move the world," a thought that occurs every day to people who are tying to pry a stubborn rock out of the ground. Many other contributions of Archimedes, less known than these but even more valuable, have been used for thousands of years. He is in fact credited with being the first person to discover that the circumference of a circle equals its diameter multiplied by the number long designated by the Greek letter π (pronounced PIE, it is approximately 3.14). Because of the irregular paths by which ancient writings come down through the ages, it is likely that even now some his contributions remain to be discovered. In 1998, a book more than a thousand years old regarding religious rituals was found to also contain, half-erased, a complete book of Archimedes that seems to include the foundations of calculus. Sometimes referred to as *The Calculus,* this mathematical system is considered to be among the major intellectual creations of all time. Previous to the discovery of Archimedes' text in the old book, calculus was thought to have been created two thousand years after Archimedes' by Englishman Sir Isaac Newton (1642–1727) and, independently, by the German Gottfried Leibniz [LEEB Nitz] (1646–1716). Today, calculus is used continually by rocket scientists and forensic scientists.

(continues on page 10)

Units Systems and Dimensions

In the discussion of Archimedes' work, weights were expressed first in pounds and then in Newtons, the pound being the way that forces are stated in the United States and the Newton being the unit for force everywhere else. This is a pattern that will be repeated throughout the book, one made necessary by the United States using a different system of weights and measures than is used by the rest of the world. In the ancient world and up to a few hundred years ago, there were scores of measurement systems. They varied from region to region in the world and from trade to trade and profession to profession. The shift to modern times began about 250 years ago in Europe when a decimal system of measurement was created. It was adopted in revolutionary France in the late 18th century before the Industrial Revolution had begun in that country. Although this would have been a perfect time for it to have been adopted as well in the United States, which had just gone through its own revolution and which also had not embarked yet on the Industrial Revolution, this did not occur. It is said that Benjamin Franklin (1706–90) was a strong advocate of the change, possibly because of his having become familiar with the decimal system through his scientific contacts with Europe. (Further descriptions of Franklin's work appear in chapter 5.) In any event, the new United States did not adopt it in the 18th century, and once the moment passed and the industrial development of the 19th and 20th centuries took place under the old system, it became progressively more difficult to shift. This explains why a system of measures based on such units as the length of the foot of an English king in the Middle Ages is still in use today in the United States. The fact that it now stands alone among the countries of the world in this regard, with the possible exceptions of Liberia and Myanmar (Burma), has many disadvantages, including hampering its international trade and burdening its citizens in their daily lives. Until a very painful transition is undertaken and carried to completion in the United States, its industry will literally be incommensurate with the rest of the world.

A decimal system is one in which units are related to one another by factors of 10. U.S. money, with its familiar units of currency—the penny, the dime, and the dollar—is such a system. It permits a simple unitary expression for a collection of dollars, dimes, and pennies. For example, three dollars, four dimes, and six pennies can be written as $3.46. It can be added to $4.13 directly to obtain $7.59. The U.S. decimal system of currency was adopted some years after the American Revolution, replacing the nondecimal penny/shilling/pound British currency, in which there were 12 pennies to the shilling and 20 shillings to the pound. A collection of British money comprising three pounds, 14 shillings, and six pence had to be written as £3 14s 6d. Adding this to £1 9s 9d was rather like adding Roman numerals (another nondecimal system).

In summary, whenever a quantity is stated numerically in this book, it will usually be given first In U.S. units (the present name of what used to be called the Imperial System of Units, a no-longer-accurate label, given that Britain abandoned the Imperial System years ago). Immediately following the quantity in U.S. units will be, within parentheses, the same information stated in the Système International (S.I.) units (sometimes referred to as the metric system).

When one says that it is 2,950 miles (4,748 km) from Portland, Maine, to Portland, Oregon, one is giving the distance (length) *dimension* between the two cities, first as a multiple of the *mile* unit and than as a multiple of the *kilometer* unit. It does not matter in what units system one chooses to express quantities as long as one is consistent and as long as one indicates which system one is using. To have said simply that the distance between the two Portlands was 2,950 would be as meaningless as saying that it was 10,384,000, a number that takes on meaning only after it is known that this is the Portland-to-Portland distance in cubits, with the cubit taken to be 1.5 feet (4.6 m). (Actually the cubit has differed from one region of the world to the next as well as with the era in which it was used. From ancient times forward, it was supposedly related to the distance between the adult human's thumb and elbow [*cubitum* in Latin].)

(continues)

(continued)

In contrast to the units in which a quantity is expressed, the dimensions of the quantity are always the same. For the subjects discussed in this book, there are only three fundamental dimensions: length (L), time (T), and mass (M). (The definition of the mass dimension awaits the discussion of Newton's laws in chapter 2.) The dimensions of all other quantities are combinations of these. For example, speed has the dimension of length divided by time. This can be stated symbolically as

$$[\text{Speed}] = L/T$$

where the square brackets mean "the dimensions of" whatever is within the brackets. The unit for length in the U.S. system is the foot, whereas in the S.I., it is the meter. Derived units for length in the U.S. system include the mile and the yard, which, characteristic of the nondecimal nature of the U.S. system, are, respectively, 5,280 feet and 3 feet. Not surprisingly, the subunit for length, the inch, also bears a nondecimal relation to the fundamental unit, being defined as one-twelfth of it. In the S.I., the most common multiple of the basic unit is the kilometer, which literally means 1,000 meters. The common subunits are the centimeter (literally, one one-hundredth of a meter) and the millimeter (literally, one one-thousandth of a meter). A sense of comparison can be maintained by remembering that one foot is approximately equal to 30 centimeters.

The unit for time in both systems is the second, and both use the minute (equal to 60 seconds) and the hour (equal to 60 minutes, that is 3,600 seconds) as multiples of the basic unit. This is an exception to the general rule that the S.I. is a decimal system. If the time were treated decimally, one might expect the minute to be 100 seconds and the hour to be 100 minutes. The reason for the exception can probably be traced to the firm place that the 360-degree circle already had in the world of navigation at the time the decimal system of measurements was first devised. In this connection it is noted that one degree contains

60 arc-minutes (usually just referred to as minutes) and that one minute contains 60 arc-seconds (usually just referred to as seconds).

Both the U.S. system and the S.I. express speed using length and time units other than the basic ones. For example, a truck's speed may be stated typically in the United States units to be 42 miles per hour. Substituting in the number of feet in a mile and the number of seconds in an hour leads to 61.6 feet per second. (Do the arithmetic to see that this is correct.) Since the original speed statement just had two digits, the appropriate expression in basic U.S. units for that speed is 62 ft/sec. This is the result of rounding off the 61.6, a topic to be discussed along with that of precision in chapter 6. In the S.I. units, the truck's speed is 68 kilometers per hour (km/hr). Doing as above and substituting in the number of meters in a kilometer and the number of seconds in an hour shows that one km/hr is 0.278 m/s. (Do the arithmetic leading to this number.) Thus 68 km/hr = 18.9 m/s is the expression of the truck's speed in the basic S.I. units, and rounding off to two digits, 19 m/s.

In addition to the U.S. and S.I. units, there are specialized systems specific to certain activities. For example, in horse racing, the common unit for the distance (length) dimension is the furlong, of which there are eight to the mile. Therefore, a horse running 40 miles per hour can be said to be running 320 furlongs per hour (f/hr). (If the horse could maintain this speed for a fortnight, how far would it go?) The fortnight (14 nights) is an archaic unit for the time dimension and is equal to 336 hours (14 24-hour days). So, the 40-miles per hour horse can also be said to be running at a speed of 107,520 furlongs per fortnight (f/f).

Summarizing, there are a number of systems of units, two of which dominate the world. One is used by the United States and will be identified as the U.S. system of units; the other, used by the rest of the world, is the Système International and will be referred to as the S.I. system. Whenever one states a quantity numerically, it is essential to provide the units in which it is stated. Without the units, the number is meaningless. However, even worse things can happen if the person reading the quantity has to guess and guesses wrong as to which units were

(continues)

(continued)

meant. A few years ago, a mission to Mars of great scientific value, one on which hundreds of millions of dollars had been spent, was lost because of lack of communication between those designing and those building the equipment as to whether certain numbers were stated in S.I. units or in U.S. units. More comic than disastrous is the not uncommon experience of a graduate science student at a U.S. university who produces a drawing for equipment to be manufactured in the machine shop. Having carefully labeled the length dimensions of the various parts of the job request, including the cm (centimeter) and mm (millimeter) units, he or she is taken aback on discovering the finished product to be approximately two-and-a-half times larger than expected. Science students operate and think in terms of the S.I. system, but the U.S. machinists are so firmly tied to the U.S. system that they look only at the numbers and take them to be inches, feet, and so on.

(continued from page 5)

Regardless of whether the story of King Hiero's crown is accurate, it provides a memorable illustration of something that recurs continually in the career of all creative people, including especially scientists. Once the mind is assigned a task, it continues working on that task even when not specifically bidden to do so, turning the problem over and over, examining it from different directions. The sudden Eureka moments one experiences long after shifting one's thoughts to other realms are one of the most exciting rewards of the scientific life. Perhaps the main difference between Archimedes' time and the present in this regard is that the Eureka thought now occurs more often in the shower than the bathtub.

RICHARD B. FEYNMAN MEETS THE *CHALLENGER* COMMISSION

One morning in 1986, millions of school children across the United States and the rest of the world were watching the launch of the space shuttle *Challenger,* awaiting the first words from high-school science-teacher Christa McAuliffe, when they saw the explosion 48,000 feet (14,600 m) above the Atlantic Ocean. Most were quickly herded back into their classrooms by their confused and upset teachers.

Following a highly publicized competition organized by the United States National Aeronautics and Space Administration (NASA), Ms. McAuliffe had been selected to be the first "Teacher in Space." She was to use her skills to describe to the nation's science students her view from Earth orbit. Instead, following the explosion that broke the crew compartment loose from the rocket, she and the other six astronauts rode the compartment as it coasted upward for an additional 17,000 feet (5,200 m) and then fell from the sky. Although at impact with the ocean (three minutes after the explosion) the compartment was falling at approximately 200 miles per hour (320 km/hr), within about one-half second it came essentially to rest. The deceleration represented by that speed reduction in a half-second was probably what killed the astronauts, rather than the explosion.

To get a sense of the size of that deceleration, bear in mind that it was approximately 25 times the deceleration one feels in a car that it is skidding to a stop. Acceleration forces will be explored in chapter 2, after which it should be clear why the weights of the astronauts fell to zero during the plunge and then, during the half-second duration of the water impact, abruptly increased to more than 20 times their normal values.

The United States public, of course, demanded to know what had gone wrong during the *Challenger* launch. In response, the White House appointed a high-profile group, the *Challenger* Commission, to investigate. Unfortunately, the chair of the commission was a political appointee with neither technical experience nor education nor, apparently, scientific curiosity. Also, with one exception, the technical people on the commission had government ties and even ties to NASA, the agency that potentially would be blamed for the tragedy. The one exception, the outsider, was Caltech (California Institute of Technology) professor Richard B. Feynman [FINE mun] (1922–88), whose presence on the commission was something of a fluke. It came about because the acting NASA administrator was a one-time Caltech student and admirer of Feynman since those days. He invited Feynman to sit on the commission. Given his field of work in high-level theoretical physics, Feynman seemed at first an unlikely choice. After working on the Manhattan Project developing the atomic bomb during World War II, he had immersed

Richard B. Feynman, professor of physics at Caltech for much of the second half of the 20th century. Although he received the Nobel Prize in physics for his landmark work with elementary particles, broad public recognition came to him for his decidedly mundane leak analysis on the *Challenger* Commission. He took umbrage at those persons not in the sciences who thought it strange that he would engage in such "non-serious" activity as bongo playing. *(the Archives, California Institute of Technology)*

himself in the world of electrons, photons, protons, and the like and how they interact with one another and with themselves. In short, he was not a rocket scientist. Feynman himself, because of a fear of becoming entangled in politics during the short time he knew he had left in life, was reluctant to accept the invitation. He was convinced to do so by his wife, Gweneth, telling him:

> If you're not on the Commission, there'll be twelve members in a little knot which will go from one place to another, figure it all out, and write a report saying nothing. If you are on this thing, there'll be eleven guys in a knot, going around, and one guy like a mosquito running all over the place. You probably won't find anything, but if there is something interesting, if there's something strange, then you'll find it and it wouldn't have been found otherwise.

Forensic investigators can do worse than to remember the image of "one man like a mosquito running all over the place."

As if to fulfill Gweneth's prediction, the commission chair announced at the first meeting that they would probably never learn what had caused the disaster, and that NASA was not to be made the villain of the accident. Also in line with Gweneth's prediction, Feynman resisted being herded into the background briefings lined up by the chair, poking around instead on his own in the areas that he thought could be fruitful. Partly as a result of this and partly because of hints from a fellow commission member who was an Air Force engineer, Feynman figured out what had caused the *Challenger* explosion. Contrary to the prediction of the commission chair, the explanation was not at all complex, and it was immediately accepted as correct. It turned out that the O-rings that were designed to provide a flexible seal on the vehicle's solid rocket boosters were made of material that lost its elasticity when the temperature fell below about 35°F (2°C) and that the air temperature at the launch site the day of the disaster was 28°F (−2.2°C). Having lost their elasticity, the O-rings permitted hot gases to escape during the flexing of the assembly. This explanation for the explosion had been suspected immediately after the disaster by engineers who were low enough in the NASA hierarchy to have actually worked on the equipment and to know its characteristics. The video images captured during the ascent of the *Challenger* that last morning, combined with knowledge of the O-rings and their role, confirmed for them and later for Feynman and the rest of the commission the cause for the fiery explosion. This was brought home for the public dramatically during a final televised press conference held by the commission where Feynman illustrated the loss of elasticity by doing the following:

- he put a clamp on a piece of material of the type used in the O-rings;

- he lowered the clamped material into a glass of water containing ice cubes;

- after waiting a few minutes, he removed the clamped material from the water and released the clamp; and

- he held the material up to the television camera, showing that the indentation caused by the clamp had not gone away and that the material had temporarily lost its resiliency (elasticity).

Although the impression made by the clamp remained only until the material had warmed up again, the impression made on the public by Feynman lasted much longer.

Feynman's work with the *Challenger* Commission had a higher profile than most forensic work. However, it was similar to many forensic investigations with respect to the role that skepticism, independence, and doggedness played in achieving a successful outcome. It also illustrated the degree to which forensic scientists are sometimes pressured to arrive at results that do not reflect the objective facts. Because these improper pressures can be brought to bear in many ways, forensic work should be undertaken only by those who feel capable of maintaining independence and objectivity in spite of this professional hazard. This subject is taken up in some detail later in the book.

In summary, forensic engineering science consists of applying the knowledge and skills of engineering and its allied sciences such as physics and chemistry to questions that may end up in a court of law. Some forensic engineering scientists collect evidence at crime and accident scenes for later analysis by themselves or others. Others develop or perfect methods used for that collection and analysis. This work, and that of all forensic scientists, provides explanations of events that have injured people, damaged property and careers, and taken lives. The attention modern society pays to forensic investigations reflects the rarity of such events—and the fact that they can be explained. This contrasts with earlier centuries when murders, accidents, and other sources of misery were so common that only in the exceptional case would a thorough investigation take place. One of the great benefits of the effort devoted in modern times to solving crimes and understanding accidents is the dramatic decline in accidental death during the past 100 years. The highways and workplaces in the United States and other developed countries are vastly safer than they were at the beginning of the 20th century. In addition, the forensic engineering sciences have played their part in improving the rate at which law enforcement agencies are able to link perpetrators to their crimes and then obtain convictions of those criminals.

The identification of unsafe conditions and designs and the corrective actions taken as a result of that identification has been a major accomplishment of the forensic engineering sciences. It may be argued that this accomplishment is a side benefit arising from the drive to determine who is responsible for injury or loss suffered by another and the effort to mount a legal case forcing the party responsible to pay. In a civil matter, that payment takes the form of monetary compensation to the injured party. In the criminal matter, the payment can also be the forfeiture of freedom by the party charged. Because the legal system is bound so tightly to forensic work, any detailed discussion of the practice of forensic engineering science must be preceded by a description of the legal system within which it resides.

RESOLVING LEGAL DISPUTES

The legal system of the United States arose from the system it inherited from England. The U.S. legal system therefore has many similarities with the systems of all the countries once dominated by England, including especially Canada. However, there are some important differences, one of which is that in the United States both sides in a civil dispute have the right to a jury trial, a right limited everywhere else to criminal defendants.

To understand the U.S. legal system, including the way in which it uses forensic science, scientific evidence, and expert testimony, there is no better starting place than the colorful systems that preceded it, especially the fact-finding methods that were used for criminal trials in those earlier systems. It is hoped that a review of this history will lead to an appreciation for the modern efforts that continue to be expended to ensure that trials are fair and just. A stronger hope is that this review will convey an ability to recognize when these efforts have failed.

The recognizable elements of our criminal trial system date back only a few hundred years. Before that time and as recently as the early colonial period in America (1609–1700), trial by ordeal was the common approach to testing the truth of criminal accusations, as it had been for perhaps thousands of years. In terms of modern legal language, it can be said that trial by ordeal was the fact-finding method employed or that the fact finder used trials by ordeal. Unfortunately for the accused under that system, a finding that the accusation was false sometimes required the death of the accused.

At the heart of trials by ordeal was the implicit or explicit assumption that supernatural forces would intervene to assist the fact finder.

Legal fact-finding during the trial-by-ordeal era *(Mary Evans Picture Library/Alamy)*

Depending on the particular ordeal chosen, this reliance on supernatural intervention took different forms. In some cases, the forces of evil were relied on either to save the accused from harm and thereby prove the truth of the accusation or to refrain from intervening, thereby establishing the defendant's innocence. In the trial of a woman (usually it was a woman) who was accused of being a witch or of practicing witchcraft, one approach called for having the woman lie on her back and then placing heavy stones atop her chest to the point where one not having access to the tools of witchcraft certainly would be expected to die. Death thereby became a verdict of innocence and survival one of guilt. Having been found guilty by surviving, the defendant was then executed by other means, such as fire, apparently an assault against which witches could not shield themselves regardless of the powers of darkness upon which they might call. Another form of trial founded on this reasoning forced the defendant to inhale water by immersing his or her face in water and holding it there. Drowning meant innocence, survival guilt. Although it would seem that the accused could not win, there was a significant benefit to being found innocent though dead. The property of the innocent dead person would not go the state (the government) but rather to the accused's family, to whom it could mean the difference between living out normal lives for the time or suffering through lives shortened by hunger and made miserable by abject poverty.

Modern society has by and large left behind trials-by-ordeal and the absurd belief that they provided truth or justice. Nevertheless, any feeling of superiority over the old ways has to be moderated by the recognition that complete fairness and justice continues to elude the modern trial system. The work of designing fair trials continues, and it is likely that some methods now used to determine guilt will one day be found as useless for determining truth and as unfair to the accused as trials by ordeal. This is particularly pertinent to the present subject matter, as the modern criminal justice system in the United States is in the midst of what could be called a revolution and the air is filled with assertions that some traditional means of determining guilt have been misapplied and, in some cases, are completely worthless.

In addition to the change in fact-finding methods, there has been a major change since ancient times in criminal-law philosophy—the acceptance of the principle that an accused person is to be presumed innocent until found guilty in a court of law. This principle is embedded in the U.S. Constitution and is one of the bedrocks of the criminal justice system in the United States and throughout most of the modern world. In spite of being considered essential to providing fair trials to criminal defendants, it was late to arrive on the scene. Previously, the rule was that the accused had the burden and responsibility of disproving the accusation. He or she was presumed guilty until that occurred. The history of the United States has fully demonstrated both the importance of the presumption of innocence and the need to fight to preserve it in practice. In every generation, there appear to be some crimes that are considered so terrible that for all practical purposes the person accused is back in the 16th century, having to prove that he or she is not guilty.

MECHANICS OF MODERN LAW

In the United States and all countries that derive their legal systems from England, there are two types of law: statutory law and common law. The former, also called black-letter law, is made by legislative bodies such as the U.S. Congress, the 50-state legislatures, the thousands of city councils, and so forth. All criminal law and a portion of civil law in the United States is black-letter law. However, it is common law that governs most aspects of noncriminal procedures, that is, civil procedures. Common law consists of principles embedded in decisions reached during hundreds of years by thousands of courts in the course of deciding disputes put before them. In this sense, it is absurd to rail against lawmaking courts as such, since that is one of the most important functions the courts in common-law countries have fulfilled. And the process still continues. In modern times in the United States, the controlling common law (sometimes referred to as "precedent") is made by the courts of appeal rather than by trial courts.

For the forensic sciences, the most important area of civil law is torts (as opposed to, for example, contract law). A tort is usually described as a "private wrong," a wrongful act committed by one private person against another, for which the injured person can seek recovery in court. (As might be guessed, the word has the same root as does *torture*.) Within the area of tort law, it is the tort of negligence that engages the most court time, the most attention in the news media, and the most time of forensic engineering scientists. When Mr. Smith claims to have been injured by the negligence of Ms. Jones, Mr. Smith is accusing Ms. Jones of having committed the tort of negligence. Since there is no statute spelling out what constitutes negligence, it is common law that governs how such claims are to be treated in court. Mr. Smith or his lawyer, before suing Ms. Jones for negligence, would look at previous cases involving facts similar to those in his claim. This would provide him with the judicial precedents governing what he can claim and also may give him an idea as to how claims like his have fared at trial in the court where he may bring it. He will also have to review any applicable black-letter law regarding details, since it always trumps common law. (Occasionally, legislative bodies conclude that some aspect of the existing common law regarding torts is unjust and enact laws overruling the common law rule in question.)

For example, common law provides no civil recovery against a person who has caused the death of another, regardless of how negligent or murderous the fatal act was or of how impoverished and sorrowful that act left the dead person's survivors. The traditional reasoning was that only the person injured by a tortious act can file a claim seeking damages, so that if the injury leads to death, "the cause of action dies with the claimant." The legislatures of all the states of the United States have long since passed wrongful-death statutes, which permit a survivor to obtain a money recovery against a person or corporation shown to have caused a person's death wrongfully. The plaintiff must prove the extent of the monetary and emotional injury for which monetary recovery is sought. The amount of money that can be recovered for wrongful death is capped in most states, in contrast with actions controlled completely by common law, where the jury or judge is not limited by statute in determining the size of the judgment.

To prove that Ms. Jones has committed the tort of negligence against Mr. Smith, Mr. Smith (usually with the assistance of his lawyer) must show the truth of all the following statements:

- Ms. Jones had a duty toward Mr. Smith.

- Ms. Jones negligently failed to fulfill that duty.

- As a result of that failure, Mr. Smith suffered an injury.

If there is no question about what Ms. Jones did, her defense would usually be that her actions—the key concept in defending against a claim of negligence were reasonable. If Ms. Jones can convince the fact-finder that, regardless of what happened to Mr. Smith, her actions about which he complained were reasonable, the verdict at trial will be in her favor, a defense verdict. Just as there is no black-letter law spelling out what constitutes negligence, there are, with few exceptions, no statutes establishing what is reasonable. One of the major reasons that parties to a negligence action look to earlier decisions, to case law, is to get a sense of what courts have previously considered to be reasonable.

Some actions can end up in trial court twice, once as a criminal action and once as a civil action. Any crime that causes individual personal loss to a person is also a tort under civil law. Therefore, the accused can be sued in civil court separately from being charged and tried under the criminal-law system. This sometimes confuses people, especially if the results of the two trials differ, such as when a not-guilty verdict in the criminal trial is followed by a plaintiff's verdict in the civil trial. The apparent contradiction lies in the different standards of proof in the two settings. The prosecution in a criminal case must show beyond a reasonable doubt that the defendant committed the crime, whereas a plaintiff in a civil action merely has to show that it is more likely than not that the defendant committed the tort. What would be really unexpected would be for the criminal trial to lead to a conviction and the subsequent civil trial to end in a defense verdict. If that ever happens, it would be important to see whether exactly the same facts were claimed in the two trials.

MODERN CIVIL AND CRIMINAL TRIALS

Apart from the respective standards of proof, most of the differences between civil and criminal trials are superficial. In each type of trial, the person against whom a claim has been brought is called the defendant and his or her lawyer the defense lawyer. In the civil trial, the claim is brought by the plaintiff, represented by the plaintiff's lawyer. In the criminal trial, the claim is brought by the government, represented by the prosecutor. However, the respective trial structures are very similar and most of the comments below apply to both the criminal and civil arenas. Most trials in the United States occur in state courts and are governed by the laws of the state in which they take place. With respect to criminal matters, by far the majority of trials take place in state courts rather than federal courts.

Both civil and criminal trials are held before either a judge and jury or a judge acting alone. The former is called a jury trial and the latter a bench trial or a judge trial. In both jury trials and bench trials, the judge decides how the trial is to be conducted, including which witnesses and information the jury will be allowed to see and hear; it is said that the judge decides the issues of law and that the jury decides issues of fact, including the most important one, the verdict. In a bench trial, the judge plays both roles. The rest of the discussion of trials will refer to jury trials. In the United States, jury trials are common for both civil and criminal matters. Other countries, including Canada, do not use juries except for criminal trials. In nearly all common-law countries, however, the verdicts have the same names and the same respective meanings. These are discussed in the following sidebar on "Confusion about Verdicts."

Confusion about Verdicts

The goal of a criminal trial in the United States and in most common-law countries is to reach a verdict of "guilty" or "not guilty." In an important sense, the two verdicts do not have equal strength, given the limitations placed on the evidence that the prosecution can introduce at trial. A guilty verdict means that the 12 jury members, after hearing the evidence, after hearing the judge define reasonable doubt, and after discussing the evidence, have unanimously concluded that there is no reasonable doubt as to the guilt of the defendant. A not-guilty verdict means that the members of a jury have unanimously concluded that the evidence presented does not establish beyond a reasonable doubt that the defendant is guilty. As with any human decision, jury verdicts are not infallible. Although a verdict of guilty establishes the defendant's guilt legally, it does not and cannot establish that the defendant is actually guilty. The defendant entered the trial either guilty or innocent and retains that status at the conclusion of the trial regardless of the verdict. It is possible, and it has been shown to occur, that a person found guilty actually was innocent. Similarly, a person found not guilty by a jury actually may be guilty. This distinction is sometimes recognized by distinguishing between facts of law—legal facts—and true facts. It is only within the context of the law that the phrase "true facts" is not redundant.

Though jury verdicts in criminal cases must be unanimous, this is not a requirement in civil trials in state court where both the jury size and the degree of unanimity required are determined by state law, and vary from state to state. A civil trial normally ends with a *plaintiff's verdict* or a *defense verdict*. News reports of a civil defendant having been found guilty, not guilty, or cleared reflect the reporter's ignorance.

In both criminal and civil trials, the party who started the process has the burden of going forward and must lead off by presenting evidence that supports its claims. Most evidence is introduced by calling witnesses to the witness stand and, after they swear to tell the truth, questioning them in the presence of the jury. When the party (the plaintiff or the prosecution, depending on whether it is a civil or criminal trial) has finished putting on its evidence, it "rests." At that point, the judge must decide whether a reasonable jury, believing all of the evidence presented, can find in favor of the plaintiff (or prosecution). This reflects the fact that the claims against the defendant are presumed to be wrong, requiring the other party to introduce enough evidence to overcome that presumption. (As mentioned previously, this contrasts with the rule that once prevailed whereby the claims or charges were presumed to be correct, with the burden placed on the defendant to disprove them.) Should the judge decide that insufficient evidence was introduced, the trial ends without the defendant having to do anything. A directed verdict will be entered, and the jury will have no role. This is such an important point that it cannot be repeated too often. The defendant has no obligation to prove anything. In particular, a criminal defendant does not have to prove that he or she is not guilty of the charges.

Directed verdicts are very rare. When one occurs in a criminal case, it suggests that the charges should not have been brought in the first place. When it occurs in a civil case, it suggests that the plaintiff had brought a frivolous claim. Under those circumstances, the plaintiff in the trial just concluded may abruptly become the defendant in a subsequent action seeking damages for the misuse of the court system, another type of tort.

In the usual case, where no directed verdict has issued, the defendant next introduces evidence countering the evidence introduced by the opposing party and/or asserts other defenses to that party's claims or charges. As with the first part of the trial, the evidence is put before the jury primarily through witnesses being called to the witness stand to testify in the presence of the jury.

Persons testifying in court are either fact witnesses or opinion witnesses. Fact witnesses testify to facts that are known to them personally, this is by direct observation. A special type of fact witness is the eyewitness, discussed in some detail in the sidebar on page 23. Opinion witnesses do not testify regarding their personal knowledge of the underlying events, but rather as to opinions they have about the evidence. It is as opinion witnesses that forensic scientists appear in court, where they are referred to as expert witnesses.

Eyewitnesses and the Harm That They Can Do

An eyewitness is a fact witness who claims to have been present at the event—a car crash, a bar brawl, a murder, whatever led to the trial—and to have seen what happened. It being human nature to believe that one can understand what is going on in front of one's own eyes and to be able to remember it, the legal system has always given great weight (influence) to eyewitness testimony. It is only in modern times that this respect has been found to be completely undeserved. Very convincing studies have shown that the ability of people to describe correctly events that occurred before their "very own eyes" is often nil, vanishing, not existent. This failure is particularly common when the events are unexpected and short-lived. Because of the implication that this discrediting of eyewitness testimony has for guilty verdicts in the past, the realization that eyewitness testimony is unreliable is causing chills in people dedicated to the proposition that our legal system is just.

One theory for the failure of eyewitnesses to correctly remember what they saw is that the failure lies not in defective memories but rather in the mind's inability to capture details of unexpected events that are quickly over. The real harm is done, however, by the mind's tendency to fill in the memory gaps resulting from this inability. In short, the unconscious mind makes up memories so as to ensure continuity in its recollection of an event. The conscious mind of the eyewitness does not realize that key elements in his or her memory of the event were produced in this manner. It is easy to see that an honest eyewitness may be the greatest obstacle to discovering what happened. With a dishonest witness, there is at least a chance that a jury will detect the lying.

(continues)

(continued)

Because of the above considerations, it is no exaggeration to say that a correct idea of what happened in an automobile crash will most likely be obtained in the absence of any eyewitnesses. The next best situation is that where there were many independent eyewitnesses. The many eyewitnesses either will contradict one another and hence be disregarded by the jury or will give the same account, supporting the conclusion that that account is probably correct. The worst situation is when a sole eyewitness comes forth. Even if the testimony of that person is at odds with the physical evidence and even the laws of physics, it will often sway a jury. To see the harm this can do, one need only reflect on the continuing parade of persons being released from long prison terms to which they had been wrongfully sentenced based on the testimony of a single eyewitness, a witness now proven indisputably wrong by DNA evidence.

All witnesses undergo direct examination during which they answer questions designed to convince the jury of the rightness of the side represented by the lawyer who called them to the witness stand. In the sense that the lawyer calling on them has usually reviewed with them beforehand the substance of the testimony they will give, this aspect of the trial is something of a staged production. But it is a staged production with an element of uncertainty since, after direct examination by the lawyer calling the witness, the opposing side gets to ask questions of the witness through cross-examination. Uncertainty enters because usually the cross-examination questions have not all been anticipated by the witness or by the side that introduced the witness. The usual goal of cross-examination is to reduce the harm that the witness may have done the cross-examining lawyer's side during direct. Sometimes it is possible to achieve this by showing that the testimony given by the witness contradicted his or her earlier statements. When the witness is an expert forensic witness, there may be an attempt to show that he or she is incompetent. Frequently, the lawyer doing the cross-examination will attempt to get the expert to agree to the lawyer's summation of the expert's opinions, a summation that will represent a slight but significant shift that favors that lawyer's client. Most expert witnesses are skilled in detecting misleading summations and also in avoiding other traps set by the cross-examining lawyer, such as those that make the expert appear uncertain or contradictory. For better or worse, the outcome of this type of trial can turn on appearances, a fact that makes it very important that the expert witness avoid being placed in a false light.

Questions are posed and answered at trial in a manner quite different than in daily dealings with friends and family. One might not have friends for long if one cross-examined them on everything they said and yelled "nonresponsive" whenever they did not answer the question asked. Also, one cannot take back an unwise comment by saying "Strike that!" Nevertheless, there are some practices of the forensic arena that can help in ordinary life. The most important of these is refusing to accept statements at face value. Not only should one not believe everything one hears or reads, one should not believe *anything* without having more reason to do so than that a friend or acquaintance said it or that it was in print. This is especially true if it is going to affect your actions or beliefs about other persons or the world in general. For the legal system to be just, it must reach verdicts based on truth rather than lies or confusion. So, too, the rational personal life is guided by truth and not confusion or lies. When a person hears something that is very important if it is true, that person needs to know the basis of the statement. Is it a fact? Unfortunately, it is common practice for people and publications to report as fact statements by others that they do not know to be true. Rarely is the statement purporting to be fact preceded by the phrase "So and so says. . . ." The listener or reader should always be alert to secondhand statements, and ask "Do you know that for a fact?"—the equivalent of asking whether the speaker or writer has firsthand knowledge of the truth of the statement. With the rise of the Internet, it is more important than ever that this question in some form be posed to people who speak in the expectation that their speech will cause others to act. The response—said out loud or not—should always be "How does this person know that?"

2

Accident Reconstruction: Getting Started

This chapter is about motor vehicle crashes—more specifically, about the investigation of motor vehicle crashes and how they can be reconstructed from the information provided by the debris they leave, the marks they make, and the damage they do. The chapter will also tie today's methods that are used to investigate crashes to the universal laws discovered by Newton and Galileo 400 years ago and will show how those laws can be used to develop new investigation techniques. The basic ideas presented in this chapter form the introduction to later chapters, especially chapters 3 to 5 since the wide range of accident reconstruction methods that are addressed in those chapters arise for the most part from these ideas. Because of its introductory aspect, this chapter emphasizes the importance of using language carefully when discussing accident reconstruction. The precise meanings of the key words used in the discussions are considerably narrower than those in common usage. For example, the terms *velocity* and *speed* are not interchangeable. While *speed* has its common meaning, *velocity* does not and should not be used in discussing motor-vehicle crashes until it has been defined, as it will be before the end of the chapter.

News stories are filled with statements such as "the car involved in the single-car crash was traveling 103.2 miles per hour when it left the road," or "the car carrying Princess Diana was going 108 miles per hour at the time it hit the bridge pillar," and "the governor's SUV was 32 miles per hour over the speed limit when it went into its skid." Where do those numbers come from? They do not generally come from jammed speedometers, which are a very poor source of impact speed information in any event. The material that follows in this and the next two chapters provides the answers—there are more than one—to this question. More important, it will identify the strengths and weaknesses of accident reconstruction techniques and will permit an evaluation of statements that appear in car-crash stories.

Crashes of cars, trucks, motorcycles, bicycles, ride-on mowers, and so forth give rise to the largest single category of forensic activity in the United States and most other countries. (Even in countries that are most notorious for terrorist activities, far more persons are injured and killed in car crashes each year than in criminal attacks.) Investigations of such crashes are usually done to assign liability (blame) to someone since they nearly always turn out to have been caused by human error of some sort, usually on the part of one or more of the drivers. Even where the immediate cause of a crash is a vehicle flaw or road defect, the ultimate cause can usually be traced to mistakes made by some person. In addition to assigning legal blame, crash investigations—numbering in the millions since the appearance of the automobile—have led to better vehicle and road designs as well as to practices that compensate for dangerous driver behavior. The relative safety of modern highway travel is the result of this work, which can claim much of the credit for the 20-fold reduction in the traffic fatality rate in the United States since the 1920s.

It is worth noting that referring to the investigation and analysis of motor-vehicle crashes as accident reconstruction effectively narrows the breadth of that phrase. As a result, it does not, for example, refer to figuring out why someone fell down a flight of stairs or what caused a chemist to blow off his hand or head accidentally. Nevertheless, since that has become the accepted label, it will be used here when referring to what is more precisely called the forensic analysis of motor-vehicle accidents. By extension, persons who do accident reconstruction are called accident reconstructionists.

The term *accident* as used in this book refers to any event causing injury or property damage that was unexpected by at least one of the persons who was directly affected. Thus, a motor-vehicle accident can be a crash caused by human error, a crash caused by mechanical failure, or a crash caused by an intentional criminal act. In this chapter and throughout this volume, *accident, collision, crash, mishap,* and similar words will be used interchangeably. It is interesting to note, however, that the U.S. Department of Transportation recently directed its offices to avoid the use of the word *accident* in favor of *crash* or *collision.*

The goal of an accident reconstruction is to obtain a numerical description, also called a quantitative description, about an accident. Obviously, saying that "The car skidded 172 feet before colliding with the wall at an angle of 40 degrees" is far more useful than saying "The car skidded quite far before slamming obliquely with the wall." The latter sentence is a qualitative statement.

Whenever a crash occurs, there is always the potential for a legal dispute. Persons who suffer injuries or money loss as the result of a crash may sue the person whom they think is responsible in civil court. In some cases, a crash leads to criminal charges being brought against one or more of the drivers. Civil claims and criminal charges are both usually settled without trial, based on what the parties believe the outcome of a trial would be. Settlements of civil claims provide primarily for the defendant paying a certain sum of money to the claimant (plaintiff). The settlement of a criminal charge involves an agreement regarding punishment that is reached between the defendant and the prosecutor and subject to approval by a judge.

As is true of all forensic investigations, accident reconstructions involve the analysis of both subjective information and objective information. Both types of information are commonly referred to as *evidence,* though strictly speaking that word should be reserved for statements and objects introduced at a trial. Subjective evidence consists of statements made by persons claiming to have knowledge about the event. They are the fact witnesses defined in chapter 1. Such evidence could include, for example, what somebody riding in one of the cars that collided says about the collision or an account by a mechanic regarding brake work that he or she had personally performed on one of the vehicles at some point before the crash. Objective evidence, more commonly called physical evidence, consists of things rather than statements, things that can be physically examined, directly or through photographs or other documentation. Examples of physical evidence include skid marks and vehicle damage.

Depending as it does on the ability and willingness of a human witness to provide correct information, subjective evidence can be unreliable and, in the case of eyewitnesses, extremely unreliable. Objective evidence is reliable—it is what it is, be it a 150-foot (46-m) skid mark or a dent 10 inches (25 cm) deep in a car door. On the other hand, objective evidence cannot speak. If it is as simple as a skid mark, its meaning—that a vehicle was braked hard enough to lock up its wheels—is quite clear even though its significance may be subject to argument. Sometimes, though, the meaning of the physical evidence—for example, whether it was even associated with the event in question—can be unclear and subject to disputes lasting right through trial. Nevertheless, the best source of information regarding a motor-vehicle crash is almost always the physical evidence associated with the crash; investigators are most likely to arrive at a correct description of events when physical evidence is abundant and eyewitnesses are absent. The worst situation is where there is a single disinterested eyewitness for the reasons set out in the sidebar on "Eyewitnesses" in chapter 1.

To give a quick introduction to the basic accident reconstruction techniques, a relatively uncomplicated accident reconstruction will be presented. It involves a pedestrian struck down by a car that fled from the scene—the classic hit-and-run. Important to understanding what accident reconstruction can accomplish is an awareness of the activities of the emergency personnel who are first at the scene, the so-called first responders. Therefore, the presentation includes a description of those activities.

THE HIT-AND-RUN

Many fatal pedestrian accidents occur along little-traveled rural roads in the vicinity of mailboxes. Because of the low traffic level on such roads, those cars and trucks that do pass tend to travel too fast for the occasional hazards that arise daily. For the same reason, residents along these roads tend not to exercise enough care before crossing these roads,

Long, curving skid marks produced by the vehicle that struck the girl and fled
(Courtesy of the author)

usually on their daily mailbox trip. It is not entirely facetious to say that the major life-limiting activity of elderly rural residents is that of collecting their mail. At any event, in the present case, the 12-year-old victim was crossing to collect the family mail when she was struck and thrown onto the shoulder of the road, which was level and with clear visibility in both directions for least 600 feet (180 m) at the mailbox. No one saw or heard the striking vehicle, which was gone by the time a neighbor found the injured girl and called 911.

The first responders—local police officers and emergency medical technicians (EMTs)—arrived approximately 10 minutes after the call. While the police officers directed traffic and recorded important aspects of the scene, such the girl's rest position near the end of the skid marks shown in the photo, the EMTs tended to the victim and quickly realized that her injuries might be fatal. Because the officers were not themselves trained accident reconstructionists, they placed a call to the state police for an accident reconstructionist as soon as they were told of the seriousness of the girl's injuries.

The state-police reconstructionist arrived on the scene within less than an hour and was able to speak with the first responders while they were still there. This was a great advantage in terms of efficient communications. Often, the first visit of an accident reconstructionist to an accident site occurs days and, in the case of civil suits, months and even years after the event. Rare is the case where the accident reconstructionist does not have to rely at least to some extent on the measurements and observations of others. It can be seen that the ultimate conclusions about an accident may rely critically on measurements made by persons not trained in accident reconstruction. It is especially frustrating when the only photographs of an accident scene do not include views of the most important features of the scene.

Arriving at the accident scene, the accident reconstructionist was shown where the victim had come to rest and what appeared to be a scuff mark on the pavement made by her sneaker. The sneaker scuff, taken to be a good indicator of where she was when she was struck, was midway between the two skid marks and a distance of 42 feet (13 m) from what appeared to be the start of the marks. The reconstructionist immediately set about determining whether the tire marks were recent, obviously a necessary condition for them to have been associated with the accident. Although skid marks can remain on pavement for weeks or even months, the opportunity to prove them to be of recent origin vanishes quickly. Fresh skid marks usually are covered by tiny black particles that are soon dispersed by wind and passing traffic. These particles tend to pile up at the downstream end of the marks, where the skidding stopped. This circumstance plus the fact that skid marks tend to be darker at their downstream end and lighter to the point of invisibility where they start can provide independent information as to the direction of the skid. The darkening occurs because the temperature of a skidding tire increases as it skids along, resulting in more rubber being transferred from tire to pavement. This variation can be seen in the twin skid marks shown in the photo. See also the illustration on page 65 in which smoke can actually be seen coming from tires heated by skidding.

Sometimes, though probably not with the marks shown in the photo on page 30, significant fading occurs within days or even within hours. Since the first to go is the light portion at the beginning of the marks, fading destroys information about where the skids started, something that is often of great importance. Any fading that shortens the length of the marks can lead to an underestimate of vehicle speed and also obscure from investigators when the driver first perceived a hazard.

Regardless of whether tire marks can be shown to be associated with an accident, good practice requires that they be measured or at least photographed. Even when the investigator is absolutely sure that a tire mark did not come from an accident under study, he or she must note its presence and the reason for not documenting it further. Otherwise, later investigators, having to rely solely on photographs, can be misled or, at least, led to waste time pondering tire marks that are irrelevant to the investigation. Although the first concern of police investigators is to determine whether a crime has been committed, they also are responsible for preserving information that may be needed in civil actions. Given that such actions may be brought up to six years following a crash, this responsibility is a significant one.

As it turned out, in this particular case, a pile of black particles was found to have accumulated at the darker end of each mark, establishing that the marks were made very recently and confirming the direction of the skidding car that made them. Since this information, along with the proximity of the marks to the victim and the location of the sneaker scuff, strongly indicated that the marks were left by the vehicle that struck her (the striking vehicle), it was essential to make detailed measurements of the marks. Even if data derived from those measurements did not lead investigators to the striking vehicle, they would be invaluable for ruling out certain vehicles.

The photo on page 30 shows the marks shifting toward the right during the course of the skid, with the shift most pronounced just before the vehicle came to a stop. Since the pavement was flat, with no sloping to either the right or the left, this shift establishes that the vehicle's rear tires made the skids. When front tires lock up, they lose all steering ability and slide along pavement like hockey pucks, leaving straight marks. In contrast, when a vehicle's front tires are rolling and its rear ones are sliding, the vehicle tends to rotate so that its rear end gets ahead of its front end because sliding tires have less traction than rolling ones. (Rotation of this sort is especially common with motorcycles in emergency situations. Their front and rear brakes are applied independently, and inexperienced operators faced with an emergency tend to lock the rear wheel

Close-up of a portion of the marks shown in the photo on page 30, the light-colored stripes corresponding to grooves in the tire-tread pattern *(Courtesy of the author)*

while applying very little brake force to the front for fear of the loss of steering associated with locking up the front wheel. Unfortunately, this strategy usually leads to loss of control anyway if the skidding continues for more than a short distance, leading to the motorcycle falling over and sliding across the pavement on its side next to its ex-rider.) Because this rotation is most undesirable, the brake systems on cars are designed so that the front wheels lock up before the rear wheels during hard braking. Pickup trucks are another matter since the braking force needed to lock up a wheel depends on the weight being supported by that wheel, and it is not possible to predict in advance the front/rear weight distribution of a pickup truck. This means that it is impossible to set the pickup's braking ratio so as to ensure that the front brakes will always lock up first; in the absence of antilock braking (ABS), the rear wheels will always lock

These are two common tire-tread patterns. The one on the left will leave a skid mark similar to that shown on page 33, whereas the one on the right will leave a solid black mark. *(Joseph Keierleber)*

up first on an empty pickup truck. The reverse is true on a loaded truck. This explains why antilock brakes were put on the rear wheels of pickup trucks very early in the ABS era.

In short, the skid mark shown in the photo on page 30 was made either by a car with out-of-adjustment brakes or by a pick up truck not carrying a load and lacking ABS, a potentially distinguishing characteristic for identifying the striking vehicle and eliminating others from suspicion.

As can be seen in the photo on page 33 and in more detail above, each of the skid marks consists of five separate well-defined black stripes, sometimes called longitudinal striations. This indicates (1) that the tires making the marks had reasonably good tread and (2) that the tread pattern included four parallel grooves. A zigzag tread would have left a much simpler pattern: a solid black mark. This photo shows the two types of tire tread side by side. The one on the left would make a skid mark much like the one shown on page 33, whereas the one on the right would leave a basically solid black mark, possibly with a little shading. In addition to the tread pattern, the marks reveal the tread width. Although many different tread patterns can be used with a particular model vehicle, each model usually has tires of a specific tread width associated with it. By their spacing, the skid marks also reveal the track width of the vehicle, that is the distance between its left- and right-side wheels.

Summing up, the tire marks reveal three characteristics of the vehicle that struck the girl: tire-tread pattern; tread width; track width. If a suspect vehicle is examined shortly after the accident, all three of these facts will be useful either for ruling that vehicle out or for examining it and its driver further. Since tread pattern can be changed simply by changing tires, and since millions of cars on the road have nearly the same tread width, the tread information is not nearly as valuable as the track width, especially as time passes. Track width—the separation between the left and right wheels—is characteristic of the vehicle.

Vehicles also can be excluded on the basis of damage since, with the exception of heavy trucks, no motor vehicle can injure a pedestrian without sustaining obvious damage itself. Needless to say, a suspected vehicle will not be excluded simply for lack of damage unless it can be established that the vehicle had not been repaired since the accident.

If there is no suspect vehicle identified soon after the event, by, for example, a tip to the police, the tire and vehicle information collected at the scene will form the basis of a more painstaking, in fact tedious, search by police investigators using motor-vehicle databases. With luck, the track width will turn out to be unusual. More commonly, however, it will fall within the narrow range about 5.4 feet (1.6 m) that is associated with hundreds of car models. Still, this information will be important in the examination of any vehicle that comes under suspicion for other reasons. If the track width for that vehicle is wrong, it will be excluded from further consideration. However, all of that work will be a waste of time if the at-scene investigation was not of sufficient quality to ensure the correctness of information being used.

The next use for the skid marks was to determine the vehicle's speed. Although one might think that this would call for skid tests with the same kind of vehicle (at this point unknown) that is equipped with the type of tires that made the skid marks, this fortunately is not the case. This is one of many lucky breaks in accident reconstruction. This particular break can be stated in the following manner: The skid-to-a-stop distance on dry roads depends only on the road and on the vehicle speed. One reason for this startling rule is profound, following as it does from the fundamental laws of the universe. The other is something of a fluke, namely that in a very important sense traction on dry roads is about the same for all ordinary car and light truck tires. In particular, the traction, better called friction, does not depend on tread design. Contrary to popular belief, all those fancy tread patterns are useful only to improve traction on wet or snowy roads. Where dry roads are involved, the variation in friction for cars and light trucks depends only on the nature of the road surface and not on the tire.

Thus, to find the speed of the car that struck the girl, it is only necessary to measure the length of the marks and the friction between ordinary tires and the road. It turns out that there is another lucky break when it comes to the friction measurement, in that the tire/road friction can be described by a coefficient of friction. The coefficient of friction concept and why it is startling will be discussed in a sidebar toward the end of this chapter.

Characteristic of skid marks, the first portion of the skid marks shown in the photo on page 30 is relatively faint. This is not just because the skidding tires had not heated up yet but also because of the manner in which tires begin to leave skid marks under hard braking. Brake application is not instantaneous when a vehicle operator slams on the brakes. For a short time—the brake lag time—the wheels continue rolling. This lag time depends on the type of brake system. In air-brake systems—nearly universal on heavy trucks and buses—the application of the brakes at each wheel depends on the build-up of air pressure, resulting in lag times of about a half-second, a significant delay for a vehicle traveling 100 feet a second (30 m/s) or faster. However, most smaller vehicles are equipped with hydraulic brakes, which transmit brake-pedal force to the individual wheels by means of an incompressible liquid (the brake fluid), resulting in a much smaller lag time, perhaps a tenth of a second or less. During that period, as the braking force at the individual wheels is rising to its maximum level, there is some tire slipping prior to full skidding. Even after the wheels fully lock up, the tires will not leave clear skid marks for a few feet. Thus, there is an area of incipient skidding resulting in a slight darkening of the pavement sometimes called ghost marks. For several reasons, one wishes to identify the point that is as close to the start of those ghost marks as is possible. This point is nearly impossible to see in photographs, which is why most at-scene investigators end up on their knees in the road peering at the skid marks from close to the pavement, often with the help of an assistant. It is usually the case that faint marks can best be detected when one is looking in the direction of travel of the vehicle that left them. Finally, the direction of the sun can make a difference in how well faint marks can be seen.

The longer mark shown in the photo on page 30 was 130 feet (40 m) in length. That provides one of the pieces of information needed to calculate the speed. Measurements of the friction are normally made at this point. However, since the road has an asphalt surface, the investigators used the typical friction that such roads present to ordinary tires to obtain an immediate value for the speed. For reasons that will be explained later in this chapter, this led them to conclude that the hit-and-run vehicle was traveling at about 55 miles per hour (88 km/hr) at the start of the skid, significantly faster than the 40-miles per hour (64-km/hr) speed limit. Because of the braking that occurred during the lag period, before full skidding began, the speed when the brake pedal was depressed would have been even higher.

It is one thing to show that the hit-and-run vehicle was speeding but another to conclude that speed caused the accident. Stated differently, it is one thing to charge a driver with violating the speed laws but a different thing—and a much more serious action—to charge that driver with aggravated assault or vehicular homicide. To support the more serious charge in this case, a prosecutor would want to show at trial that the difference between the girl being struck and the girl not being struck lay with the vehicle traveling at 55 miles per hour (88 km/hr) instead of 40 miles per hour (64 km/hr).

Although it is very likely that the injuries to the victim were more serious than they would have been had she been struck at a lower speed, it remains to be determined whether the excess speed (55 mile per hour v. 40 miles per hour) (88 km/hr v. 64 km/hr) made the difference between an accident and no accident. If she ran into the road just a few feet in front of the approaching vehicle, she would have been struck regardless of the speed. In fact, there is a considerable range of distances in front of the vehicle for which the impact would be unavoidable for a 40 miles per hour (64 km/hr) vehicle. The key question then becomes whether she was within that range or farther away when she stepped into the road. Answering this question brings in interesting physics as well as aspects of human behavior that are not commonly understood. A lucky break for the investigator of this particular accident is that there was apparently a mark made on the pavement indicating where the girl was when she was struck, the sneaker scuff. (It is most common in pedestrian impacts that the point of impact along the roadway is known only to within a broad range.) That mark does not indicate how long she had been in the road nor whether she was walking along the road prior to being struck. There are always limitations to what one can figure out through accident reconstruction, and the correct approach, where there is doubt, is to give the benefit of the doubt to the person who may end up being charged. Therefore, in this case, the assumption was made that the victim entered the road at the point where she was hit, where the sneaker scuff was found.

The question as to whether the injury would not have occurred but for vehicle speed is a typical but-for question. Its answer would seem to rely on how far away the girl was from the vehicle when she entered the road. Actually, the best that can be done is to estimate the distance between the vehicle and the girl when the hazard of the girl entering the road or being in the road first entered the driver's field of vision. This estimate can be obtained from two pieces of physical evidence—the position of the sneaker scuff and the starting point of the skid marks— and a consideration of the driver's perception-reaction time (PRT). The significance of the perception-reaction time was foreshadowed above by the use of the phrase "entered the driver's field of vision" and instead of the phrase "could be seen by the driver." The fact is that in the context of accident reconstruction the simple statement "The driver saw the girl" is so ambiguous as to be useless. As will be explored in the following sidebar, it turns out that before an observer "sees" something a time-consuming sequence of events involving the eyes and brain of the observer must take place. Therefore, instead of saying, for example, that "The driver could have seen the danger when he rounded the curve," one must say that "The danger could have entered the driver's field of vision when he rounded the curve." Seeing is not instantaneous. For this reason, the word *perceive* is used in its place, and the time interval between the image of an object entering a person's field of vision and the instant that the person correctly identifies the object is called the perception time. Where that object is a hazard requiring action on the part of the person perceiving it, such as a girl running in front of the person's car, another important interval, the reaction time, must pass following perception before an action to avoid the hazard such as braking or swerving can be taken. Following the sidebar, the answer to the threshold question—How far from the impact point was the vehicle when the hazard first entered the driver's field of vision?—will be calculated. That distance will then be used to find the answer to the but-for question, and the significance of that answer will be evaluated in the context of a criminal prosecution.

Perception-Reaction Time

Think about what it means to see something. Most people, when they consider the subject at all, think of the eye as a camera. In that model, the lens of the eye plays the role of the camera lens and the retina the role of the film or digital sensing array. This model is not only boring, but it is also of little value, failing as it does to explain the most exciting thing—how the image on the retina is created in the mind. It is this last step that permits a person to see the image. Consider what led to that point. The retina is in a real sense a portion of the surface of the brain, that portion where millions of points of light that make up an image of the world are focused by the lens. Those points of light are then carried to another part of the brain by the optic nerve, which is a bundle of fibers, each connected to a single "pixel" of the retina. How the brain then interprets those many data points so as to produce a sensation of seeing has been studied for a very long time. It has been established that seeing consists of the brain matching up signal patterns received from the optic nerve with patterns that it (the brain) has encountered previously and stored. For the brain to interpret visual data correctly, it must be trained to identify a particular pattern with a particular type of object. Pattern acquiring is one of the most important things a baby is

(continues)

(continued)

doing while looking at and handling toys and other objects. A lifetime of such interactions with the outside world results in the brain containing many, many patterns. This is the image database to which it refers when presented with a signal from the optic nerve, trying to match that signal to one of its stored images, be it a friend's face, a running child, or a vertical post. Analogous to email software using previously stored information to complete automatically email addresses after one has typed a few characters on the address line, the brain quickly conjures up an image as soon as it has processed the first small amount of visual information received. Just as does the address-completing email software, it makes errors. Thus the first thing a person thinks he or she sees can be incorrect partially (a face, but the wrong one) or incorrect completely (an alligator instead of a tree branch). It should be clear, then, why careful users of language, in describing a forensic investigation, avoid the word *see* as in "at this point the driver could first see the tree." Generally, the location that the uninitiated would identify as the point where the driver could first see the tree is merely the location at which the tree could first have entered the driver's field of vision. That location would be the first place where, if the driver was looking in the direction of the tree, an image of the tree would first be focused on the retinas of the driver's eyes. The time interval between the instant an object enters the field of vision of a person and the instant the person correctly sees the object is the perception time. In general, the word *see* in its various forms should be replaced by *perceive* in its various forms.

The next surprise to those who have not thought about the perception mechanism is the length of the perception time. It should not be surprising, however, that an unexpected object will take longer to be perceived than an expected object and that an object that is very much unexpected will take much longer to be perceived. A simple, well-known and well-lit hazard, will require three-quarters of a second (0.75 sec) to be perceived by most drivers. This is about the time that it takes for a pencil to strike the floor after being dropped from a height of 9 feet (2.7 m). While seeming very short, it is enough time for a 40 miles per hour (64 km/hr) car to travel 45 feet (13.7 m). When the hazard that enters the field of vision of the driver is unfamiliar or is difficult to make out because of low light, the perception time can be five seconds or longer!

Even after perceiving a hazard, a driver takes a finite time deciding how to react, that is, deciding what action to take to avoid the hazard and then to take it. During this period, the reaction time, the vehicle continues moving, usually at a constant speed. Between the instant a hazard enters the field of vision of an automobile driver, and the instant the driver takes evasive action such as swerving or braking, the vehicle travels a distance equal to its speed multiplied by the perception time plus the reaction time: the PRT. Just as with perception time, the reaction time varies depending on the circumstances. The easier the decision, the shorter the reaction time. Once one perceives a child dashing in front of one's car, the decision as to what to do does not require much of a thought process, and the reaction time may be three-quarters of a second or even shorter. Thus, when the hazard is simple and the proper reaction obvious, the total PRT can be as short as 1.5 seconds. Most police investigators take this number as a rule of thumb in doing their accident reconstructions. However, since perception time can be much longer than 0.75 seconds and reaction time can also be longer than 0.75 seconds, it is important not to automatically use 1.5 seconds as the PRT for an accident reconstruction. At the very least, one must be aware that in using it that one is making a key assumption that may not be correct.

A final word on the subject is directed to the skeptic who insists that he or she can spot and react to something in a much shorter time than 1.5 seconds, citing, for example, his tennis game. It is of course true that for objects that are expected to a very high degree and that require a simple, well-practiced reaction, the PRT can be much less

(continues)

(continued)

than 1.5 seconds. Under such circumstances, the reaction as well as the perception is an automatic process. The champion tennis player returns the blazing shot across the net in a tenth of a second or faster, his or her brain having matched up the reaction required with the speed and angle of the ball, drawing on information stored from practice and previous matches. That does not have any relevance for the operation of a motor vehicle. Thousands of tests have demonstrated that most drivers cannot perceive and react to even simple hazards in less than 1.5 seconds.

In summary, it is wrong to say that a driver saw or should have seen a hazard simply because there was a straight line of sight between the driver and the hazard. It is wrong because of the impossibility of instantaneously perceiving an object that enters one's field of vision. Further, an objective accident reconstructionist recognizes that a good driver continually changes the direction of his or her gaze and that it is only when the driver's gaze is directed toward the hazard that the hazard enters the driver's field of vision.

PLACING THE HIT-AND-RUN VEHICLE

To determine where the vehicle was when the hazard first entered the field of vision of the hit-and-run driver, the investigator worked backward from the start of the ghost marks. Given the obviousness of the hazard, the time of day, and the straightforward reaction required, it was reasonable to use the rule-of-thumb value for the PRT: 1.5 seconds. It was also reasonable and standard practice to assume that the vehicle traveled at a constant speed during that 1.5 seconds. At a speed of 55 miles per hour (80 feet per second) (24.5 m/s), the vehicle traveled 120 feet (37 m) during the 1.5 seconds between the hazard entering the driver's field of vision and the instant that the first ghost mark was put down on the road. Note that this says nothing about when the hazard *could* have entered the field of vision. Because of the straight, clear road, that might have occurred much earlier.

Given the 120 feet (37 m) covered during the PRT and the 130-foot (40-m) skid distance, the vehicle traveled a total of 250 feet (76 m) between the instant that the hazard entered the driver's field of vision and the instant that the vehicle came to a halt—approximately 88 feet (27 m) after striking the girl, as marked by the sneaker scuff about 42 feet (13 m) into the skid. The conclusion is that when the hazard entered the driver's field of vision, the girl was 250 − 88 = 162 feet (49 m) from the car.

Now for the crux of the but-for question. Would the girl have been hit had the vehicle been traveling 40 miles per hour (59 ft/sec, 18 m/s) instead of 55 miles per hour (80 ft/sec, 24.5 m/s) at the instant that the hazard entered the driver's field of vision? During the 1.5-second PRT, it would have traveled only 87 feet (26 m) instead of 120 feet (37 m). How far would it have skidded starting at the lower speed? As will be shown later, the skid-to-a-stop distance is proportional to the square of the vehicle's speed. This means, for example, that if the starting speed is cut in half, the length of the skid will be one-fourth as long. Similarly, given a skid of 130 feet (40 m) starting at 55 miles per hour (88 km/hr), the skid starting at 40 miles per hour (64 km/hr) will be $(40/55)^2$ times 130 feet: approximately 69 feet (21 m).

Therefore, had the vehicle speed been 40 miles per hour (64 km/hr), the total distance traveled between the instant that the hazard entered the field of vision of the driver and the instant the car halted would have been 87 feet + 69 feet, which is 156 feet (48 m). The police accident reconstructionist concludes, therefore, that had the driver been operating at the speed limit, the impact with the girl would not have occurred since she was 162 feet (49 m) away when the sequence began. He believes that the driver, when caught, should be charged with aggravated assault or vehicular homicide, depending on the outcome of the victim's treatment.

There are two things wrong with the reconstructionist's conclusion. The more important is that given the assumptions made, especially about PRT, the difference between 162 feet (49 m) and 156 feet (48 m) is not enough to support a criminal prosecution for aggravated assault or vehicular homicide. Recall from the discussion in chapter 1 that the prosecutor, to obtain a conviction on those charges, must prove beyond a reasonable doubt that but for the speeding, the girl would not have been struck. The fact that the reconstructionist recommended such prosecution probably reflected inexperience. However, he made an error that if not caught by his reviewing officer has the potential for serious embarrassment. Throughout the calculations reported above, the unstated assumption was that, at any given instant of the skid, the position of the front of the car was defined by where the skidding tires were marking the pavement. In fact, the rear tires made the skid marks, and the front bumper presumably struck the girl. Typically, the front bumper is 10 to 12 feet (3 to 4 m) ahead of the rear axle of a car or light truck.

As an exercise, take the role of the police supervisor and redo the calculation assuming that the front bumper is 10 feet (3 m) in front of the rear tires. Note all of the changes that follow in the numbers calculated above. For example, what is the distance between the girl and the front bumper of the vehicle when the hazard entered the field of vision of the driver with the vehicle going 55 miles per hour (88 km/hr)? By assumption, in the actual case, the front bumper of the vehicle ended up 10 feet (3 m) beyond the end of the skid marks when the vehicle came to rest. Where would it end up had the vehicle been going 40 miles per hour (64 km/hr)?

Before leaving the hit-and-run case, the key evidence and assumptions will be summarized. The main pieces of physical evidence were (a) the skid marks, (b) the sneaker scuff, and (c) the victim's point of rest. From the skid marks, a reconstructionist could determine the following:

1. the direction of the skid;

2. that the rear tires and not the front tires were skidding, suggesting a car with out-of-adjustment brakes or an empty pickup truck without antilock brakes;

3. the distance between the right and left rear tires on the vehicle;

4. the tread pattern and tread width on the rear tires of the vehicle; and

5. the speed of the vehicle at the point when the tires started skidding.

From the sneaker scuff, the reconstructionist could draw a reasonable conclusion as to where impact occurred. From the distance between the sneaker scuff and the victim's rest position, the reconstructionist could make an estimate of the vehicle speed at impact. The reconstructionist chose not to do this, but the technique he could have used will be discussed in the next chapter.

The assumptions used in the calculation of speed were that the friction between the tires and the road had its typical value for an asphalt road. For reasons to be explained in the sidebar on "Coefficient of Friction," the calculated speed will not be wrong significantly even if the actual value of the friction was somewhat different. The key assumption used in examining the "but-for" question was that the perception-reaction time of the driver was equal to the rule-of-thumb value of 1.5 seconds associated with simple hazards and simple reactions. Whenever the answer obtained for the "but-for" question is close, a range of values for the PRT must be used to see whether the answer changes; that is, calculations should also be done using a PRT of 1.3 seconds and a PRT of 1.7 seconds.

BACK TO BASICS

Throughout the hit-and-run discussion, both fundamental laws and not-so-fundamental circumstances were alluded to without further discussion. For example, there was no justification provided for the remarkable assertion that that one need not know anything about the vehicle that left the skid marks to calculate the speed of that vehicle. Furthermore, the assertion remains remarkable even if one accepts the statement that all tires used on cars and small trucks are made of material that in some sense have the same traction on a given road. It means, for example, that a 6,000-pound (26,700-N) Hummer rumbling down the road on huge deep-treaded tires at 60 miles per hour (96 km/hr) will take the same distance to skid to a stop as an 1,800-pound (8,000-N), skinny-tired Volkswagen (VW) traveling at 60 miles per hour (96 km/hr) will, provided only that the road is dry. How can this be? It can be for the same reason that the Hummer and the VW, driven off the edge of the Grand Canyon (or any other high place), will hit the bottom at the same time. That reason was revealed 500 years ago by the work of Galileo

Galilei (1564–1642) as built on by Sir Isaac Newton (1642–1727). After a sidebar on Galileo and a discussion of units and dimensions, Newton's laws of motion, which underlie all accident reconstruction and nearly everything else, will be introduced, all of the explanations deferred above will be seen to follow from them.

Since the time of Galileo, it has been accepted that, neglecting air resistance, freely falling objects accelerate at a constant rate that is the same for all objects, regardless of weight. For hundreds of years, that acceleration rate g has been known to be 32 ft/sec^2 (9.8 m/sec^2). The speed in feet per second of an object that has been falling for T seconds is therefore

$$V = 32T$$

But what on earth does the sec^2 term in the g = 32 ft/sec^2 (9.8 m/sec^2) expression mean? Everyone is familiar with units such as square miles or square meters since these are often used in describing the area of a farm or a city, such as in the statement "The island is nearly one square mile." But what can a square second be? Be assured that there is no such thing, that this form is just a handy way of writing the units in a compact manner. By reviewing the meaning of dimensions and units, first mentioned in the Introduction, the following sidebar on "Dimensions and Acceleration" should explain this and somewhat more.

Born the year of Galileo's death, Sir Isaac Newton (1642–1727) built on the work of Galileo to create his first masterpiece: the laws of motion. Newton's first law of motion can be stated as follows:

> An object will move at a constant speed in a straight line as long as no force is applied to the object.

Before Newton began to publish his ideas, the informed view regarding the motion of things was the Aristotelian one: Any object in motion slows down and stops of its own accord if there is nothing to keep it moving, an object's natural state being that of zero speed, that is, being at rest. This view prevailed even following the work of Galileo and the realization that planets and the Moon were individual objects moving

(continues on page 52)

Galileo Galilei (1564–1642): One of Newton's Giants

Galileo had the great good fortune of being able to introduce to the world a radically new view of a common event that had been observed as long as there had been creatures on Earth who were capable of observing objects falling to the ground. For all the generations before Galileo, people who thought about the subject of falling objects at all were convinced that the heavier the object, the faster it fell to the ground. The common people believed this because it seemed to make sense that the more effort it took to lift a rock, the faster the rock would fall back down again. The learned people had a more detailed belief but less justification for it. They believed that a two-pound rock falls to the ground in half the time required by a one-pound rock. More generally, they believed that any object's speed of fall V was directly proportional to its weight W, meaning that

$$V = KW,$$

where K is called the proportionality constant. Another way to state this is to say that the time taken to fall to the ground T is inversely proportional to the weight, that is, that

$$T = C/W$$

where C is a different proportionality constant. These learned men (they were all men) thought that they believed this for having been convinced by the pure reasoning of Aristotle (384–322 B.C.E.). Actually, they believed it to be true because Aristotle said so.

It is hard to fault the common view. But for being told that it was wrong, most people today would think that the heavier the object, the faster the fall. On the other hand, consider the detailed belief of the learned. It did not require much learning at all to see that it was absurd to think that a one-pound (4.45-N) weight takes 10 times as long to fall to Earth as a 10-pound (44.5-N) weight. Just look at the two objects fall. However, the common people did not have time for such things, if they even knew the learned theory, and the sages did not believe in studying

(continues)

(continued)

a phenomenon by actually observing it. Even greater than Galileo's contribution to the knowledge of how things fall was his emphasis on observation of nature as the path for understanding nature. The major interest here, however, is in what he concluded.

Just as Archimedes's memory is plagued by his cartoon self shouting "Eureka!," Galileo has his own cartoon memorialization, he being thought of as a man dropping things off the Leaning Tower of Pisa. Though he never mentioned the tower in his writings, he did report dropping objects from a height of 100 cubits (150 feet, 46 m) and finding negligible difference in the times that objects of different weight took to fall. For example, the following passage is translated from his book *Two New Sciences:*

> . . . The variation of speed in air between balls of gold, lead, copper . . . and other heavy materials is so slight that in a fall of one hundred cubits a ball of gold would not outstrip one of copper by as much as four fingers. Having observed this, I came to the conclusion that, in a medium totally devoid of all resistance, all bodies would fall with the same speed.

The Tower at Pisa tops out at 183 feet (56 m) but also provides lower points from which to drop things.

Having disproved the Aristotelian idea that the speed of fall is proportional to the weight, Galileo took a giant step further and theorized that in the absence of air resistance, the speed of fall would be completely independent of weight. This is very important. Contrary to common belief, Galileo did not prove that weight has no effect on the speed at which objects fall. In fact, given the limited scientific devices available at that time, he could not have proven this. But he did something much greater. From an experiment that suggested certain ideas to him, he developed a theory that (1) led to testable predictions and (2) opened up a new field of study, to be further advanced by others.

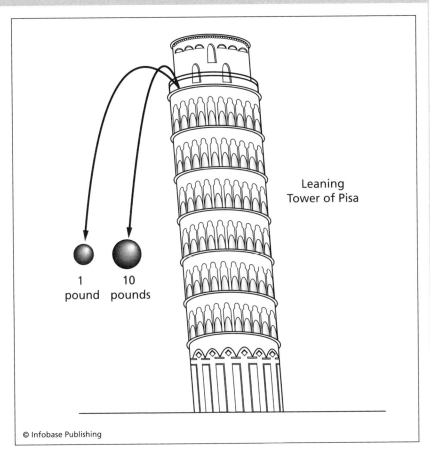

Leaning
Tower of Pisa

1
pound

10
pounds

© Infobase Publishing

The Tower of Pisa, from which Galileo is thought to have demonstrated that the speed of fall is independent of weight

Galileo makes clear in his *Two New Sciences* that he was not the first person to reveal Aristotle's error regarding falling objects. However, he had the influence, and he did the detailed work necessary to drive this lesson home, even for the sages. Moreover, based on his experiment, he theorized that for each second that an object falls, its speed

(continues)

(continued)

increases by the same amount. Thus, after falling for 20 seconds, an object's speed V will be 20 times what it was at the end of the first second of fall. This is the same as saying that the speed V is directly proportional to T, the time elapsed since the falling started.

$$V = gT$$

where g, a number, is the proportionality constant.

Something increasing in speed is said to be accelerating or under acceleration. Thus, Galileo's theory can be stated as follows: A freely falling object accelerates at a constant rate. The rate is the proportionality constant in the above equation, g. Galileo did not have the means to measure g precisely, but that did not stop him from making the effort. The value he reportedly obtained from observing falls of 100 cubits (183 feet, 46 m) was low by a factor of more than two from the actual value.

One very important conclusion can be drawn from the hypothesis that a falling object has a constant rate of acceleration and this is that the distance that the object falls in a given time interval is proportional to the square of that interval. That this is so can be seen as follows. If the acceleration of an object is constant over a time interval, the object's average speed during that interval is one-half the sum of its starting speed and its ending speed. In the special case where its starting speed is zero, Its average speed will be one-half its ending speed. In particular, an object starting from rest and falling for a time T with the acceleration due to gravity, g, will attain a speed of gT, and its average speed during that period will be $1/2gT$. It is a very general statement that a car or anything else that travels at an average speed V_{AVE} for a time T will travel a distance S equal to that average speed times the time that it traveled. That is, $S = V_{AVE}T$. So, when $V_{AVE} = \frac{1}{2}gT$, then $S = \frac{1}{2}gT^2$. There is nothing special about the acceleration rate for a falling object, which means that anything accelerating at a constant rate A, starting from a speed of zero, will, in a time T, travel a distance

$$S = \frac{1}{2}AT^2$$

Dimensions and Acceleration

The sidebar on "Units Systems and Dimensions" in chapter 1 introduced a topic that needs to be explored more fully at this point. Recall that, in contrast to the units chosen to express the size of a quantity, the quantity itself and its dimensions are fixed. They remain unchanged as one switches from one system of units to another. In particular, the dimensions of speed are always the length dimension over the time dimension, as indicated by the following dimension equation:

$$[\text{speed}] = L/T$$

where the square brackets mean "the dimensions of" whatever is within the brackets. L and T stand for the dimensions of length and time, respectively. Since speed has dimensions of length divided by time, a *change* in speed also has dimensions of length divided by time. For example, if a Volkswagen (VW) Beetle changes its speed from 50 miles per hour (80 km/hr) to 60 miles per hour (96 km/hr), the change is 10 miles per hour (16 km/hr). Since acceleration is not just a change in speed, but the rate at which speed is changing, the dimensions of acceleration are the dimensions of change of speed (the same as the dimensions of speed) divided by the dimension of time, namely,

$$[\text{acceleration}] = [\text{speed}]/T = (L/T)/T$$

Compound dimensions are simplified in the same way that fractions are. Just as $(8/13)/2 = 8/(13\times2) = 8/26$ and $(a/b)/b = a/bb = a/b^2$, $(L/T)/T = L/(T\times T) = L/T^2$. Thus, in the U.S. units, acceleration can be expressed in ft/sec^2 and in the S.I. as m/sec^2. This is where the peculiar form sec^2 arises. It does not imply that somewhere there are square seconds.

The value of g, the acceleration of a freely falling object, has a convenient size compared to the accelerations associated with motor vehicles and accident reconstruction. Therefore, those accelerations are often expressed as a multiple of g. For example, the 14.7 ft/sec^2 (4.5 m/sec^2) acceleration of the VW described above is slightly less than one-half g,

(continues)

(continued)

namely, 0.46*g*. Thus, it would be said that the VW considered above accelerated from 50 miles per hour (80 km/hr) to 60 miles per hour (96 km/hr) at an average rate of 0.46*g*. One benefit of this approach is that it eliminates the need to express acceleration numerically in both U.S. units and S.I. In this particular example, it also reveals immediately to persons familiar with VWs the implausibility of the statement. No VW Beetle traveling 50 miles per hour (80 km/hr) could accelerate so rapidly. A figure of 0.10*g* would be more like it, which, during one second, would cause the car to increase in speed by 3.2 ft/sec (0.98 m/s), which is 2.2 miles per hour (3.5 km/hr), taking it from 50 miles per hour (80 km/hr) to 52.2 miles per hour (84.0 km/hr).

(continued from page 46)

in orbits rather than being fixed on some kind of backdrop that rotated around Earth. As a consequence of that realization, a major intellectual challenge during the era following Galileo was to explain what kept the Moon and other celestial bodies moving. According to Aristotle, they should all be slowing down and stopping as they used up their motion.

Newton's first law effectively rephrased the question by asserting that it was natural for a free object such as the Moon, once it was set in motion, to continue in motion without slowing. Now the question became that of why that motion was not in a straight line, why it deviated so as to carry the Moon around Earth. The first law of motion implied that there must be a force on the Moon for this to occur. Determining the nature of that force led Newton to his second great creation: the theory of universal gravitation.

As with Archimedes and Galileo, Newton has associated with him legendary imagery lacking an historical basis. Archimedes had his bath, Galileo had his Leaning Tower, and in connection with his Theory of Gravitation, Newton has the apple tree. He is sometimes depicted of "discovering" gravity when an apple hit him on the head as he dozed

Newton is inescapably associated with falling apples, even though his discovery of the universal law of gravitation had no more to do with apples than it had to do with chipmunks. *(Hulton Archive/Getty Images)*

beneath the tree. If an apple entered Newton's thoughts it was in connection with his realization that the same force that pulled the apple down was what pulled on the Moon and the planets to keep them orbiting, the realization that put the "universal" in the theory of universal gravitation. Newton asserted that the only difference in the gravitational force between that on the apple and that on the Moon arose from the difference in their respective distances from the center of Earth. The fact that the force caused things to "gravitate" toward one another was what led Newton to label it *gravity* or *gravitation.* (Ponder the fact that until that time, not only did this sense of gravity not exist, its very concept was absent from human thought. It makes one wonder whether pre-Newtonian people even saw the same thing when they looked at the Moon as those coming afterward did and do.)

In a display of modesty unusual for him, Newton said that he had stood on the shoulders of giants to see a bit farther than others in his discoveries. The giants included not only Galileo but also Johannes Kepler (1571–1630) and Tycho Brahe (1546–1601), who had assembled earlier the precise orbital data needed to confirm the theory of universal gravitation.

VELOCITY

The first law of motion was said to require an object to continue to move at a constant speed in a straight line if no force is applied to it. This is a correct statement. However, it does not give the full strength of the first law, which is now stated as follows with more of its information content:

> An object will not be accelerated in a particular direction if there is no force applied directly to the object that pushes or pulls it in that direction.

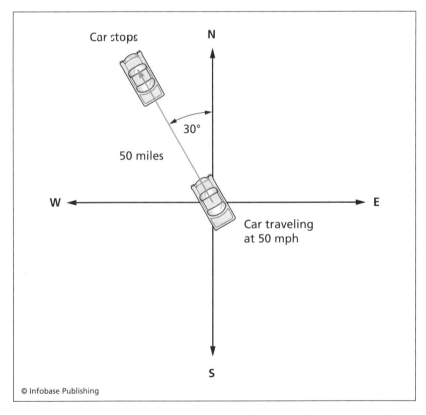

Illustration of the movement through space of a car traveling at a particular speed in a particular direction

To help convey the significance of the first law stated in this fuller manner, velocity will now be introduced. Earlier it was remarked that *velocity* and *speed,* though words used interchangeably in common speech, have different meanings. A car's speed is the size (magnitude) of its velocity. To state the velocity of a car, it is necessary to state the car's direction of motion as well as its speed. The symbol representing velocity is usually written in boldface as *V* to distinguish it from *V,* used to indicate speed. The figure shows the starting and ending points of a car that traveled at 50 miles per hour (80 km/hr) in the direction shown by the arrow. The arrow makes an angle of 30° with respect to straight north, a direction called 30° west of north. If the car has traveled for an hour at this velocity, it will have gone 50 miles (80 km) in that direction. It will therefore be 25 miles (40 km) west of its starting point (the sine of 30° is 0.50) and 43.3 miles (69.7 km) north of its starting point (the cosine of 30° is 0.866.)

In a sense, the speed of the car to the west was 30 miles per hour (48 km/hr) and its speed to the north was 43.3 miles per hour (69.7 km/hr). These directions are perpendicular to one another. Newton's laws of motion operate in each direction independently. Therefore, instead of being a single rule, the first law of motion is two rules if one is dealing with two dimensions and three laws if one is dealing with three dimensions. It translates into the following:

> An object will not undergo acceleration to the west unless acted on by a force directed to the west or to the east

and

> An object will not undergo acceleration to the north unless acted on by a force directed to the north or to the south.

Throughout this discussion and what follows, the word *acceleration* means a change of speed and not just an increase in speed, though occasionally the word *deceleration* will be used to indicate a reduction in speed, following common usage.

Think what this means. If a car is heading straight north at 50 miles per hour (80 km/hr) when a force begins pushing it to the east, it will begin to have motion to the east, resulting in a change in its velocity. However, since there was no force in the direction of its original motion, its speed to the north remains unchanged at 50 miles per hour. Since it is now moving at some speed to the east, its velocity will no longer be straight north but will be to the east of north to some extent. It can be said that the component of the car's velocity in the north direction remains at 50 miles per hour but that the velocity now has an increasing component in the east direction as well. Since velocity has direction as well as magnitude, so does acceleration, the rate at which the velocity is changing. Hence, acceleration in general is written with a boldface symbol such as **A**.

Although one can talk of the force in a particular direction, in general one describes a force by its magnitude (strength) and its direction. This is exactly the pattern used for describing velocity, and the symbol for force is also in general written in boldface, for the same reason: **F**.

From the definition of velocity, it is seen that a car's velocity changes whenever its direction of motion changes, regardless of whether the speed changes. With this in mind, the first law can be written yet again, with more content:

> An object has a constant velocity If And Only If it has no force applied to it.

Going one step further than the first law, but not as far as the second law, it can be said that:

> An object with force **F** applied to it will be accelerated in the direction of **F**.

Although the Moon's speed is essentially constant, its velocity continuously changes. It is constantly being accelerated as a result of the gravitational force. Newton introduced the word *centripetal* for a force causing an object to follow a curved path and the term *centripetal acceleration* for the acceleration occurring as a result of such a force. Centripetal force and centripetal acceleration play very important roles in accident reconstruction and underlie one of the most powerful techniques for determining speed: the Critical-Speed Scuff Mark technique to be presented in chapter 4.

Newton's second law of motion can be stated as follows:

A force *F* applied to an object accelerates the object in the direction of *F* at a rate directly proportional to the strength of the force and inversely proportional to the mass of the object.

Using **F**, **A**, and *M* to represent the force applied to an object, the acceleration of the object, and mass of the object, respectively, the second law can be written very simply, as follows:

$$A = F/M$$

As stated, the symbols for force and acceleration are made boldface to emphasize that they represent direction as well as magnitude.

Multiplying both sides of the above equation by *M* yields:1

$$F = MA$$

Newton's laws of motion form the rock on which all accident reconstructions rest. Describing (or controlling, depending on one's point of view) how the motion of cars and everything else changes when they are pushed or pulled, these laws combine three basic concepts: acceleration, mass, and force. *Acceleration* was first discussed in terms of the rate of change of speed and now in terms of the rate of change of velocity. *Force,* not defined yet apart from how it appears in Newton's laws of motion, is in fact defined by those laws. It is defined in connection with what it does. It is a push or a pull on something. Metaphysical or metaphorical uses of the word such as "he is a force for good in the community" and "may the force be with you," have no place here. Some examples of correct usage: The skidding tires applied a force on the car causing it to slow down; the force of the rear-end collision on the small car accelerated it forward into the intersection; the force of gravity on the "airborne" car caused it to fall to Earth; the truck's trailer hitch applied the force to the trailer that made the trailer follow the truck.

MASS

Mass, the remaining actor in the laws of motion, is often mistakenly thought of as just another word for *weight.* It is not weight, though an object's mass determines the object's weight on Earth, where weight is the force pulling an object toward the ground (actually toward the center of the Earth, but the ground gets in the way). A heavy object is referred to as "massive." However, an object can be massive and yet will have no weight at all in the absence of gravity. Mass is that property of an object that makes it difficult to change its velocity, to accelerate it. This is the essence of the second law stated above. Along with length and time, mass is one of the three fundamental dimensions of nature. In the U.S. system, the unit for mass is given the name *slug*. From the relationship $F = MA$, the force dimension can be stated in terms of the fundamental dimensions. From the earlier discussion of dimensions, this can be stated as $[F] = [M][A] = [M]L/T^2$. Substituting U.S. units, in which the unit for force is the pound, the equation relating the dimensions becomes

$$pound = slug\text{-}ft/sec^2$$

The *pound* is defined as the force that when applied to an object having a mass of one slug causes that object to accelerate at one foot per second per second. Thus the definition can be stated as follows:

A force of one pound applied to a object having a mass of one slug accelerates the object one foot per second per second.

In the S.I., the name for the mass unit is the kilogram (kg). Recalling that the unit for force in the S.I. is the newton, the S.I. definition corresponding to that just stated for U.S. units is as follows:

A force of one newton applied to a mass of one kilogram accelerates the mass one meter per second per second.

Many modern cars can accelerate from rest to 60 miles per hour (96 km/hr) in 6 seconds, an average acceleration of 10 miles per hour per second (16 km/hr per second), which is 0.46g. A typical weight for a midsize U.S. car is 3,200 pounds (14,234 N), a weight corresponding to a mass of 100 slugs (1460 kg). What is the force F in pounds needed to accelerate this car at 0.46g? From $F = MA$, $F = 100 \times 0.46 \times 32 = 1,472$ pounds or, with rounding, 1,470 pounds. Alternatively, working in the S.I. the result in Newtons can be found similarly: $F = 1,460 \times 0.46 \times 9.8 = 6,582$ N or, with rounding, 6,580 N. To convert the numerical expression for force in Newtons to a numerical expression of the same force in pounds, multiple by the conversion factor 0.2248 pound/N; to go the other way, multiply by the inverse conversion factor 4.448 N/pound. For example, a ton of coal weighs 2,000 pounds (8,896 N).

In addition to force, mass, and acceleration, there is a fourth concept—*energy*—associated with the modern application of Newton's laws. Its significance was not realized until centuries after Newton. Energy will be dealt with in the next chapter, where it will be shown to greatly simplify a number of accident reconstruction calculations.

Following the sidebar on "Coefficient of Friction," Newton's laws of motion will be used to show why a vehicle skids to a stop in a distance proportional to the square of its speed and why that distance does not depend on the weight of the vehicle; that is, the skid-to-a-stop formula will be derived from Newton's laws.

Coefficient of Friction

Everyone becomes familiar with friction in earliest childhood. Friction leads to scuffed knees; friction warms one's hands when they are rubbed together; reducing friction by icing over the tennis court allows one to slide across it and to ice skate; and so on. The familiarity that everyone has with friction makes it seem to be of a lowly and uninteresting nature compared to other sights and events one encounters in the physical world. Actually, it turns out to be not only one of the most important forces but also to be startlingly interesting.

Friction is a surface thing. It is a force that resists one surface sliding across another surface. Its twofold nature can be illustrated by a brick resting on a horizontal tabletop, in which case the surfaces are respectively the bottom of the brick and the top of the table. Once someone tries to slide the brick by pushing on it parallel to the tabletop, friction between the two surfaces prevents the brick from moving until the pushing force has exceeded a certain threshold level. The reason it does not start sliding is that the frictional force opposing the

(continues)

(continued)

movement is exactly equal to the force applied by the person and in exactly the opposite direction. As the person increases the force on the brick, the frictional force increases at exactly the same rate and continues to do so as long as the brick does not move. This automatic adjustment is one of the interesting things about the frictional force. Eventually, the person increases the force to the point where the brick starts moving. What happened is that the external force became greater than the maximum frictional force that could be generated between the bottom surface of the brick and the top surface of the table. Once the sliding starts, the frictional force resisting the sliding remains constant, and equal to the maximum frictional force available.

One often describes two surfaces in contact with one another as creating an *interface*. The frictional force arises at the interface between the bottom of the brick and the top of the table. Although these two surfaces look very simple, they are not simple at all when examined at a microscopic level, the level at which the frictional force is generated. Instead of being smooth, each consists of many tiny pits and peaks, and much of the frictional force is due to the peaks of one surface descending into the pits of the opposite surface, in a microscopic interlocking. This continues to be the case once the brick starts sliding, so that the tiny peaks on one surface plunge into and are dragged out of pits on the other surface. At any instant, only a small fraction of the total surface areas will be in direct contact. Although one might conclude that this complicated behavior would make the description of the friction force equally complicated, it does not. In fact, the friction forces at a wide range of interfaces display the same simple behavior, one characterized by a coefficient of friction. For all interfaces describable by a coefficient of friction, it is possible through a single measurement to determine what the frictional force will be for a wide range of conditions.

What does this mean? And what does a wide range of conditions mean in this context? To say that the sliding of an object across a particular surface is characterized by a coefficient of friction means that the maximum frictional force resisting the sliding (1) is directly proportional to the weight of the object, (2) does not depend on the area of contact between the object and the surface, and (3) does not depend on the speed with which the object is being pushed across the surface. These three statements boil down to saying that the force resisting the sliding—the frictional force F_f—is directly proportional to the force F_N pressing the two surfaces together, and that it depends on nothing else. To see how this works, consider again the brick on the table. If the brick weighs 20 pounds (89 N) and one must push on it parallel to the table with a force of 10 pounds (44.5 N) to make it slide across the table at a constant speed, the coefficient of friction for the brick/table interface is 0.5. Furthermore, if one grinds a pattern into the bottom of the brick so that when the brick is returned to the table it is supported by only a small fraction of the original surface, one will find that the force required to slide it has not changed (presuming that the grinding did not significantly reduce the brick's weigh). In short, the frictional force does not depend on the area of contact. Next, assume that one places an eight-pound (36-N) piece of lead on top of the brick. Now, the frictional force (F_f) will be 14 pounds (62.3 N), namely the total weight (F_N) multiplied by the brick/table coefficient of friction, 0.5.

Consider what it means that the tire/pavement interface is subject to a coefficient of friction. It means, for example, that the frictional force resisting the slide of a tire skidding across dry pavement depends not at all on how fancy the tread pattern is. The frictional force will be the same for a new snow tire as it is for a bald tire. It will depend on the weight that the tire is supporting and nothing else. The fact that tread does not improve dry-road traction should be no surprise to those familiar with NASCAR events, where "racing slicks" are the tires of choice.

Another amazing thing is the simple dependence of the frictional force F_f on the force F_N pressing the surfaces together. (The subscript in F_N comes from the reference to "normal force," the word *normal* used to mean perpendicular to the interface, as opposed to the frictional

(continues)

(continued)

force, which is parallel to the interface.) Given the complex interaction between the surfaces, one might expect a more complicated change in frictional force as F_N increases strongly. However, in the case of vehicle tires, the force F_N pressing the tire against the pavement can increase by a factor of 100 or more without a change in the simple proportionality. If the frictional force on a sliding tire supporting 30 pounds (130 N) is 24 pounds (107 N)—which is the case for a coefficient of friction of 0.8 (24/30), the frictional force when that tire is supporting 1,000 pounds will be $0.8 \times 1,000 = 800$ pounds (3,560 N) and so on.

Yet another unexpected and useful aspect of coefficient of friction is that it does not depend on the speed of the slide.

Since the coefficient of friction is independent of weight, one need not have a car with the weight of the unknown car to obtain the coefficient needed to calculate the speed of the car that left skid marks of interest. One just needs to measure the tire/pavement coefficient of friction on the road where the marks were made, and this can be done with any car.

The coefficient of friction is usually represented by the Greek letter μ (written in Latin letters as "mu") [myew] or, less often, by the letter *f*. The frictional force can then be stated in terms of the normal force as

$$F_f = \mu F_N$$

For the frictional force of most interest here, the normal force is the weight supported by the individual tire. Thus the frictional force resisting the skidding of tire 1 is $F_{f1} = \mu w_1$, w_1 being the weight supported by tire 1. But the total frictional force acting to slow the vehicle is the sum of the frictional forces against the individual tires. Therefore, the total frictional force F_f on a four-wheel vehicle with all its tires sliding is

$$F_f = \mu (w_1 + w_2 + w_3 + w_4)$$

The term in parentheses is the sum of the weights supported by the individual tires, which is, of course, the total weight *W* of the vehicle. Therefore, the frictional force on the sliding vehicle is simply

$$F_f = \mu W$$

From the sidebar on "Coefficient of Friction," a skidding car will be acted on (slowed) by a frictional force F_f proportional to the weight of the car,

$$F_f = \mu W$$

This force will continue as long as the car is skidding and will fall abruptly to zero once the skid stops. Since the weight is proportional to the mass M of the car, $F_f = \mu gM$. This is the force slowing the car. But from Newton's second law, the car of mass M with force $F_f = \mu gM$ acting on it will display an acceleration A, where A must satisfy the equality

$$\mu gM = MA$$

Therefore $A = \mu g$. So, without going farther, it has been demonstrated that the deceleration of the skidding car is independent of the car's mass, which means that it is independent of the car's weight. Since the deceleration is constant, the average speed during the skid equals one-half the sum of the speed at the start of the skid (V) and the speed at the end the skid (zero). The average speed during the skid is ½ V. But the average speed multiplied by the time t of the skid will be the distance the car goes while skidding, the car's skid distance. With an acceleration of g, the time t required for the speed to change by an amount V is $t = V/\mu g$. The skid distance S is equal to this time multiplied by the average speed, or

$$S = (V/2)(V/\mu g) = \tfrac{1}{2}V^2/\mu g$$

Rearranging, the expression becomes one for V in terms of S, that is,

$$V = (2S\mu g)^{1/2}$$

(Recall that a superscript one-half means that the square root is to be taken of the number inside the parentheses.)

Thus, the statements made during the discussion of the hit-and-run vehicle are shown to have been correct. The skid distance is proportional to the square of the speed and inversely proportional to the coefficient of friction, and the speed calculated from the distance is proportional to the square root of the coefficient of friction. The expression for S shows that the smaller the value of μ, the farther the car will skid. On a slippery road, a car takes a long distance to stop, as everyone knows. In contrast, not everyone is so familiar with the way S varies with speed. The above relation shows that a car traveling 80 miles per hour (130 km/hr) will skid sixteen times as far as a car traveling 20 miles per hour (32 km/hr). Thus, even without taking into account the much greater distance the car will travel during the PRT, it can be said that the faster car requires sixteen times the stopping distance as the slower one once the brakes are fully on—typically 320 feet (98 m) instead of 20 feet (6 m).

In manuals used by accident reconstructionists, and especially those in the police agencies across the United States, a modified form for the skid-to-a-stop expression is often given, one that directly gives the speed in miles per hour (V_{mph}) when one inserts the skid distance in feet:

$$V_{mph} = (30S\mu)^{1/2}$$

By substituting in the value for g in the U.S. system in the earlier equation, show how this form for V_{mph} can be obtained. Hint: to change an expression in miles per hour to one in feet per second, use the fact that a mile is 5,280 feet and an hour is 3,600 seconds.

The counterpart in S.I. is obtained directly after substituting in the skid distance in meters, namely

$$V_{km/hr} = (19.6S\mu)^{1/2}$$

where $V_{km/hr}$ is the starting speed in kilometers per hour.

MEASURING THE COEFFICIENT OF FRICTION

The final point to be addressed is the method for measuring the tire/pavement coefficient of friction μ at accident sites. The simplest technique uses a sled constructed so as to present to the pavement a segment of tire tread. A fish-scale-like device is used to measure the force required to drag the sled across the pavement of interest. It is important, and somewhat difficult, to ensure that the pulling force is exerted parallel to the pavement. Assuming that that is done, the tire/pavement coefficient of friction equals that force divided by the weight of the sled, which is typically about 30 pounds (133 N). Thus, if 24 pounds (107 N)

Tire/pavement coefficient of friction tested by skidding to a stop, the smoke suggesting how hard this test method is on tires *(Joseph Keierleber)*

is required to drag a 30-pound (133-N) sled across the pavement, the tire/pavement coefficient of friction is 24/30 = 0.8. Good practice dictates that the investigator make several runs with the sled to ensure that the readings are reproducible.

Done with care, drag-sled measurements usually provide sufficiently precise values for μ. Occasionally, dirt or other material on the road surface can skew the reading from a drag sled. A more dependable approach overall is to do test skids using a car or light truck. Years ago, such tests involved skidding to a stop from measured speeds of 30 to 35 miles per hour (48 to 56 km/hr), after which the skid length was measured and the skid-to-a-stop formula used to calculate μ. This method had two serious drawbacks. It was destructive of tires, since several test skids would be done each time, and it severely complicated the work of investigators who arrived later to find the accident site crisscrossed with skid marks from police cars. More important, however, was that it gave the wrong results, with calculated μ values as high as 1.2 being obtained on pavements where the true tire/pavement μ was 0.7 to 0.8. The error came from ignoring the distance over which braking occurred before skid marks began. Currently, the preferred method involves doing a one- to two-second test skid in a car containing a simple accelerometer. The accelerometer measures and records the deceleration of the test vehicle every tenth of a second or less. Combining Newton's law, $F = MA$, and the expression for the frictional force $F_f = \mu W$ leads to $\mu W = MA$. Then, since $W = Mg$, a further combination leads to : $g = A$ and

$$\mu = A/g$$

In short, the coefficient of friction, μ, is the deceleration in units of g of the skidding vehicle.

Although the accident reconstructionist always prefers to have a measured value of μ, it is not a disaster to the reconstruction if that number is not available. This is fortunate since often an investigator is brought in on a case where the original investigator failed to measure μ and the road was resurfaced after the crash. From the expression created above, it can be seen that the speed calculated from skid marks is relatively "insensitive" to μ, that is, it does not change rapidly as μ changes since it is proportional to the square root of μ:

$$V = (2gS\mu)^{1/2}$$

Essentially no dry concrete or asphalt road surface exists that results in a tire/pavement value for μ outside the range 0.6 to 1.0. Furthermore, the vast majority of roads lead to a μ value of between 0.7 and 0.9. Reflect now on the hit-and-run case that opened this chapter and the reference to "the typical friction for a highway like this." What that statement meant was that 0.8 was being used for μ, resulting in a calculated speed of 55 miles per hour (88 km/hr) from the 130 feet (40 m) of skid marks. By how much would this result be in error if the actual value of μ was 0.7? Since the calculated speed varies with the square root of μ, the answer with: $= 0.7$ will be $(0.7/0.8)^{1/2} = 0.94$ times the value obtained taking $\mu = 0.8$. That is, it will be 52 miles per hour (84 km/hr) instead of 55 miles per hour (88 km/hr). Similarly, if the correct value was 0.9 instead of 0.8, the correct speed will be $(0.9/0.8)^{1/2} = 1.06$ times 55 miles per hour (88 km/hr), which is 58 miles per hour (93 km/hr).

Thus, it has been shown that around a µ of 0.8, an error of approximately 12 percent in µ will lead to an error in the calculated speed of only about 6 percent. One would say that the expression for speed is "robust" against errors in µ. This is true within the limits by which µ can reasonably expected to be wrong, that is, for dry pavement. However, one can end up with a huge overestimate of speed if one assumes µ to have been 0.8 whereas in fact at the time of the accident the road was covered with a thin film of ice. The opposite error is not possible because of the upper limits on the tire/pavement coefficient of friction. Although the soft tires used on some racing vehicles can be higher, it never exceeds 1.0 for normal automobile tires on the roads of the United States and Canada.

STATIC VERSUS SLIDING FRICTION AND ANTILOCK BRAKE SYSTEMS

In all of the discussion so far, there has only be one type of tire/pavement coefficient of friction referred to—that of the sliding tire. It turns out that for most pairs of surfaces, a little more force is required to start them sliding than is required to keep them sliding. In terms of the coefficient of friction language, one says that the static coefficient of friction is greater than the sliding coefficient of friction. If the coefficient of friction for car tires sliding on a particular stretch of road is 0.75, it might be found that the force required to start the sliding reflects a coefficient of friction of 0.80 or even a bit higher. Antilock brake systems (which have received the unfortunate acronym *ABS*) take advantage of that difference by seeking to ensure that the vehicle's tires are always on the verge of sliding. When the driver of an ABS-equipped car pushes down hard on the brake pedal, the brakes applied to each wheel increase in force up to the point where the tire starts sliding. At that point, the system causes the brake force at the wheel to be reduced. With the wheel again rolling normally, the system permits the brake force to increase again to the point of the tire sliding, then reduces it and so forth. This cycling of the brake force occurs many times a second and in this way maintains the wheel just at the point of sliding, thereby taking advantage of the higher coefficient of friction at that point to achieve a higher deceleration of the car. Depending on the ABS system, the driver may be able to detect this cycling in the form of a pulsing of the brake pedal. ABS systems seem to be particularly beneficial for straight-line stopping on surfaces made slippery by rain or snow.

Because of the way in which ABS systems pulse the brakes, a hard-braked car no longer leaves such nice visible skid marks, as shown in the figures early in this chapter. On the other hand, they usually do cause some kind of tire mark on the road. Recall that they operate by sensing when each tire just starts to slide, at which point they back off on the braking on that wheel. Thus, during hard braking, many ABS-equipped cars leave tire marks made up of a series of short, faint, black segments. Usually, the black segments are not very black. These marks will continue for the duration of the hard braking, their total length reflecting the distance along the road that the vehicle took to come to a halt. In other words, the skid-to-a-stop method of determining vehicle speed has not been made totally obsolete by the arrival of ABS. However, the faintness of the marks that are left means that time is even more of the essence in getting the measurements done. Actually, some versions of ABS contribute a new approach to the determination of speed, namely the ones that cycle with a constant frequency. If the braking cycles up to slip and then backs off ten times a second, the speed in feet per second or meters per second will be equal to ten times the distance—in feet or meters, respectively—between the onset of two successive black segments.

SUMMING UP

In this chapter, the basic elements of at-scene accident investigation were set out, including the measurements that are made for later use in identifying a car from its skid marks. In addition, the skid-to-a-stop formula was used in a real case. Next, as part of describing Galileo's use of the experimental method to show that the speed at which an object fell did not depend on weight, it was shown that when an object starting from rest and moving at a constant acceleration A will reach a speed VT after a time T at which point it will have traveled a distance one-half AT^2. Combining Galileo's work with the results of Newton's universal law of gravitation and the laws of motion, the universal skid-to-a-stop formula

$$V = (2g\mu S)^{1/2}$$

was derived. This was done by using:

1. Newton's second law of motion: $F = MA$,

2. the frictional force between pavement and sliding tires,

3. the fact that tire/pavement friction satisfies the coefficient-of-friction condition, and

4. the uniformity of modern automobile and small-truck tires with respect to friction.

It was therefore shown that the following skid-to-a-stop distance

$$S = \tfrac{1}{2}V^2/g\mu$$

is

1. the same for all cars and light trucks traveling at the same speed,

2. proportional to the square of the initial speed, and

3. proportional to $1/\mu$, where μ is the tire/pavement coefficient of friction on that road.

The chapter introduced perception-reaction time, nearly always a factor in an accident reconstruction, and emphasized the care one must take with the meaning of seeing.

Along the way, a number of details were alluded to, such as brake-lag time, air brakes, hydraulic brakes, and ABS brakes. Also, mention was made of important topics to come, including energy and centripetal acceleration.

3

Accident Reconstruction: Moving into High Gear

Much of chapter 2 was devoted to laying the groundwork for more serious ventures into the accident reconstruction field. It included a description of a fictitious hit-and-run case, in part for the purpose of introducing the skid-to-a-stop formula for calculating speed. After Newton's laws of motion were presented, the idea of force associated with those laws was used to show why the skid-to-a-stop formula has the form it does. This chapter will show how the speed of a car that went off a cliff can be found quickly by using the simplest of the ideas developed in chapter 2. The chapter will next introduce energy and work in their forensic form and demonstrate their strength by deriving once again the skid-to-a-stop formula. Then, moving from theory to the highway, several types of physical evidence will be examined. This evidence, though its creation follows directly from the laws of physics, is specific to motor-vehicle crashes and goes under such labels as signature marks, scuffs, gouges, hot shock, and cold shock. After that break from theory, Newton's third law of motion, the most important, will be presented and explained, thereby completing the picture of how cars and stars and everything else move and affect one another. At that point, attention shifts naturally to the momentous conservation of momentum, an absolute rule that follows directly from the laws. The power of conservation of momentum is then applied to accident reconstruction and other interactions between physical entities. Finally, the chapter concludes by de-mystifying black boxes, those electronic recorders in modern cars that are said to spy and inform on their owners.

HOW TO READ EQUATIONS

Describing the behavior of objects or persons with words requires the creation of sentences that must follow certain structural rules so as not to be confusing. Equations are statements about objects or persons that use symbols rather than words and which have many fewer rules to obey than do sentences. Although until one becomes comfortable with the equation way of speaking and writing it may seem hard to believe, the truth is that equations provide a much easier way than words to send and receive ideas and conclusions. Even if that was the only value of equations, they would still be worth using. The fact is, they provide much more. The equation rules allow the statements they represent to be moved about in such a way that surprising new ideas can arise from statements of obvious fact. Those who make the effort needed to become comfortable with equations will experience repeatedly the surprise and pleasure of discovering what may arise from their own equations. This chapter provides help in developing the needed "comfort" to understand how in some cases equations can replace an entire paragraph of sentences. Most people, including those who are old hands at equations, find it useful to read them while holding a writing device poised above paper. If the equations appear in a book they own, they prefer to write in the book's margins, continually checking the validity of the equations and the calculations produced by them. The best way to read calculations and statements based on calculations is to *do* the calculations, continually checking whether what the text says the equations stand for is correct. There are many ways in which this benefits the scholar. Confirmation reinforces the knowledge, which is good but not as useful as failing to find confirmation. This means either that the book is wrong—always a possibility—or that one has a misunderstanding that needs to be sorted out before reading further. As an aid to entering the world of physics, equations, and numbers, the forensic case immediately following requires only simple equations, yet uses them to come up with significant conclusions.

SMART CAR MYSTERY

The "smart car" is a relatively new entry into the North America automobile population. Characterized by a length that is not much greater than its width, this type of car has great appeal for urban drivers, who continually are in search of parking spaces. Given these cars' natural advantages in cities and their supposed lack of comfort on long trips, a pair of hikers in rural Montana were quite surprised to find a new smart car "parked" at the bottom of a sharp drop-off bordering a narrow mountain roadway. From the appearance of the terrain, it appeared to them that once the car left the shoulder of the road it had not been in contact with anything until it slammed into the flat horizontal surface where they found it. They were able to deduce the impact point from a collection of scratches and pitting they found near to where the car came to final rest. They found no one in or near the car, nor any indication that anyone had been in the car when it crashed. Finally, there was no note or any writing to explain what happened nor to identify the owner of the vehicle, which bore Nova Scotia license plates. Having completed their "forensic investigation" in short order, the hikers called the nearest police department, that of a small town 35 miles (56.3 km) away.

The law-enforcement officers who arrived in response to the call first spent time scouting around the road and roadside area above where the car rested. In the thin layer of dust alongside the road, they found two parallel tire tracks leading up to the edge of the drop-off. Looking in the book of vehicle specifications they had with them, they found that the separation between the tracks was consistent with the unusually narrow track width that was one of the defining features of smart cars. The tracks were perpendicular to the cliff edge and displayed the pattern associated with tires that are rolling, not skidding.

To make their measurements of the tire tracks most useful to later investigators, the police officers needed reference points for their measurements of the tracks. Since the surrounding region was remarkably

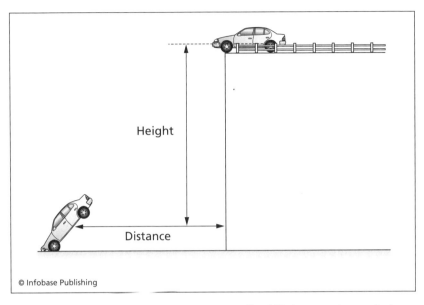

Schematic representation of a car plunging off a cliff, showing the vertical and horizontal distances traveled through the air by the car's center of mass during flight

empty of landmarks of even a semipermanent nature—such as utility poles, storm drains, pavement edges, and the like—the officers drove a number of nails into the hard surface, marking each with a letter created with a can of spray paint. After recording the track positions and orientation and photographically documenting them, the investigators turned to figuring out the speed of the car. They realized that they had a near-perfect situation for determining speed and, moreover, that having a figure for the speed would permit them to eliminate a few possible reasons for the car being so far below the road. They just needed two measurements: the vertical distance that the car fell and the horizontal distance that it traveled while falling that distance. In short, by measuring the vertical and horizontal distances from the car's take-off point to its impact point, they could quickly assess its speed. They figured that that speed would be quite low if the car had simply been shoved off the cliff, a manner of vehicle disposal not unknown in the region. Since there was no sign of a driver, they were hoping that that would be their finding. Only a few years earlier, the measurements they needed would have required a skilled surveyor and the delay and the expense to the county that that would entail. However, their department having equipped them with a total station and the equipment that went with it, the measurements could be made with ease and precision. The sidebar on "Total Stations" shows why.

Total Stations

When accident reconstructionists adopted the electronic surveying equipment known as the total station a few years ago, the mapping of accident sites was revolutionized. Scale diagrams that previously required four or five hours of tape-measure work followed by tedious, error-prone calculations can now be created by spending an hour at the site with a total station followed by a computer-assisted drawing session that lasts as little as a half-hour. With the total station, hundreds of position measurements precise to within a small fraction of an inch (centimeter) can be

The total station used to do forensic surveys, especially in accident reconstruction cases *(Joseph Keierleber)*

made within an hour. From its first use by accident reconstructionists, the total station has now spread throughout the forensic field to wherever position measurements are required. This includes the mapping of a wide variety of crime scenes both indoors and outdoors.

Usually, measurements with a total station are done by a two-person team. One person will hold a retro-reflecting target at each of the points that needs mapping. (Something is retro-reflecting if it reflects light back in exactly the direction from which it came. An important example is the tape used on clothing to make it especially visible at nighttime in automobile headlights.) The other person operates the total station. With the target at a desired location, which may be from a few feet up to thousands of feet away from the total station, the operator orients the total station on its swivel mount so that the target is centered in the

The police investigators found that the vertical distance of the impact marks from the take-off point was 120 feet (36 m) and that the horizontal distance was 40 feet (12 m). This was all the information they needed to determine take-off speed using nothing more than Galileo's

total station's telescope crosshairs. The operator then presses a button to take the measurement. This causes two things to happen. The two angles defining the target direction are recorded, and a laser beam having an intensity that varies regularly with time is directed to the target. The intensity of the reflected beam when it arrives back at the total station is different from that of the outgoing beam by an amount depending on the time required for the round-trip. The beam's travel distance, twice the separation of total station and target, is the round-trip time multiplied by the speed of light, c. In outer space (that is, in a vacuum), the speed of light is

$$c = 983{,}571{,}056 \text{ ft/sec (299,792,458 m/s)}$$

In air, it is slightly less, varying with the temperature of the air. At 60°F (15°C), speed of light in air is 983,298,564 ft/sec (299,435,082 m/s). These numbers with their many digits are given here to indicate the very high precision with which they are known. If the total station is 1,000 feet (305 m) from the target, the laser beam travels 2,000 feet (610 m) in its round-trip out to the target and back to the total station. Therefore, the time required for that trip is 0.00000204 seconds. Expressed in words, that time interval is two millionths of a second.

Each time the operator of the total station presses the button to measure a point, the total station registers the two angles that define the direction of the point of interest. It also registers the distance of the point. This is sufficient to locate the point in three-dimensional space. As soon as a second position is measured, the positions of those two points with respect to one another is known. Later, all of

(continues)

(continued)

the measured points are entered in a computer program that produces a scale diagram of the scene. Then, from measurements made by the police investigators at the scene, relevant objects that they recorded at the scene can be placed into the diagram, using the same computer process. For example, in the hit-and-run described in chapter 1, the police investigators measured the position of the victim's body relative to fixed objects such as the road edge and a utility pole. By ensuring that the total station mapping included those fixed objects, the body can be put into the scale drawing. It is usually the case that the site mapping is done long after the key physical evidence has been removed. However, if the scene investigation was done carefully, and the total station work includes the position of the same fixed points that the scene investigators used for references, that physical evidence can be placed accurately on the scale diagram.

observation that all free-falling objects have the same downward acceleration, *g*. From the discussion in the sidebar on Galileo in chapter 2, one knows that the relation between the distance the car fell, represented by *h*, and the length of time that the fall took, *t*, is the following:

$$h = \tfrac{1}{2}gt^2$$

Rearranging this equation, one can say that the time required to fall a distance *h* is

$$t = (2h/g)^{1/2}$$

(Recall that the exponent of ½ means that one is to take the square root of the term inside the parentheses. Recall also the multiplication convention being used, where symbols that are adjacent to one another on a line are to be multiplied together. Thus, gt^2 is to be read as "*g* multiplied by *t* squared" or "*g* times t^2." Finally the backslash is used to indicate division; so h/g means "h divided by g.") Replacing the symbols h and g by their numerical values, one finds that the smart car was falling for t = 2.74 seconds. Air resistance was neglected, as it normally can be with high-density objects.

But what about the fact that the car was also moving horizontally? Would that not have affected the fall time? Well, no, as can be seen from Newton's laws of motion and the discussion in chapter 2 and from what follows below.

Let F_V represent the force in the vertical direction on an object (more briefly stated, the vertical force) and F_H the force in the horizontal direction on an object (the horizontal force). Also, let A_V represent the object's acceleration in the vertical direction (the vertical acceleration) and A_H represent the object's horizontal acceleration. Recall from chapter 2 that an object's speed in a particular direction is not affected by a force that is perpendicular to that direction. Then, Newton's second law of motion provides the following two general equations for any object of mass M:

$$A_V = F_V/M$$

and

$$A_H = F_H/M$$

For the falling car, the vertical force is the gravitational force, $F_V = Mg$, so that the first equation above reduces to $A_V = F_V/M = g$. In contrast to Wile E. Coyote, who sometimes seems to be able to scramble horizontally back to the cliff edge without touching anything but air, the car, once it is off the cliff, has no horizontal force acting on it (that is, $F_H = 0$). $F_H = 0$ means that $A_H = 0$.

With no horizontal acceleration ($A_H = 0$), the car's horizontal speed remains the same for the entire trip down from the drop-off to the impact. To repeat, while the car is accelerating vertically downward, it is continuing to travel horizontally at a constant speed. Once its horizontal travel distance is determined, since its fall time calculated, its speed at take-off follows immediately. In this case, the fall time was t = 2.74 seconds, as shown above. During that time, the car traveled 40 feet (12 m) horizontally. If something travels a distance S in a particular

Roadrunner might well wonder why gravity was suspended for Wile E. Coyote running off a cliff (*Looney Tunes* characters, names, and all related indicia are trademarked, Warner Brothers Entertainment, Inc.)

direction during a time *T* at a constant speed, that constant speed must be *S/T*. Thus, for the smart car in this case, *V* = 40/2.74 = 14.6 feet/sec (4.45 m/s). In more familiar terms, the speed of the car as it left the cliff was 10 miles per hour (16 km/hr).

The problem seemed solved, but the investigators were not entirely pleased with the result. Given the narrowness of the road from which the car departed, it was doubtful that a person or persons pushing the car could have accelerated it to a speed of 10 miles per hour (16 km/hr) before it went over the edge. Also, since this happened on a curve in the narrow road, it seemed unlikely that the pushing could have been done by a vehicle. Pondering this, the police investigators returned to the take-off point—and realized that they had overlooked something significant. The run-up to the edge was not horizontal. In fact, the surface was such that the car would have been moving on a 15° incline as it approached the drop-off. What difference would that make? What errors were introduced by not taking that slope into account? The sidebar on the "Fall Formula" answers these questions while providing a fuller discussion of vehicles that fly through the air.

(continues on page 84)

Fall Formula

From the discussion of the smart car case, the time T required to fall a distance h is as follows:

$$T = (2h/g)^{1/2}$$

$$3-1$$

If the car's speed is V the instant that its tires lose contact with the ground, the car will move forward a horizontal distance $S = VT$ during that time T, which means that $T = S/V$. Replacing T by S/V in Equation 3–1 and then multiplying both sides by V yields for S the following expression:

$$S = V(2h/g)^{1/2}$$

In the usual situation, S and h are known, and it is the value of V, the vehicle speed, that is sought. Therefore, one would like to have an expression for V in terms of the known quantities. This is easily obtained by dividing both sides of the last equation by the term in parentheses, leading to the following:

$$V = S(g/2h)^{1/2}$$

$$3-2$$

This is the general expression for V in terms of the horizontal and vertical travel distances, S and h, respectively, when the take-off surface is horizontal. By seeing the source of this expression, one knows the conditions under which it will give the right answer for the speed V. One sees, for example, that S, the horizontal travel distance, will be the distance between the cliff face and the impact point only if the vehicle was moving perpendicular to the face of the cliff at take-off. Also, one must take care that S and h are measured to the first impact point, which in general will not be where the car comes to rest. Finally, though not stated previously, the horizontal and vertical travel distances refer to the vehicle's *center of mass* and not to the point on the vehicle that first hits the ground. This latter need not be a large matter of concern

(continues)

(continued)

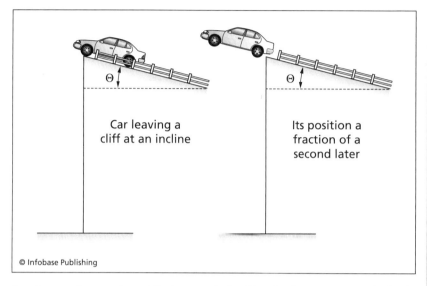

Car leaving a
cliff at an incline

Its position a
fraction of a
second later

A car's upward momentum at the instant of takeoff carries the car up a ways before it starts its final plunge

since h and S for the center of mass usually can be determined from the shape of the car once the vertical and the horizontal distances from the take-off point to the first impact point have been measured. For vehicles with their engines in front, the center of mass (CM) is nearly always 0.40WB back of the front axle, where WB is the vehicle's wheel base (separation between the axles). Also, it is midway between the vehicle's left and right sides. Its height above the ground depends on vehicle height but is typically about two feet.

Estimate the location of the center of mass for the car in the figure on page 73. Placing a mark at that point, estimate how much the values for h and S will differ from those used in the earlier discussion. How much will it change the calculated value V if these center-of-mass values are used for h and S?

Often, the vehicle will be traveling on an upgrade or downgrade immediately before going off the cliff. This changes the problem since it changes the path the vehicle follows. For example, if the car was on an upward slope, it will continue to rise for a short time after its tires have left the ground. Even as it rises, the force of gravity is accelerating it at the rate $-g$, causing its vertical speed to decrease to zero and then become negative under the continuing acceleration of $-g$.

If the surface leading to takeoff makes an angle Θ with the horizontal plane, the velocity of the car can be divided into a vertical speed $V_{V0} = V\sin\Theta$ and a horizontal speed $V_{H0} = V\cos\Theta$. (The Greek letter Θ—pronounced [THAY da] in most places outside of Greece—is the most common symbol used to represent angles in physics discussions.) Although the image in the figure above shows the slope to be upward (Θ positive), the following discussion is equally true when the slope is downward (Θ negative).

As before, the vertical speed of the car is affected by gravity, and the horizontal speed is not affected by anything and so remains constant. The up direction is defined here as positive, and the down direction as negative. All vertical positions above the takeoff point are taken to be positive, and all below it negative. This means that the vertical position of the impact point is negative h and that the acceleration of the car for the entire time between take-off and impact will be $-g$, as stated above. Finally, time $t = 0$ is taken as the instant the car's front tires leave the cliff.

What is the vertical speed V_V of the car after a time T? As shown earlier, the change in speed as the result of constant acceleration for a particular interval of time equals that constant acceleration multiplied by the time interval. In this case, this will be $-gT$. Since the vertical speed at $t = 0$ is being represented by V_{V0}, the vertical speed at time $t = T$, after a speed change of $-gT$ will be:

$$V_V = V_{V0} - gT$$

If the total time to reach the bottom is T_{Tot}, then impact occurs at $t = T_{Tot}$, and the vertical speed at impact will be $V_{V0} - gT_{Tot}$.

(continues)

(continued)

To find T_{Tot}, the total time that the vehicle is in the air, one proceeds just as in chapter 2, using the fact that whenever an object's speed is changing at a constant rate, the average speed for any time interval is the average of the starting speed and ending speed. That average, in turn, is the sum of the two speeds divided by 2. This is very important. (This is not true for accelerations that change with time, as discussed in chapter 4.) Here, the starting value for V_V, the vertical speed, was V_{V0} and its final value (at impact) was $V_V = V_{V0} - gT_{Tot}$. (Note that at this point, the value of T_{Tot} has not been determined.) Therefore, the average vertical speed $<V_V>$ during the time between the instant of take-off and the instant of impact will be

$$<V_V> = \tfrac{1}{2}(V_{V0} + (V_{V0} - gT_{Tot}))$$

This can be simplified to read $<V_V> = V_{V0} - \tfrac{1}{2}gT_{Tot}$.

The vertical position of the car at $t = T_{Tot}$ has been stated to be $-h$. Therefore, $-h$ can be set equal to the average vertical speed ($<V_V> = (V_{V0} - \tfrac{1}{2}gT_{Tot})$) multiplied by T_{Tot}; that is,

$$-h = (V_{V0} - \tfrac{1}{2}gT_{Tot})T_{Tot}$$

This equation simplifies to the following:

$$-h = V_{V0}T_{Tot} - \tfrac{1}{2}gT_{Tot}^2$$

Through the interval from $t = 0$ and $t = T_{Tot}$, the car's speed in the horizontal direction continues at a constant V_{H0}, carrying the car horizontally a distance $S = V_{H0}T_{Tot}$. Therefore, $T_{Tot} = S/V_{H0}$. Substituting this expression for T_{Tot} into the previous equation leads to a statement for V, the original forward speed of the car in terms of S and h, which can be measured directly from the physical evidence at the scene. Thus,

$$-h = V_{V0}(S/V_{H0}) - \tfrac{1}{2}g(S/V_{H0})^2$$

and so

$$h = \tfrac{1}{2}g(S/V_{H0})^2 - V_{V0}(S/V_{H0})$$

Going back to the definition for V_{V0} as $V\sin\Theta$ and the definition of V_{H0} as $V\cos\Theta$ and using them to replace V_{V0} and V_{H0} in this equation leads, after a slight rearranging of the second term on the right, to the following:

$$h = \tfrac{1}{2}g(S/V\cos\Theta)^2 - S(\sin\Theta/\cos\Theta)$$

Completing the rearranging so as to arrive at an expression for V^2 leads to

$$h(V\cos\Theta)2 = \tfrac{1}{2}gS^2 - S(V\cos\Theta)^2(\sin\Theta/\cos\Theta)$$

$$V^2\{h(\cos\Theta)^2 + S(\sin\Theta\cos\Theta)\} = \tfrac{1}{2}gS^2$$

and, finally,

$$V^2 = \tfrac{1}{2}gS^2/\{h(\cos\Theta)^2 + S(\sin\Theta\cos\Theta)\}$$

Finally, taking the square root of both sides yields the general expression for V:

$$V = S\{(g/2)(h(\cos\Theta)^2 + S(\sin\Theta\cos\Theta)\}^{1/2}.$$

Do not be confused with the multiple parentheses in Equation 3–3. This is an illustration of nested parentheses, which are used to shorten the statement of an expression. The equation can be expanded so as to be clearer, though longer, as follows:

$$V = S\{gh(\cos\Theta)^2/2 + ghS(\sin\Theta\cos\Theta)/2\}^{1/2}$$

or, going farther, as:

$$V = \{gh(S\cos\Theta)^2 + ghS^3\sin\Theta\cos\Theta\}^{1/2}/\sqrt{2}$$

Since $(\cos\Theta)^2$ can also be written as $\cos^2\Theta$, the equation may be expressed in yet another form, as:

$$V = \{ghS^2\cos^2\Theta + ghS^3\sin\Theta\cos\Theta\}^{1/2}/\sqrt{2}$$

(continues)

(continued)

Confirm that the changes in form of Equation 3–3 just carried out are correct.

Equation 3–3 is known as the *fall formula.* Because S, h, and Θ are all measured or measurable quantities, this expression easily can be evaluated for V; in spite of the somewhat messy appearance of the equation. When Θ = zero (horizontal take-off surface), cosΘ = 1 and sinΘ = 0 for. Thus, it can be seen that Equation 3–3 reduces to Equation 3–2 when Θ is zero, as it should, that being the condition under which the simpler Equation 3–2 was worked out.

(continued from page 78)

MORE DIMENSIONS

At the conclusion of a several-step derivation, it is always a good idea to take a look at the result to see whether it is dimensionally correct. The term on the right side of Equation 3–2, the fall formula, must have the dimensions of speed, L/T. If it does not, then the formula is wrong, and one must go back to find where the error crept in. Making use of the ideas set forth in the "Dimensions, Units, and Acceleration (DUA)" sidebar of chapter 2, and using the square-bracket notation defined there (for example $[V] = L/T$ is to be read, "The dimensions of V are length divided by time"), the dimensional analysis of Equation 3–2 is as follows:

The term on the left side of the equal sign is V. $[V] = L/T$. Therefore, the term on the right side must also have dimensions of L/T. Since sine and cosine terms are dimensionless, as are all numerical factors, the expression for the dimensions of the term within the outer parentheses can be stated as follows: $[g/(h + S)] = [g][1/(h+S)] = [g]/[h+S]$. But $[g] - L/T^2$ and $[h] = [S] = L$. Therefore $[g]/[(h+S)] = L/T^2/L = T^2$. Since $[T^2]^{1/2} = T$, the dimensions of the complete term on the right are $[S]T = L/T$. This was the required result and, therefore, the condition that the dimensions on both sides of the equation be those of speed is seen to be satisfied.

APPLICATIONS OF THE FALL FORMULA

Using the relationship developed in the "Fall Formula" sidebar, the question posed in the smart car case can be answered. Substituting the values of $h = 120$ feet (36.6 m) and $S = 40$ feet (12.2 m) into the fall formula along with $\Theta = +15°$ leads to $V = 14.4$ ft/sec (4.39 m/s). (Check that this is correct, using the fact that $\cos 15° = 0.97$ and $\sin 15° = 0.26$.) Compare this with the result when $\Theta = -15°$. (Hint: $\cos(-\Theta) = \cos\Theta$, and $\sin(-\Theta) = -\sin\Theta$)

Cars probably go off cliffs more often in the movies than in life. Nevertheless, it is fairly common for a vehicle involved in a crash to fly through the air at some point during the crash sequence. Thus, reconstructionists have ample opportunity to use the fall formula. Sometimes a vehicle is launched as the result of drifting at high speed off a road and across a drop-off formed by a drainage ditch. (See chapter 5, the burning-car case.) Sometimes, a high-speed, out-of-control vehicle is launched by uneven terrain in a field in which it was traveling after departing the road. Whatever causes a vehicle to be launched, the faster it is going, the farther it will travel before returning to the surface, and this flight often provides all that is needed to calculate its speed using the fall formula. What is needed is the launch angle (that is, the slope of its take-off surface) and its horizontal and vertical travel distances from take-off to impact. Some reconstructionists refer to such launches as the vehicles having "gone airborne," an unfortunate phrase. Airplanes and hot-air balloons are airborne because they are borne by the air. A falling vehicle is not airborne any more than is a falling rock.

A particularly sad application of the fall formula is called for in the aftermath of a fatal one-car crash caused by a driver deliberately "grabbing air" by driving so fast over a crest in the road that the car's tires momentarily leave the road surface. This lift-off is due partly to the vertical speed given to the car on the way up and partly to the sharpness with which the road drops away on the down side of the crest. At any event, when the car rejoins the road one to a few seconds later, its downward speed can place great force on its tires and suspension system, even to the extent that mechanical failure occurs. Also, this downward force may be distributed irregularly because of the nature of the take-off surface, or depending on the nature of the take-off, the vehicle may return to earth moving in a direction that is not lined up with the direction of its wheels. Any of these circumstances can lead to loss of control, sometimes followed by a sudden rollover or end-to-end flip of the vehicle. Rollovers and flips are associated with a very high occupant-fatality rate. Such crashes usually create all the physical evidence needed for a reconstructionist to use the fall formula to determine speed, and vehicle speed is always key in the manslaughter trial of a driver who has survived a crash fatal to someone else in the vehicle that "caught air."

MORE NEWTON'S LAWS

Recall Newton's first two laws of motion from chapter 2. Reflection will show that the first law is the second law for the special case where the force on the object is zero. *Force on an object* means the total force (which is also called the net force). A 10-pound (44.5-N) brick at rest on a table is acted on by a net force of zero. Gravity is exerting a 10-pound (44.5-N) downward force on it, and the table is exerting a 10-pound (44.5-N) upward force on it. Defining the up direction as positive and the down direction as negative, one can write the sum of these two forces as the total force, F_{TOT} = +10 pound −10 pound = 0 pound. The total force is zero. The fact that the brick is not accelerating in the vertical direction follows from either the first law or the second law.

In describing the brick, the phrase used was "not accelerating," even though the temptation might have been to say "not moving," given the circumstances described. It is important to be careful with term such as *moving*. To see why, think about the fact that a brick can be at rest with respect to the Earth, even though it is being accelerated. Alternatively, and more importantly for present purposes, it can be moving with respect to the Earth without being accelerated. The latter should be no surprise at this point. However, explain how the former statement can be true.

By the definition of *acceleration*, a brick having zero acceleration is moving at a constant velocity. The statement about the brick on the table continues to be true even if the table is in an elevator that is going up or down at a constant vertical speed. It has been known since the time of Galileo that motion at a constant velocity does not affect any of the forces that may be applied to an object. In general, however, when stating an object's

(continues on page 92)

Newton's Third Law

In view of the fundamental and pervasive role it plays in the world, it is most unfortunate that Newton's third law is so misunderstood, even by those who think that they understand it. Failure to understand the third law leads to confusion so profound that it is best described as floundering when one attempts to describe one of the most powerful tools of accident reconstruction, the Critical-Speed-Scuff Method for determining speed, the topic to which chapter 4 is exclusively dedicated. This circumstance may be the result of how most people first encounter the law, how they hear it stated. Therefore, this discussion will sidle up to it and avoid stating it outright until after several of its consequences are examined.

Jim cannot push Mike without Mike pushing Jim back with equal strength, not because Mike refuses to be pushed around but because Newton's third law commands it. For the same reason, Jim cannot pull on a tree branch without the tree branch pulling back on Jim just as hard. Or, going back to the apple tree which Newton is contemplating the photo on page 53, it can be said that an apple on that tree is being pulled toward the Earth by the force of gravity but that, because of the third law, the Earth is being pulled toward the apple with just as much strength. The tree to which both are attached serves to keep them apart. Just so long as the twig to which the apple is connected pulls up on the apple with a force equal in magnitude to the gravitational force on the apple, the apple is not accelerated. This is consistent with Newton's first and second laws, since the net force on the apple is zero. Once the apple's connection to the tree breaks, the apple accelerates downward at a rate described by the second law and the gravitational force. But the third law states that the Earth is accelerated upward toward the apple at a rate given by the second law and the gravitational force. From the second law, it can be seen that the Earth's acceleration upward is equal in magnitude to the rate of apple's acceleration downward (g), multiplied by the ratio of the apple's mass

(continues)

(continued)

Space shuttle

Door to the shuttle

Rope

Piece of heavy equipment

Astronaut tugging on rope

© Infobase Publishing

A schematic illustration of forces being applied in a weightless situation

to the Earth's mass. That makes the Earth's upward acceleration due to the apple to be tiny, to say the least. The Earth and the apple do not meet in the middle.

When a boy jumps off a 10-foot-high ledge and hits the ground hard with his feet, that hard hit is the force of the Earth pushing up on the bottom of the boy's feet to make him stop, to decelerate his downward motion. The third law ensures that the boy's feet are pushing down just as hard on the Earth. Furthermore, the two forces will be exactly equal in strength at each instant of the impact. Just as was the case with the falling apple, the difference in masses makes the Earth's acceleration due to the impact force so small as to be immeasurable. The situation is quite different when the object exerting the decelerating force on the boy is something closer to him in mass, for example, a swimming float. When he jumps onto it from a pier 10 feet above it, the float, having a mass not much different from his, will at first accelerate downward at approximately the same rate as his upward acceleration (deceleration) during the impact.

To sharpen further the effects of the third law, picture a male astronaut performing a task outside of his orbiting vessel. He has undertaken an EVA (Extra-Vehicular Activity), commonly called a space walk, to haul in apparatus having a mass of 15 slugs (219 kg). Previously, the vessel had maneuvered so as to be traveling at the same velocity as the apparatus. As shown in the figure, the astronaut has to use a rope to pull the apparatus toward the point on the vessel marked with the D. The total mass of the astronaut along with his suit is 5 slugs (73 kg). The rope when taut is parallel to the long dimension of the vessel, and everything is at rest with respect to everything else in the vicinity (even though all are moving at about 18,000 miles per hour [29,000 km/hr] with respect to Houston). Initially, the astronaut is located 25 feet (7.6 m) forward of D, and the apparatus is 25 feet (7.6 m) aft of D. Defining locations forward of D to be positive and locations aft of D to be negative, the astronaut is initially at +25 feet (+7.6 m), the equipment is at −25 feet (−7.6 m). By definition, D is at 0. The astronaut then pulls on the taut rope for exactly two seconds with a force of 25 pounds (111 N), and then does nothing more.

Since the astronaut is pulling in the positive direction, the force on the apparatus is +25 pounds (+111 N). From Newton's third law, there is a corresponding pull of the same strength on the astronaut as well, but in the negative direction. The force on the astronaut is therefore −25 pounds (−111 N). What happens to the apparatus and what happens to the astronaut during the two seconds? The second law gives the

(continues)

(continued)

answers. They are stated below, where all directions and movements are stated with respect to D.

(a) the Equipment
  i. Acceleration during the two seconds is A_E = +(25/15) = +1.67 ft/sec^2 (0.5 m/sec^2).
  ii. Acceleration at A_E for two seconds leads to a speed of +3.34 ft/sec (1 m/sec).
  iii. Average speed during the two seconds is ½(0 + 3.34) = 1.67 ft/sec (0.5 m/sec).
  iv Two seconds at this average speed moves it +3.34 ft (1 m).
  v At end of two seconds, its position is therefore −25 + 3.34 = −21.66 ft (-6.60 m).

(b) the Astronaut
  i. Acceleration during the two seconds is A_A = −(25/5) = −5 ft/sec^2 (−1.5 m/sec^2).
  ii. Acceleration at A_A for two seconds leads to a speed of −10 ft/sec (3 m/s).
  iii. Average speed during the two seconds is ½(0 − 10) = −5 ft/sec (−1.5 m/sec).
  iv. Two seconds at this average speed moves him −10 ft (−3 m).
  v. At end of two seconds, his position is therefore +25 − 10 = +15 ft (4.6 m).

Since the astronaut is applying no force to the equipment or anything else after the end of the two seconds, he and the equipment will approach each other at a constant closing speed. This speed will be the speed of the equipment relative to D minus the astronaut's speed relative to D: +3.34 − (−10) = 13.34 ft/sec (4.06 m/sec). Since they are 35.66 feet (10.87 m) apart when the force between them ceases, they will collide in another 2.67 seconds (35.66 feet divided by 13.34 ft/sec). Where will the collision occur with respect to D?

After checking that the numbers given above are correct, reflect on the fact that there was no mention of the weights of the astronaut and the equipment. Did they have any weight? This scenario will be revisited, especially with respect to what happens when astronaut and equipment collide, after the discussion of momentum later in this chapter.

There are many ways of stating Newton's third law. Here, it will be stated in two parts plus a third part summarizing the first two.

1. If an Object A is exerting a force of strength F on Object B, then Object B is simultaneously exerting a force of strength F on Object A.

2. The force being exerted on Object A by Object B is in the opposite direction from that of the force being exerted on Object B by Object A.

3. Taking the force being exerted by Object A to be in the positive direction so that it can be stated as $+F$, the force being exerted by Object B is $-F$.

Object A and Object B in these statements can be replaced by any two things, such as Jim and Mike, respectively. However, the other words should not be changed. For example, *being exerted* emphasizes that the third law applies at each instant during which the force is applied; it is not some kind of average effect. It applies, for example, for every *nanosecond* of a 50-millisecond vehicle collision.

Anyone claiming to quote the third law by saying that "For every action, there is an equal and opposite reaction" should be asked to define *action* and *reaction* and then asked how something can be equal and opposite at the same time. Such sloppy statements of the third law sabotage students' efforts to obtain knowledge. In contrast, once armed with a correct understanding of Newton's laws of motion, practically anyone can become a rocket scientist.

(continued from page 86)

velocity or speed, one includes a reference. For example, instead of saying that an apple was moving 10 feet (3 m) per second vertically, one says that it was moving 10 feet per second vertically with respect to the Earth. Here, the Earth is the reference. In this context, the phrases *relative to* and *with respect to* appear frequently; their meanings are identical. If the identification of the reference is clear, it is often left unstated. In reporting that a car was moving west at 60 miles per hour (96 km/hr), it is usually left unstated that the 60 miles per hour is its speed with respect to a road or with respect to the Earth. However, in describing a rear-end collision, the key information is the speed of the bullet car with respect to the target vehicle, and a typical statement would be, "The red car was traveling at 30 miles per hour (48 km/hr) with respect to the blue car when it slammed into the blue car's rear bumper." The blue car might have been traveling 20 miles per hour (32 km/hr) and the red one at 50 miles per hour (80 km/hr), but the important fact for the investigator, at least initially, is the relative speed.

Understanding Newton's third law of motion, the final one, is essential to grasping how the physical world operates. For those who do not understand it, the confusion about the physical world continues to be as great as it was for everyone before the time of Newton. One of the most important, probably the most important, rules controlling the way in which physical objects interact with each other, be they cars, stars, or galaxies, is conservation of momentum. The sidebar on Newton's third law provides the last bit of material needed to see why conservation of momentum is so important and also to see why it is such an ironclad rule of the universe. The sidebar also identifies inertial forces, permitting the subsequent discussion of "fictitious forces" and, later, in chapter 4, the introduction and explanation of the Critical-Speed-Scuff Method of estimating speed.

CONSERVATION OF MOMENTUM

For physicists and those who think like physicists, the word *conservation* means something different than it does for most of us. The following story illustrates this meaning.

As it departs the third floor of the Research Institute, an elevator is occupied by a physicist and an engineer headed for the eighth floor.

They share the car with seven men and four women. At the fourth floor, three men and two women exit and one man and two women enter. At the fifth floor, five men and one woman exit and six men and one woman enter. As the elevator again rises, the physicist turns to the engineer and says, "I'm working on a new conservation law, namely that this elevator conserves women, but does not conserve men." At the sixth floor, everyone except the physicist and engineer exits and no one enter, leading the physicist to say, "My new theory just became more restricted. This elevator conserves women as it travels from the third floor to the sixth floor."

In the language of science and engineering, to say that something is conserved is to say that it remains constant. Saying that the momentum of a truck and a car that collide is conserved means that the total momentum—the sum of the car's momentum and the truck's momentum—does not change during the collision. Although the momentum of each will change, the total momentum will not. It has the same value immediately after the collision that it had immediately before the collision. (Note the care with which this is stated in terms of the momentum immediately before and after collision. As the seconds go by following the collision, both truck and car are affected by frictional forces with the road and their total momentum changes.) This is a particular case of the universal rule of conservation of momentum.

What is a car's momentum? It is the car's velocity multiplied by the car's mass. Velocity has direction as well as magnitude (the magnitude of velocity being called speed). Mass is simply a number. Therefore, a car's momentum will have direction as well as a magnitude, the direction being the same as that of its velocity. A car of mass M headed west at a speed V has a momentum to the west of magnitude MV. The letter P is often used for the magnitude of momentum. When direction as well as magnitude is intended, the symbol is usually written in boldface, $\textbf{P}$. The same convention is used for velocity and force, using $\textbf{V}$ and $\textbf{F}$, respectively.

Taking west to be positive and east negative, the momentum along an east-west line of the westbound car just described is $P_1 = +MV$. Imagine that there is a second car moving in the opposite direction on a collision path with the first car, a car with mass m and speed v. Its momentum is along the east-west line and is $P_2 = -mv$. Before their collision, the two cars' total momentum is thus $P_{TOT} = MV - mv$, and it is along the east-west line. (Since the direction of motion has been stated and is all along the same line, it is not necessary to use boldface here. For the sake of the example, it is assumed that, after the collision, the motion continues to be limited to the east-west direction.) Immediately after the collision, each car will have a lower speed than it had before and, therefore, a momentum different from its preimpact momentum. In this particular collision, the cars stick together as a result of the collision and thereafter move together along the east-west line at a velocity V_{COMB}. (When cars become locked together in this fashion, rather than springing apart after they collide, the collision is said to be completely *inelastic*.) V_{COMB} can have either a negative or positive sign; determining the sign is part of the analysis. If the postimpact movement is to the west, V_{COMB} will be positive, and if to the east, it will be negative. From the definition of momentum, the momentum immediately postimpact is $(M + m)V_{COMB}$. Because momentum was conserved, this must equal the momentum immediately preimpact, leading to the equation:

$$(M + m)V_{COMB} = MV - mv$$

This can be solved for V_{COMB}, yielding:

$$V_{COMB} = (MV - mv)/(M + m)$$

(Equation 3–3)

This equation shows that if the magnitude of the eastbound car's momentum was greater than that of the westbound car before the collision, V_{COMB} will be negative; the combined cars will be moving to the east immediately postcollision and vice versa. But that could be seen without solving any equations. If the total momentum preimpact is to the east, then, because momentum is conserved, the total momentum will be to the east postimpact also and vice versa.

Suppose that the two cars had the same mass (that is, the same weight) and the same speed. In such a case, the precollision momentum would be zero, requiring V_{COMB} to be zero. This follows regardless of how fast the cars were going at impact. Even if the cars were not of the same weight and speed preimpact, the preimpact momentum, $P_{TOT} =$

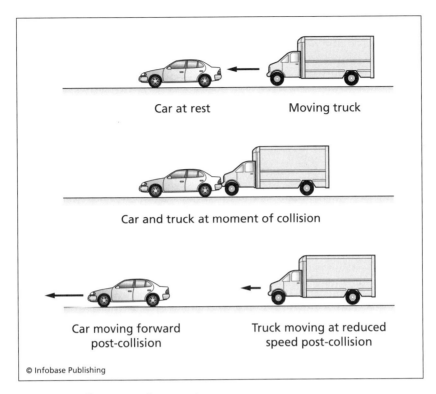

Car at rest   Moving truck

Car and truck at moment of collision

Car moving forward   Truck moving at reduced
post-collision   speed post-collision

© Infobase Publishing

A schematic illustration of rear-ender

$MV - mv$ could be zero. All that is necessary is for the momentums of the individual cars to cancel each other out. This would be the case, for example, if the westbound car weighed 5,000 pounds (22,240 N) and had a speed of 40 miles per hour (64 km/hr), while the eastbound car weighed 2,500 pounds (11,120 N) and had a speed of 80 miles per hour (128 km/hr). (Recall that mass is proportional to weight.)

Consider one more example to see what follows from momentum being conserved during a collision. Let a truck of mass 500 slugs (7,300 kg) traveling at a speed V_{TK} squarely rear-end a car of mass 100 slugs (1,460 kg) that is stopped at a traffic light so that the car is knocked straight forward, with the truck continuing to move in that direction also. Assume that the reconstruction established that immediately after being rear-ended, the car was moving at 40 miles per hour (64 km/hr), followed by the truck at 32 miles per hour (48 km/hr). Since momentum was conserved, the truck's speed at impact V_{TK} can be calculated easily. The precrash momentum came entirely from the truck, the momentum of the car at rest having been zero; that is, $P_{TOT} = 500V_{TK}$ before and therefore after impact. From the postimpact speeds determined from accident reconstruction, the total momentum immediately postimpact can be written as $P = (500)(32) + (100)(40) = 20,000$ slug-miles per hour. Conservation of momentum leads to the following equation:

$$500V_{TK} = 20,000 \text{ slug-mph}$$

Solving the equation gives $V_{TK} = 40$ miles per hour (64 km/hr). Note the strange units used, slug-miles per hour. Since the end result was going to be stated in miles per hour, there was no need to do conversions back and forth. To see what this means in terms of saved steps, state the preimpact momentum in correct U.S. units (slug-ft/sec), solve the problem for V_{TK}, and then convert the answer to miles per hour. As a further exercise in units manipulation, show that in the U.S. system the momentum units can be written *pound-sec*.

Momentum is always conserved by any set of physical objects as long as forces from outside the set do not affect any of the objects. When the set consists of two colliding vehicles, the outside forces—the tires/road forces—are completely negligible during the 50 to 100 milliseconds of a collision compared to the forces between the vehicles. (Only for collision speeds of one or two miles per hour is this not completely the case. Then, the Earth has to be included within the group, and conservation of momentum does not assist the analysis.)

Consider the power of conservation of momentum. Among other marvels, it applies equally to bowling-ball collisions and marshmallow collisions. It applies to collisions between icebreakers just as much as to collisions between ice skaters. It applies in the laboratory, and it applies on the back roads of New Jersey. Because of the pervasiveness and usefulness of conservation of momentum, it is important to see why it is such a robust rule of nature. It flows directly from the second and third laws of motion. Recall the second law as last stated in chapter 2:

A Force **F** Applied to an Object Accelerates the Object in the Direction of **F** at a Rate Directly Proportional to the Strength of the Force and Inversely Proportional to the Mass of the Object

It was shown that by using symbols A for acceleration and M for mass, all the expression in words boils down to the following:

$$A = \mathbf{F}/M$$

which can be solved for F, as follows:

$$F = M\mathbf{A}$$

Since momentum P of an object of mass M and velocity V is $P = M\mathbf{V}$, and A is the rate of change of the velocity V, $M\mathbf{A}$ is the rate of change of the momentum. Then the second law can be articulated as the following:

> An object's momentum changes at a rate equal to the force F applied to the object

The universality of the conservation of momentum rule follows directly from the universality of the second and third laws of motion. This can be seen working with a simple collision between a Hummer of mass M and a VW of mass m. At each instant of the 50 to 100 milliseconds that the two vehicles are engaged with one another, the third law requires that the force that the VW is exerting on the Hummer is equal in magnitude to the force that the Hummer is exerting on the VW. Therefore, if the force on the Hummer at each instant is F, then the force on the VW will be $-F$. Next, it follows from the second law that the rate at which the momentum of the VW is changing during the collision is $-F$, and that the rate at which the momentum of the Hummer is changing is F. At every instant of the collision the change in momentum of the Hummer exactly cancels the change in momentum of the VW. Obviously, all the statements made about the VW and Hummer in this illustration are equally true of any two colliding objects. Therefore, the conservation of momentum law is seen to be as valid as the second and third laws of motion.

ENERGY AND CONSERVATION OF ENERGY

Nearly as important as conservation of momentum is the conservation of energy. As above, the meaning of conservation in the conservation of energy is that the total energy of a system does not change. Unlike conservation of momentum, which has just been shown to be required by the laws of motion, conservation of energy is an experimental fact. For the 200 or so years that all types of energy have been recognized to be just different forms of the same thing, the conservation-of-energy rule has never been found to be violated. If such a violation were ever to be found, say, in some newly discovered type of physical phenomenon, it would be extremely interesting, but it would not upend the scientific view of the way the world works. In contrast, if the conservation-of-momentum law ever is discovered not to be applicable universally, a revolution would occur in the scientific world comparable to that which occurred when Galileo and Newton overthrew the Aristotelian world view 400 years ago.

To understand what it means to say that energy is conserved when two vehicles collide, it is necessary to understand what is meant by the word *energy*. Of all the words used in describing the workings of the universe, *energy* has suffered the most from being hijacked by those who, lacking knowledge of the way the physical world works and often hostile to science, nevertheless wish to benefit from the prestige of scientific words by using them to describe their ideas. To make actual use of the power that the conservation-of-energy rule provides, one must root out from one's thinking, the fuzzy meanings of *energy* reflected by statements such as "She heals by locating the negative energy areas," "He's a crystal energy therapist and can reprogram you using crystal energy," and "What a lot of negative energy there was in that room!"

Humans were aware of and made use of various forms of energy for centuries before they realized that they were working with different forms of the same thing. This realization only occurred in the early 19th century. As a consequence, language for the different forms of energy developed. That language is still in use, resulting in many different words for energy, even in the technical realm. There is heat (energy), noise (energy), electrical energy, magnetic energy, kinetic energy, and so forth. In addition, some forms of energy but not others are referred to as potential energy. The important thing to remember is that, although energy may be moved around among these various forms, every indication is that energy is never destroyed. Energy is conserved. (Until the 20th century, another conservation law reigned supreme, only to be

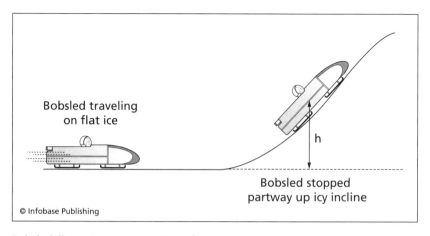

Bobsled traveling
on flat ice

h

Bobsled stopped
partway up icy incline

© Infobase Publishing

Bobsled illustrating conservation of energy

shown to be invalid. It was the conservation-of-mass rule, which grew out of the work of chemists.) Mass is now known to be a form of energy. If mass were not a form of energy, then neither mass nor energy would be conserved when an electron and an antielectron collide. The mass of the two particles vanishes completely in the collision, and energy in the form of radiation appears. By stating that mass is yet another form of energy where the energy associated with mass M is equal to M multiplied by the square of the speed of light, namely Einstein's $E = Mc^2$, the conservation of energy rule is saved. On the other hand, this marked the end of the conservation-of-mass rule.

The most important form of energy for accident reconstruction is the energy that a car (or anything) has simply because it is moving. This is called kinetic energy (K.E.); it is proportional to the square of the speed of the object:

$$K.E. = \tfrac{1}{2}\,MV^2$$

that is, the kinetic energy of a car is equal to one-half the car's mass multiplied by the square of the car's speed.

Imagine a bobsled of mass M moving at a speed V along a horizontal track so slippery that the friction between the track and the sled can be neglected and that air resistance can also be neglected. With no horizontal force on it, the bobsled continues at a constant speed along the track. Everyone knows, however, that when the track slopes upward, the sled will slow down and eventually come to a stop. Where did the kinetic energy go? It was converted into an increase in gravitational energy. Gravitational energy is one of those energy forms that is called potential. It is always described in relative terms. On Earth, if an object of mass M is raised by a vertical distance h, its gravitational energy is increased by an amount Mgh. If, in the example, all of the kinetic energy of the bobsled was converted to gravitational energy when the bobsled increased in elevation by h, it follows from conservation-of-energy that $Mgh = \frac{1}{2} MV^2$. Is this just a bookkeeping trick to avoid having the conservation-of-energy law violated? No. The potential energy that the bobsled gained as it gave up its kinetic energy can all be converted back to kinetic energy if the sled slides back down to it original level. Finding h from the fact that $Mgh = \frac{1}{2} MV^2$ leads to the following:

$$h = V^2/2g$$

(Equation 3–4)

This is yet another example where the mass of the object drops out of the final equation, leading to a valuable intrinsic link between the other variables. Show that Equation 3–4, which might be called the Roller Coaster Equation, satisfies the ironclad condition that both its terms have the same dimensions.

Consider that, instead of losing its kinetic energy to gravitational energy by going uphill, the bobsled continued to slide horizontally until it suddenly ran out of ice and friction brought it to a halt. Again the kinetic energy falls to zero. Where did it go? This time it would have gone into heat energy in the sled's runners and in the track, which would have increased slightly in temperature as a result. By considering this situation, one can appreciate why the gravitational energy was described as potential. It was easy to shift that gravitational energy back to kinetic energy. However, once the kinetic energy has gone into heat, it cannot be recaptured. Because of this, it is sometimes said that the energy has been dissipated. It is not destroyed, even though it has been changed into a form that for all practical purposes removes it from further use.

What are the dimensions of energy? To find the answer, it is sufficient to look at a single form of energy. Kinetic energy has the form K.E. = $\frac{1}{2}$

MV^2. A dimensional equation can be formed from this expression, as follows:

$$[\text{K.E.}] = [\tfrac{1}{2} MV^2] = M[V]^2$$

$$[\text{K.E.}] = M(L^2/ T^2)$$

This means that in the U.S. system, energy can be expressed in units of slug-ft²/sec² and in S.I. as kg-m²/sec². Energy is considered to be such an important entity that in the S.I. it is given its own unit name, the Joule (J) (pronounced "jewel" in America, but "jowl" in Great Britain, presumably the form preferred by Englishman James Joule [1818–89], in whose honor the S.I. energy unit was named).

In the U.S. units, the combination slug-ft²/sec² can also be stated as ft-pound, and this is the form generally used for energy in the U.S. units. (Show that one slug-ft²/sec² equals one ft-pound. Hint: first express the slug in terms of the force units using the expression $F = MA$.)

It is important to obtain a feel for the quantities with which one works. To obtain a feeling for the energy units and for kinetic energy, consider the 3,200-pound (14,200-N) car traveling at 60 miles per hour (96 km/hr). From the definition of kinetic energy and the fact that the car has a mass of 100 slugs and that 60 miles per hour is 88 ft/sec, the kinetic energy of the car is seen to be as follows:

$$\text{K.E.} = \tfrac{1}{2}(100)(88)^2 = 387{,}200 \text{ slug-(ft/sec)}^2 = 387{,}200 \text{ ft-pounds}$$

To express this in S.I., recall that the S.I. unit for energy, the Joule, is equal to one m-N. Since one meter is 3.28 feet and one newton is 0.225 pounds, one m-N equals 0.738 ft-pound. Therefore one ft-pound equals 1.355 J, so 387,200 ft-pounds is 524,656 J. The final number must be rounded off, leading to 525,000 J. Compare this kinetic energy with the kinetic energy of a 25-pound (111-N) lead brick dropped onto one's toes from a height of 3 feet, just before it hits.

Because of the long history of dealing with energy in different forms, there are different units in use for energy in its different forms, even in the technical community. For example, the calorie is a unit of energy. It is often defined as the energy by which one gram (0.001 kg) of pure water is increased when its temperature is increased from 3.5°C to 4.5°C (38.3°F–40.1°F). (Because it appears in the definition, this is one instance where the S.I. temperature unit, the degree Celsius, must be stated before the U.S. temperature unit, the degree Fahrenheit). One calorie equals 3.1 ft-pounds (4.2 J). Because, in some contexts, the word *calorie* has come to mean 1,000 of the calories just defined, careful usage requires the terms gram-calorie and kilogram-calorie to be used. In the context of weight-loss schemes, calorie means kilogram-calorie. It is a quirk of history that the calorie, defined in S.I. terms, is the standard unit used in the United States in discussions of dietary matters. Other quirky energy units include: erg, BTU (British Thermal Unit), kilowatt-hour (kWh), horsepower-hour, electron-volt, barrel of oil, ton of TNT (the last listed being 4.2 billion joules).

When that 60-miles-per-hour (96-km/hr) car introduced above brakes to a halt, whether gradually or with brakes locked and tires skidding, all of its kinetic energy is transformed into other kinds of energy noise (screeching tires, squealing brakes) and heat (as the brakes and tires increase in temperature) being the major ones for the skidding car, though some also goes into making those little balls of asphalt that lie atop the skid marks.

When cars collide, there is another energy account that receives deposits from the kinetic energy fund, that of the energy that goes into crushing the vehicles. Look back at the example used to illustrate conservation of momentum, where the 40-miles per hour (88-km/hr) truck rear-ended the car stopped at the light. Calculate the total kinetic energy of the two vehicles after the collision, and compare it with the kinetic energy before the collision. Find the quantity of kinetic energy converted to other energy forms during the collision. Express this quantity in ft-pounds and in Joules. Discuss where it went.

When two vehicles of roughly equal weight traveling at roughly the same speed collide head-on, they often come to rest just about where they came together on the road, after partially rising into the air and then settling back to the pavement. In such collisions as these, the largest part of the original kinetic energy goes into crushing the vehicles, the *energy of crush*.

In an example used above to illustrate conservation of momentum, two colliding vehicles ended up stuck together—the completely inelastic

Work

In its scientific sense, if a boy does work or has work done on him, something was accomplished. The change can either be an increase or decrease in the boy's energy, or it can be a conversion of one form of his energy into another form. If there is no change in energy, no work in the sense of the word as used here has been done. One may think that Atlas was doing a great deal lot of work by holding the whole world on his head. However, as long as the world does not move, Atlas does no work. The same thing is true of two evenly matched tug-of-war teams pulling against each other through a nonstretchable rope. The same thing is true of the woman pulling unsuccessfully on a stump or root to remove it from her garden. In contrast, the classic example of work is the boy who climbs a hill holding a brick in his hand. If the mass of the brick is M and the vertical height of the hill is $h,$ the boy has done work on the brick by increasing its gravitational energy by $Mgh.$ He, of course, did work on his own body as well, increasing its gravitational energy.

Though Atlas holds up the whole world, he is performing no work *(Bettmann/CORBIS)*

Because of conservation of energy, the gravitational energy increase given to the brick and to the boy's body came from somewhere. It was not just created. In this case, the work was done by the boy's muscles which, to walk him up the hill, consumed chemical energy stored in the boy's body, energy that had in turn come from the food he had eaten previously. Because of inefficiencies in the energy conversion process, the stored energy coming from his body to drive the muscles

(continues)

(continued)

that enabled him to reach the top of hill would have been greater than the increase in gravitational energy of the boy and the brick. Where did that extra energy go? It would have gone primarily into the waste heat (energy) that increased the boy's body temperature. In turn, that heat energy would have been carried away, to prevent a rise in body temperature harmful to the boy, through the evaporation of the perspiration called forth by the temperature increase.

The work done by the climbing boy is an illustration of the general rule that the quantity of work W done by a force on an object is equal to the distance the object moves with or against the force. To increase the elevation of the brick, the boy had to exert an upward force. If the slope of the hill was such that, for every 500 feet (152.4 m) he walked, his elevation only increased by 300 feet (91.4 m), he would have lifted the brick by 300 feet (91.4 m) for every 500 feet (152.4 m) he walked. It is the 300 feet (91.4 m), parallel to the gravitational force that determines the work he is doing on the brick. This can be stated generally by defining S_F as the distance moved either parallel to or opposite (antiparallel) to the force F. Then, the definition of the work done on or by the object is as follows

$$W = FS_F$$

This makes clear why, with work as defined this way, the woman who pulled unsuccessfully on the root did no work on the root, no matter how great was the force she applied. S_F was zero.

Work is a number; it does not have a direction. Note the choice of words used in the definition above. The work depends on the object's movement in the direction of or opposite to the direction of the force. That was why the subscript was used in stating the distance moved S_F. An equivalent definition would be that $W = F_S S$, where F_S is the force in the direction of the movement S. To appreciate what this means, reflect on the fact that if a force is applied to an object that is perpendicular at all times to the direction the object is moving the work being done

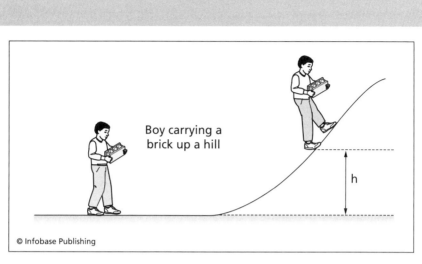

Boy carrying a
brick up a hill

h

© Infobase Publishing

Only the distance that the boy moves against the force of gravity counts
toward the work that he does in climbing the hill

on the object by the force is zero. This would be the case for a gravitational force keeping a planet revolving around a star in a circular orbit.
It applies to the example of the boy climbing the hill as well. Since the
hillside is not vertical, the boy's path will not be parallel to the direction of the gravitational force. Only that part of his movement that
increases his elevation enters into the expression for the work done
against gravity.

When a force is applied to an object in a direction opposite from the
object's velocity, the work done reduces the object's kinetic energy. The
bobsled going uphill was an example of this. It was moving upward,
opposite in direction from that of the gravitational force that was acting on it. The work done by gravity reduced the sled's kinetic energy,
ultimately to zero, converting it to gravitational energy.

collision. As could be seen from that example, completely inelastic collisions greatly simplify calculations using conservation of momentum.
In a completely elastic collision, kinetic energy is conserved along
with momentum and is the same immediately postimpact as it was

immediately preimpact. This provides an even better situation from the point of view of calculating speed. Unfortunately, completely elastic motor-vehicle collisions never occur, it being practically impossible to avoid converting some kinetic energy into vehicle crush. It is only with collisions of billiard balls, bowling balls, hockey pucks, and other very hard objects that the kinetic energy is conserved. Those cases come very close to being completely elastic even at high speeds, a fact that that billiards players, whether they realize it or not, rely on when setting up their shots. Only at very low speeds, when the chance of permanent crush is very low, near-elastic conditions hold in the collision of motor vehicles. They are pretty much limited to parking lots. Unfortunately, at those very low speeds, one can no longer count on the momentum of the two vehicles being conserved since the tire/pavement forces no longer can be ignored. In any event, there is not much call for the reconstruction of vehicle collisions in parking lots.

To organize the examination of how energy changes form, the framework of work was developed. This framework can be useful in considering how, during motor-vehicle collisions, kinetic energy changes into heat, crush, and gravitational energy. The following sidebar "Work" explains this.

Return to that 3,200-pound (14,230-N) car—the 100-slug (1,460-kg) car—being accelerated by a force of 1,470 pounds (6,540 N). In the example, the car starts at rest and soon is accelerated by the force to 60 miles per hour (96 km/hr). Since the kinetic energy at that speed was shown above to be 387,200 ft-pounds (525,000 J) and since that energy must be equal to the work done by the force, one can determine immediately the distance S the car moved under the effects of that force. Since FS = 387,200 ft-pounds, $S = 387,200/1,470 = 263$ feet (80 m). Most satisfyingly, this conservation of energy argument leads to a general expression connecting force, distance, mass, and speed:

$$FS = \frac{1}{2}MV^2$$

REVISITING THE SKID-TO-A-STOP FORMULA

Recall in chapter 2 the skid-to-a-stop formula relating skid distance, coefficient of friction, and starting speed:

$$S = V^2/2g\mu$$

After Newton's laws of motion were introduced, it was shown why this relationship was true. The skid-to-a-stop formula was derived earlier from a force and time perspective. It will now be derived from the point of view of energy and work. (The act of proving the relationship between different quantities is called deriving an equation.)

The force slowing the skidding car is μMg. If the car stops in a distance S, the force applied over that distance performs work on the car as follows:

$$W = FS = -\mu MgS$$

where the negative sign is used because the force is in the opposite direction from the direction of motion; the force is taking kinetic energy out of the car. At the end of the skid, the change in the kinetic energy of the car, ΔKE, is $-\frac{1}{2} MV^2$ where the negative sign is used because the change is a decrease in kinetic energy. The Greek letter Δ (delta) is often used to indicate a change in something. ΔKE should be read as "the change in kinetic energy." Since this change must be equal in magnitude and sign to the work done on the car by the frictional force,

$$-\mu MgS = -\frac{1}{2} MV^2$$

Solving this for S produces once again the skid-to-a-stop formula,

$$S = V^2/2g\mu$$

It is worth repeating that the skid distance depends on the initial speed V and the coefficient of friction μ and not on the mass of the vehicle (and hence not on the weight of the vehicle).

REVISITING THE SMART CAR CASE

Recall that using the fall formula with the smart car case showed that the car left the cliff at a speed of about 14.4 ft/sec (4.4 m/s). The investigators puzzled over the mechanism by which the car had attained that speed since it appeared that it had had no driver at that point. Although the key

Photograph of a collision scuff occurring at the end of a skid mark,
corresponding to the position of the skidding tires at the moment of impact
(Courtesy of the author)

was in the ignition, the damage caused by the impact made it impossible
to determine whether the engine was running at that point or even what
gear the car was in. The puzzlement occurred because they reasoned
that if the car was simply pushed over the edge, it would not have had
a forward speed of more than one or two miles per hour, in contrast to
the forward speed of nearly 10 miles per hour that was indicated by the
fall formula and the position of the impact point.

The smart car had a weight of 1,600 pounds (7,117 N) and so a mass
of 50 slugs (730 kg). At 14.4 ft/sec (4.4 m/s), its kinetic energy would
have been ½(50)(14.4)² = 5,184 ft-pounds (7,029 J). From the terrain
alongside the road at the top of the cliff, the investigators found that the
greatest distance the car could have been pushed in a straight line was
20 feet (6.1 m), and it would have been up a 15° incline. This meant that
as the car went forward 20 feet (6.1 m), the height of its center of mass
would have increased by 20 times the sine of 15 degrees, which is 5.2
feet (1.6 m). Therefore, the gravitational energy (*Mgh*) would increase
by 8,320 ft-pounds (11,280 J) meaning that, while the car was being
pushed 20 feet (6.1 m), its total energy would increase by 13,504 ft-
pounds (18,309 J). (Check this.)

Ignoring for a moment the incline, what force would have to be
applied to the rear of the car for 20 feet (6.1 m) to increase its kinetic

energy by 5,184 ft-pounds (7,029 J). The force times the distance equals the change in K.E. $\Delta KE = FS$. Since ΔKE is 5,184 ft-pounds, the force required is $F = 5,184/20 = 259$ pounds (1,152 N), assuming that there is no resistance from the engine and that the frictional resistance of the car is essential zero. This force would have to be maintained for 20 feet. If done by a person pushing the car, that person would have to be running 10 miles per hour (16.1 km/hr) by the end. What about the gravitational energy increase? That is different in that the force required to produce it is constant, just as it was a constant force that the boy carrying the brick to the top of the hill had to exert. Here, the force to move the car up the 15° incline against the force of gravity is equal to the weight of the car multiplied by the sine of 15°, namely 0.26. This means that to move the car at all, the person pushing it must exert a force of 416 pounds (1,850 N). To accelerate it to 10 miles per hour (16.1 km/hr) in 20 feet (6.1 m), the pusher has to exert an additional 259 pounds, for a total of 675 pounds (3,000 N). The conclusion was that this was impossible.

Notice that the general use of the force definition yields the same result with a single calculation; that is, the total increase in the car's energy, the sum of the K.E. and gravitational energy increase is 13,504 ft-pounds (18,309 J) as it is pushed the 20 feet (6.1 m) forward. The general work equation thus becomes

$$13,504 = 20F$$

$$F = 675 \text{ pounds (3,000 N)}$$

SIGNATURE MARKS

The term *signature mark* is sometimes used in accident reconstruction as the label for localized physical evidence indicating a specific event, as opposed to evidence such as skid marks or vehicle crush profiles. A distorted steering wheel, for example, would be a signature for the steering wheel having been loaded during impact by the driver's upper body. It might be taken as evidence that the driver was not wearing a shoulder belt. Marks on seat belt webbing would be a signature of the seat belt having been loaded during a crash and hence in use by the occupant. When air bags have deployed, there may be marks on the bag fabric made by

Photograph of bounce scuffs made when the tires of a car involved in a collision contact the pavement a short distance from the impact point *(Courtesy of the author)*

portions of an occupant's face or by make-up worn by an occupant. A technique for observing marks on deployed air-bag marks is to fill them with ping pong balls or packing material to cause the bags to take on the shape they had when struck by the occupant's face. Other important signature marks within a crashed vehicle include the image of a shoe sole on a brake pedal, or of the pattern of the brake pedal or accelerator on the bottom of a shoe. Similarly, there may be prints resembling patterns on clothes worn by the occupants on plastic padding at the front of the occupant compartment or doors that give information about the respective locations of the occupants of the vehicle at the time of the crash. This can be very important when there is a dispute as to which one had been driving. Yet others within the occupant compartment would be clothes patterns impressed into the plastic under the instrument panel. These last-named signature marks can be very useful in determining the respective positions of the vehicle occupants during the crash.

A separate category of signature marks are the scuff marks made by tires when knocked sideways, often just called scuffs. These include collision scuffs, which can help pinpoint where the vehicles were at the instant of impact. Collision scuffs may occur at the end of a skid, appearing as an abrupt change in the direction of the skid mark. Not only the tires closest to the collision point on the vehicle, but also other tires can make collision scuffs useful in figuring out what happened. Collision marks can also be made by a tire pushed forcefully down on the pavement as a result of impact. Intersection collisions, T-bone collisions, are one of the more common urban collisions. The sudden blow against the side of the struck vehicle always knocks it sideways a few inches, resulting in one or more of its tires printing a short black mark on the pavement. If it is moving slowly when struck, this scuff will be perpendicular to the car's initial travel direction, in contrast to the angled mark that is left if its speed was higher, as depicted in the photo on page 110. The striking car also may also leave scuffs marking its front tires' position at the instant of impact, especially if it skidded into the collision. Because of front overhang, these collision scuffs will be 1–3 feet short of where the metal-to-metal collision occurred.

Sometimes when a skidding car strikes something while braking, it will continue skidding past the object, past the collision point. This will occur when the object stuck is much less massive than the car, such as a pedestrian or a motorcycle, though this is not a necessary condition. It can happen regardless of the mass of the struck object when the collision occurs at a glancing angle. In all such cases, there may be, and usually is, a little wiggle in one or more of the skid marks caused by the impact. The wiggle in the skid mark shows the location at the instant of impact of the tire making that skid mark. This always happens when a motorcycle or another vehicle is struck. However, when the struck object is much lighter than the car, the impact signature may be hard to detect. Nevertheless, it should always be looked for. It often has the greatest importance in the cases where it is hardest to find, especially in connection with a pedestrian being struck. There usually is no other physical evidence indicating where the pedestrian was when struck. As was seen in the hit-and-run case of chapter 2, the exact point at which the pedestrian was struck was key to analyzing the driver's fault. As in that case, it occasionally happens that the *pedestrian* leaves a scuff mark. Even in low-speed impacts, the force of the front of the vehicle tends initially to shove the pedestrian forward as a unit so that the pedestrian's shoes slide forward without leaving the pavement. Such scuffs are most likely when the pedestrian is wearing sneakers, hence, the sneaker scuff.

When two cars collide head-on, it often happens that the front end of one is lifted so that its tires leave the pavement. When this occurs, the lifted car will not leave collision scuffs, but may leave scuffs when its tires again come into contact with the pavement, something that may happen several feet from the point of impact. When they touch down, they may cause "bounce scuffs," even if they are free to roll, for they will rarely be lined up in the vehicle's travel direction. The photo shows such a mark made by a car when its tire struck the pavement a distance from the impact point. One must be on guard to avoid identifying such a mark as a collision scuff. The curved stripes in the scuff mark shown in the photo suggest that the car was spinning about its vertical axis at the time the mark was being made and that the tire making it was free to rotate on its own axis. This is important information for identifying what was happening with the car at that point since some of the wheels are usually bound up by collision damage and are not free to rotate as the car moves from collision to rest.

In summary, a scuff mark is caused by a tire slipping in a direction other than the one in which it was rolling or skidding. Most types of scuff marks are only a foot or so in extent, in contrast with skid marks, which can continue for hundreds of feet. One exception is the critical-speed scuff, to be described in chapter 4, which also can continue for hundreds of feet and create confusion if investigators mistake them for skid marks. Scuff marks literally mark the presence of a vehicle at a particular location on the pavement and otherwise provide information about the movement of the vehicle at impact and immediately afterward.

Gouges in the pavement are made in much the same way that collision scuffs and bounce scuffs are made. When the collision is between vehicles differing in height or weight, the larger vehicle often will push the smaller vehicle down hard enough that some portion of its underside digs into the pavement. Because of the short duration of the collision, the pushed-down vehicle generally springs back up immediately after punctuating the pavement so that the collision gouge is very good indicator of where the collision took place, better than tire scuffs. Some civil lawsuits arising from motor-vehicle collisions have their outcomes turn on which side of a road's centerline the collision occurred. Often, collision scuffs or collision gouges can settle this question immediately. Also, just as bounce scuffs can be made by cars lifted off the pavement by the collision, so can bounce gouges. Both provide information about the trajectory of the car on the way to its rest position.

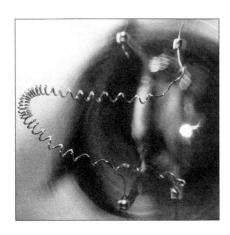

Illustration of hot shock, indicating that this filament was hot at the time of impact *(Triodyne, Inc.)*

ELECTRIC-LIGHT FILAMENTS AND WHAT THEY RECORD

A common reaction when one is struck while pulling into an intersection after dark is that the unseen oncoming vehicle did not have its headlights on. The other driver denies that he or she was driving without headlights. Determining which driver is correct turns out to be one of the few questions that accident reconstructionists can answer quickly and correctly. The light filaments tell the story, and they tell it in terms such as *hot shock* and *cold shock.* Not only can they be used to establish after a collision whether a car's headlights were on, but they can also be instrumental in addressing the question of whether the car's turn signals were activated or its brakes applied at impact.

Even though motor-vehicle lighting is undergoing great changes, the large majority of vehicles continue to rely on tungsten-filament-based incandescent lights. Lighting by incandescence requires the light source to be raised to a high enough temperature that it emits light. This is the origin of such phrases as *red hot* and *white heat.* It is a very inefficient way to provide light since 96 to 98 percent of the electric energy consumed goes into waste heat rather than into light. However, it has been the standard for lighting for 120 years and for nearly 100 years of that period, the light sources have been tungsten filaments. (Nonincandescent lighting includes gaseous discharge lights such as fluorescent tubes with a light-producing efficiency of about 20 percent and systems based on light-emitting diodes, which achieve efficiencies close to 100 percent.)

Unless they are raised to high temperatures, tungsten filaments are very brittle. Therefore, if they are not in use at the time they undergo the high acceleration pulse associated with the collision of the vehicle in which they are installed, they can snap. This is called cold shock and is very easy to detect postcollision. In contrast, when the tungsten filament is at the temperature at which it is serving its light-emitting function, it is soft and, if exposed to an acceleration pulse, can become wildly distorted. This is hot shock. In its most pronounced form, the stretched out filament coil that is the talisman of hot shock is also easy to detect, though there are some situations where it, unlike cold shock, its appearance can be ambiguous. Absence of hot shock cannot be taken as evidence that a light was not on and absence of cold shock cannot be taken as evidence that it was on.

When the glass envelope on a light bulb breaks as the result of a crash allowing air to rush in, the filaments provide information in a different way. A hot filament will oxidize, as the oxygen in the air combines with the hot tungsten making up the filament. An oxidized filament displays a number of colors, in dramatic contrast with the uniform gray color of tungsten metal, a positive indication that the light was lit at the time of the crash or within a couple of seconds before the crash. If the filament in a bulb broken in a crash does not show this change of color, it is a positive indication that the light was not lit.

In summary, examining the light bulbs of a vehicle that has been in a crash can provide information about whether the headlights were on, whether the brakes were applied, and whether the driver was signaling a turn at the time of the crash. Even though turn-signal lights blink on and off rather than being continuously lit, the filaments do not cool off sufficiently between blinks to prevent hot shock from occurring when the car crashes. An important aspect of this filament evidence is that it retains its information indefinitely.

"BLACK BOXES" AND WHAT THEY RECORD

A modern car contains a number of small, dedicated computers used to control various aspects of the car's operations. The particular computer at the heart of the system controlling the car's air bags has an especially demanding task to perform. It must decide during an extremely short time whether the car is in the midst of a crash that is serious enough to justify air-bag deployment, and if it decides that that is the case, the computer has to choose the nature of the air-bag deployment. As the technology has advanced, the air-bag system has become more and more responsive to the particular circumstances both of the crash and of the occupants that are to be protected. For example, the speed at which the bag is directed toward the occupant (100 to 275 miles per hour [161 to 443 km/hr]) is based on the estimated seriousness of the crash, seat-belt use, occupant size, and other factors. Emphasis is placed on the system not being "fooled" into deploying the air bags when they are not needed since the air bags themselves can inflict injuries that are sometimes fatal. Both for the deployment decision and for the decision regarding the nature of deployment, the computer examines the shape of the deceleration that the car is undergoing as the result of something having happened. This is complicated since both serious and nonserious crashes can display a variety of deceleration shapes. Therefore, the air-bag computer has a database with a huge number of deceleration shapes that it compares to the deceleration that the car is going through. There is an Arabic word for a method of mathematical analysis. The word is *algorithm.* The air-bag computer is equipped by its designers with an algorithm and a database, on both of which it relies to perform its task. The average air-bag computer may go for years without being called on to perform. However, should a vehicle undergo a frontal deceleration exceeding a certain threshold—typically 2*g,* twice the acceleration due to gravity—the computer wakes up and does its job very fast. This awakening is called Algorithm Enablement (AE). Following AE the air-bag computer must decide within a few milliseconds (thousandths of a second) whether to deploy the air bags. As stated earlier, the usual crash pulse lasts, depending on the nature of the crash, for 50 to 100 milliseconds. Dropping a penny is one way to get a feeling for 50 milliseconds. It is the time required for the penny to fall the first half-inch (0.013 m) after being dropped. The decision to deploy, and also the decision regarding the nature of the deployment, must be made in one-tenth that time.

Because of the stringent demands on the air-bag computer, it is continually being fed information about the vehicle and the vehicle occupants. Approximately once a second, it receives such data as (1) vehicle speed, (2) percent of throttle (that is, the degree to which the driver has the accelerator depressed), (3) brake status (on or not), and (4) engine speed. The computer retains only the last five readings of each type of information, with the oldest information being erased each time a new piece of that type of data arrives, that is, approximately once a second. When deceleration of the vehicle exceeds the threshold for algorithm enablement, the computer freezes all of the data then in the memory and begins its analysis of the high-resolution acceleration data. This is what leads to those statements in the news reports about the vehicle's speed five seconds prior to the crash, statements that may leave people wondering how the system could know five seconds before the crash that the crash was going to occur. If the computer, following algorithm enablement, decides that it was a false alarm, there is no deployment. Nevertheless, the data that was frozen in memory remains there and is identified as being associated with a nondeployment event. With most existing systems, only the latest nondeployment event is retained in memory.

Since 1996, for millions of cars and light trucks on the U.S. and Canadian highways, this information has been available to anyone with the relatively inexpensive device needed to download it from these Electronic Data Recorders (EDRs). The data appears in both graphical and tabular form. The table on page 117 is the graphed data from a nondeployment. The vehicle was involved in a crash immediately after the nondeployment event. However, the crash itself was not head-on and so was not appropriate for air bag deployment. The event that led to the loss of control and crash was that of "grabbing air" as described earlier in the chapter where a car lifted off the pavement after clearing a crest in the road; that is, it was going fast enough that it did something like the maneuver depicted in the figure on page 80. Instead of going off a cliff, however, it just returned to the road but was misaligned so that the landing threw it out of control. Review what the graph on page 117 is showing. The speed appears to change in a remarkable manner, and it is only through knowing the other aspects of the car's behavior that one can make sense of it. The data shows that five seconds prior to algorithm enablement, the speed (shown by the squares) was more than 60 miles per hour (96 km/hr), but that one second later it had fallen to less than 25 miles per hour (40 km/hr), and that it remained at approximately that level for the next several seconds. What type of acceleration would be required for the speed to drop by 40 miles per hour in one second?

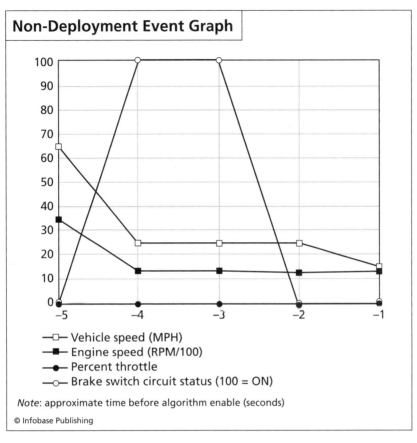

Non-Deployment Event Graph

- —□— Vehicle speed (MPH)
- —■— Engine speed (RPM/100)
- —●— Percent throttle
- —○— Brake switch circuit status (100 = ON)

Note: approximate time before algorithm enable (seconds)

© Infobase Publishing

Graph forming part of the download from an event data recorder, displaying five types of operating data collected approximately every second during approximately five seconds before algorithm enablement (AE).

That number is easy to calculate but impossible to achieve simply by braking. (Show that it is nearly 2 g, at least twice the deceleration that can be achieved by locking up the wheels.) Note what else happened between −5 seconds and −4 seconds. The brakes were applied. The brake data does not provide information as to how hard the brakes were applied. It indicates only whether the brake pedal was depressed or was not depressed. At −5 seconds, there was no braking. At −4 seconds and −3 seconds, there was braking but at an unknown level. Then, for the final two seconds, there was no braking. Although in the graph of the data, lines are drawn between the points at the second marks, this can be misleading since it indicates that there is knowledge of the values in between the points, whereas in fact there is not. For example, in the second between −4 s and −3 s, the brakes could have been applied and released two or three times. Also, although the graph shows a straight upward-sloping line for the brake status between −5 s and −4 s, the driver may have had no braking braked between −5.0 seconds and −4.1 seconds, depressing the brake pedal only an instant −4 seconds, when the brake-status was recorded.

The information available from the EDRs becomes more detailed and varied with each new model year. Accident reconstructionists being very interested in what can be learned from this automatically recorded information, most police departments and private reconstructionists began to purchase the devices needed to download the data just as soon as there were any vehicles with which the devices could be used, namely in the late 1990s. Essentially all GM cars and trucks manufactured since 1996 and sold in the United States and Canada provide EDR crash information. As of late 2008, this is true to a lesser extent for Ford vehicles since 2000 and for Chrysler vehicles starting in 2007.

While EDRs can be very useful sources of information for those seeking to learn what happened in a crash, it should be clear by now that a proper "reading" of their data requires an understanding of how the data are collected and stored. For example, one needs to know that the speed readings provided by the EDRs are equal to the car's speed at the reference times only if the car's drive wheels are rolling without slipping. If they are spinning, either because the driver is peeling out or accelerating on ice, the speed recorded will be too high. On the other hand, if the wheels are being braked hard so that the tires are skidding partially or fully, the recorded speed will be lower than the car's speed. Both effects follow from the fact that the EDR gets its speed readings from the car's drive train. In summary, as is the case with all the methods used in a forensic investigation, the strengths and weaknesses of the EDRs must be understood if they are to be useful to the investigation rather than a source of confusion.

EDRs in cars have been criticized by persons and organizations concerned with personal privacy, especially because of the ease with which anyone with access to a car can extract the car's EDR data. The image that they evoke in some is that of cars spying on, and then informing on, their owners. This fear may be heightened by calling the EDRs "black boxes," a labeling error reflecting the same error made with flight data recorders in airplanes. The EDRs in cars are usually housed in unpainted aluminum containers (very not black in color) located between the two front seats and connected to an electrical receptacle under the instrument panel next to the steering-wheel shaft. The flight data recorders in planes are also not black but rather are bright orange to enhance their visibility at a crash scene.

4

Speed from Critical-Speed Scuffs

his chapter is dedicated to a single accident-reconstruction technique—the Critical-Speed-Scuff-Mark (CSSM) method. The method does not require that one know anything at all about the vehicle that made the marks. The CSSM method accounts for many and perhaps most of the puzzling statements about speed that appear in accident reports. For example, "The 1978 Chrysler was traveling 103.8 miles per hour just before leaving the road." This type of statement alone would justify a separate chapter on the subject. An additional reason for raising its discussion to this level is that most students find it incredible when they first are told of it. Yet another reason for devoting an entire chapter to the CSSM method is the opportunity it provides to revisit the laws of motion and to integrate them into the broader accident-reconstruction framework. This in turn leads to the introduction of inertial forces, a major element in accident reconstruction, and to the demonstration that inertial forces are not forces at all but the result of acceleration. Centrifugal force is an inertial force associated with centripetal acceleration. The chapter presents a convincing demonstration that centripetal acceleration and a new, simple, proof of its dependence on speed and curvature.

CSSMs are made by a vehicle traveling around a curved path at a high rate of speed. In contrast to the vehicle leaving skid marks as the result of its wheels being locked-up, the vehicle leaving CSSMs has all its tires rotating. As discussed in chapter 2, the longitudinal striations in skid marks have an appearance determined by the tire's tread pattern. In contrast, the *lateral striations* of CSSMs have little or nothing to do with the tread pattern. Furthermore, the lateral striations are not exactly lateral, that is, not exactly perpendicular to the direction of the mark. Rather, they are slanted. One says that they are oblique. This obliqueness indicates the direction in which the vehicle was traveling when it made the marks. Since CSSMs are always curved marks, one can speak of their concave side and their convex side. Alternatively, one can use the descriptive words *inside* and *outside,* referring to the curve. As the marks are laid down, the tire is slipping not just laterally but also in the direction of motion of the vehicle. Therefore, looking from the inside of the curve to the outside of the curve, one will see the lateral striations slanted forward in the direction of the vehicle's direction of travel.

Sometimes, CSSMs are called yaw marks because a car in the course of beginning to make them rotates slightly about its yaw axis so that its rear tires, which had been tracking inside of the front tires, slide outward and begin to track outside the front tires. What does it mean to say that the rear tires track inside the front tires? It means, for example, that, as a car follows a right-turning curve at a reasonable speed, its left rear tire follows a path with a smaller radius of curvature than the path followed by the left front tire and similarly for the right-side tires. When the maneuver is made in mud or snow, one can see this effect quite clearly. The car's yaw axis is the vertical line passing through its center of mass. (The center of mass was discussed in chapter 3 in connection with the fall formula.)

Chapter 2 outlined how frictional forces stop a skidding car, how once the car's brakes had stopped its wheels from rotating so that the tires began to skid, the car comes to a halt with a deceleration equal to the tire/pavement coefficient of friction μ multiplied by g. On dry pavement, μ is approximately 0.8, causing a skidding car to have a deceleration of

0.8g. Recall that g is the acceleration of a freely falling object. In U.S. units, it is 32 ft/sec^2, and in S.I., it is 9.8 m/sec^2. Recall also that the force required to cause an acceleration A in an object of mass M is equal to M multiplied by A. A car of mass 100 slugs (1,460 kg) skidding to a stop on a dry road will be subject to a frictional force between the four tires and the road of

$$F = MA = (100)(0.8)(32) = 2,560 \text{ pounds (11,400 N)}$$

(Since a car's weight is its mass multiplied by g, the 100-slug car weighs 3,200 pounds (14,200 N).

Most people drive cars for years without slamming on the brakes and skidding. Nevertheless, these drivers call on friction every time they stop. A typical deceleration as a car approaches a traffic light is 0.1g to 0.2g. For the 100-slug car, a 0.2g deceleration requires a retarding force between tires and road of 640 pounds (2,850 N). If the brakes are applied a bit harder so as to slow down at a rate of 0.4g, the frictional force will be 1,280 pounds (5,700 N). As the driver applies greater force to the brake pedal, the car's deceleration will continue to increase—but only to the point where the wheels lock up. After that, no matter how much the force to the brake pedal is increased, there will be no increase in deceleration. The brakes are doing all that they can do once the tires start skidding. The point at which the wheels lock up is determined by the tire/pavement coefficient of friction. In some cases with heavy trucks, it is not possible to apply enough braking force to the wheels to cause them to lock up.

Both positive and negative acceleration (the latter commonly called deceleration) introduce effects known as inertial forces. The following example of a boy riding in a closed van and restrained by a seat belt provides a simple illustration of what might be called linear inertial effects since they all take place in a straight line.

INERTIAL FORCES: LINEAR EFFECTS

A boy is seated in the rear of a closed van traveling west on a smooth road at a constant speed of 60 miles per hour (96 km/hr). The boy is at rest with respect to the van but is moving west at 60 miles per hour with respect to the Earth though, being unable to see out, he may not realize it if the road is smooth and the noise insulation effective. Suddenly, the van brakes hard, and the boy feels himself thrust forward, halted only by his seat belt from colliding with the front of his compartment. What the boy sees as a force trying to pull him forward out of his seat is an inertial force. It is not a true force but only an effect caused by the deceleration of the van. Nevertheless, he cannot distinguish it from the forward force which he would feel if the van had been at rest all along and suddenly had its rear end lifted up. To the outside, all-seeing observer, of course, it is clear that the boy is not being thrust forward but in fact is having his forward speed reduced. His motion with respect to the van just results from his obeying Newton's First Law. He continues to move with the velocity that he had been given until a force is applied to him to change that velocity. When his seat belt slack is taken up and he is held back by the belt, the inertial force is applied to the belt as called for by Newton's Third Law. It is the reaction to the belt applying the force necessary to decelerate the boy; that is, in accord with the third law, the boy exerts a force in the opposite direction of equal magnitude on the belt.

After the van carrying the boy had slowed nearly to a halt, it rapidly accelerates, continuing on its westward journey. If the boy is not to be left behind, something must accelerate him as well. In accord with Newton's second law of motion, a force equal to the boy's mass multiplied by the van's acceleration must be applied his body. Initially, however, this does not happen, as he is sitting in a well-padded seat. Until his seat back compresses to the point of bottoming out, the boy does not accelerate along with the van. His speed lags behind that of the van. Only when the seat back has become fully compressed can it exert the force required to make the boy's acceleration equal that of the van.

The force that compressed the seat back is another inertial force, an effect of the acceleration of the seat back while the boy's speed did not at first change. Once the seat back is accelerating the boy forward, the third law requires that the boy exert a rearward force on the seat equal to the forward force exerted by the seat back on the boy. That force on the seat back is another inertial force, an effect of the acceleration. If the acceleration is so great that the inertial force exceeds the strength of the seat back, it will collapse rearward. This is a common effect when a vehicle is struck from behind, a so-called rear-ender. Occupied seats in rear-ended vehicles often collapse as a result of the inertial forces generated by the impact.

In summary, the force with which the boy pushes on the seat back is another example of an inertial force, an apparent force arising as the result of acceleration. The real force is the force that accelerates the boy forward. As soon as that real force stops, the inertial force stops as well. Most people have no trouble understanding that principle in an example such as this where everything is in a straight line. However, when the acceleration involves a change in the direction with no change in speed, the average person has a difficult time understanding what is causing the apparent force on the moving object. Inertial forces associated with motion such as a car going around a curve are taken up next.

INERTIAL FORCES: CIRCULAR EFFECTS

The model shifts now from the boy in the closed van to a girl on a merry-go-round who can look around all she wants. The merry-go-round rotates at a constant rate that is high enough that the girl has to hold on tightly so as not to be thrown off. She may think that she is holding on so as to "overcome the centrifugal force," and those people standing on the ground and watching her may agree. Indeed, they may have given her the phrase about overcoming centrifugal force. Nevertheless, what they all call centrifugal force is just as much an inertial force—a fictitious force—as the one discussed with the boy in the van.

The key facts are these. The girl is moving, and she is not moving in a straight line. Therefore, from Newton's first law, she must have a force applied to her. The fact that she is moving not in a straight line means that her velocity is changing. If her velocity is changing, she is being accelerated. Any object that is being accelerated must have a force applied to it. The force applied to the girl, the force that is continuously accelerating her, comes from the grip that her fingers have on the rails of the merry-go-round.

The figure shows a merry-go-round rotating within four posts, each labeled with one of four directions—east, west, north, and south. Because the merry-go-round is rotating in a clockwise sense, after the girl passes the W post she passes the N post, then the E post, and so forth. As she passes W, the direction of her velocity is straight north. (Show that her speed at any instant is equal to $2\pi R$ multiplied by the number of times per second that the merry-go-round rotates.)

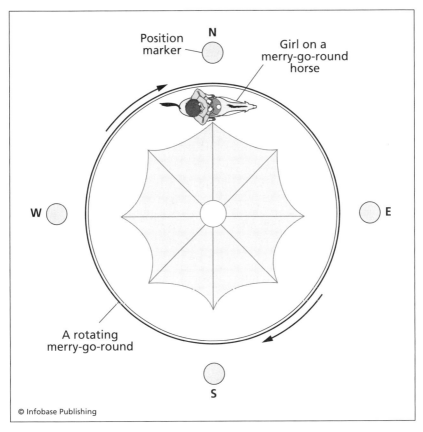

Girl riding merry-go-round and holding on so as to overcome "centrifugal force"

Passing W, with a speed *V* directed straight north, the girl will say that the centrifugal force is pulling her straight west. Then, as she goes by N with her velocity directed to the east, she will feel a pull purely to the north and so on. At each point, the centrifugal force is pulling straight out from the merry-go-round. This direction can be described as being along a line joining her to the hub of the merry-go-round. If the merry-go-round had spokes and she was sitting in line with one of them, the centrifugal force would always be directed out along the spoke. The centrifugal force is revealed for the fictitious force it is by what happens if the girl releases her grip and flies off the merry-go-round. Say that she does this while passing the W post, at which point the centrifugal force will be pulling her west. Which way will she fly? Probably to her surprise, it will not be to the west. On the other hand, if she has a good understanding of the laws of motion, an understanding that allows her to overcome her intuitive feelings, she will realize that, of course, she will fly to the south. This is because at the instant she released her grip, her velocity was to the south, and until some other force causes her velocity to deviate from that direction, she will continue heading that way as required by Newton's first law of motion. The fact that she will also be falling toward the ground will not affect her motion to the south since the force accelerating her toward the ground is perpendicular to the southward motion.

The thought experiment just described is a good demonstration of the fictitious nature of centrifugal force, which is an inertial force that exists only as long as a real force is causing the girl's velocity to change. Nevertheless, it leads to a very important conclusion. From the third law, it is known that the real force must be in the opposite direction from the centrifugal force. Therefore, the force causing her to go around with the merry-go-round is directed toward the hub of the merry-go-round, toward her center of rotation. If there is a spoke running out to her from the hub, the force will be directed inward parallel to that spoke. It is the centripetal force first named by Newton. Understanding that the force keeping someone or something moving on a circular path is a centripetal force is very important. Since acceleration is parallel to the applied force, the acceleration is also centripetal. Anyone or anything traveling on a circular path at a constant speed is undergoing centripetal acceleration.

If the merry-go-round increases its rate of rotation, the girl will have a higher speed; the magnitude of her velocity will be increased. For example, if the rate is doubled, the girl's speed must also be doubled since she will now take half as long to go around. She will have to hold on tighter since the centripetal force will have increased. What happens if she moves in closer to the hub so that the radius of the circle she moves about is smaller? Does the centripetal force on her increase? If so, by how much? Does it decrease? Same follow-up question. (Hint: her speed will be lower the closer she is to the center.)

Whatever is true of the centripetal force on the girl on the merry-go-round is also true of the centripetal force required to keep a car moving along a circular path as it increases in speed from 50 miles per hour (80 km/hr) to 60 miles per hour (96 km/hr) while still following the same curve. How strongly does this centripetal force increase with speed? Is it proportional to V so that it doubles when V doubles? Is it proportional to V^2 so that it quadruples when V doubles? Is it proportional to V^3 so that it goes up by a factor of 8 when V doubles? Also, it is clear that if the driver of a car that is traveling 50 miles per hour (80 km/hr) on a curve steers so as to direct the car around a tighter curve (one with a smaller radius of curvature, R), the required centripetal force will increase. How does the increase depend on R? Does the centripetal force double when R is cut in half? Does it quadruple? The sidebar on "Centripetal Acceleration" answers those questions and more.

(continues on page 132)

Centripetal Acceleration

It has been shown that a girl or a car moving on a circular path is continually accelerating toward the center of curvature of the path; it is undergoing centripetal acceleration. The traditional discussion used to convince students of the way in which centripetal acceleration depends on speed and the radius of curvature makes use of moveable vectors and the concept of limits as used in calculus. The discussion here will not do that and, as a result, may be more convincing.

To begin the discussion, picture a car represented by a dot traveling around a circle of radius R at a constant speed V, as shown in the figure on page 128. The car is shown in the figure at three different points around the circle. At all times, it is subject to the centripetal acceleration represented by the arrow directed toward the circle's center, the center of curvature of the car's path. The magnitude of the centripetal acceleration will be represented by a_c. (When both magnitude and direction of the centripetal acceleration are meant, a boldface symbol a_c will be used. Recall that acceleration, like velocity, has direction as well as magnitude.)

The most important characteristic about centripetal acceleration is that it is always changing direction. It is this that makes it initially a

(continues)

(continued)

Centripetal Acceleration

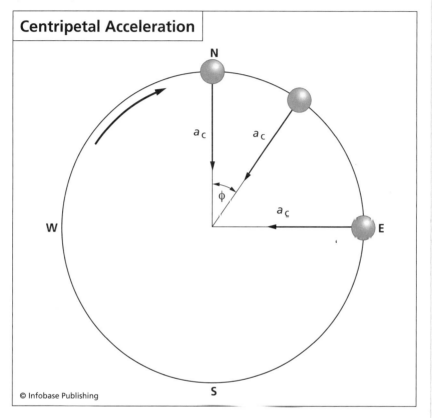

© Infobase Publishing

Car traveling on circular path, depicted at three points around the path

little difficult to grasp. One of the positions for the car depicted in the figure is at N, the northernmost point on the circle. At that point, a_c will be pointed straight south. When the car is at E, a_c will be pointed straight west, and when it is at S, a_c will be point straight north. When it is at the point shown in the figure partway between N and E, a_c will be pointing somewhere between south and west.

The figure on page 129 identifies two perpendicular lines: an east-west line and a north-south line. These lines will be used to describe

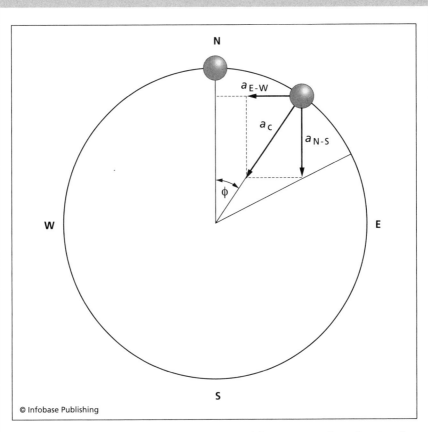

© Infobase Publishing

Showing the resolution along two directions of the centripetal acceleration for the car at a particular point

how the centripetal acceleration changes with time. When the car is at one of the positions marked by a direction sign, as depicted in the figure on page 128, a_c will be parallel to one or the other of the lines. By taking east as the positive direction along the east-west line and north the positive direction along the north-south line, some definite statements can be made about the direction of a_c at various points

(continues)

(continued)

around the circle. When the car is at N, $\boldsymbol{a}_c$ will have a value of $-\boldsymbol{a}_c$ along the north-south line and zero along the east-west line. Similarly, when the car is at E, $\boldsymbol{a}_c$ will have a value of $-\boldsymbol{a}_c$ along the east-west line and zero along the north-south line. When the car is at the point shown in the figure on page 128 between N and E, a_c will have a direction somewhere between the south direction and the west direction. The figure on page 129 shows this intermediate position, with $\boldsymbol{a}_c$ shown to have those two directions. To carry the discussion forward, the symbols a_{E-W} and a_{N-S} are now defined as follows: a_{E-W} is the part of the acceleration that lies along the east-west line and a_{N-S} the part that lies along the north-south line. They are defined so that they can be either positive or negative. Thus, for the car at the N point, a_{N-S} equals $-a_c$ and a_{E-W} equals zero. For the car at the E point, a_{E-W} equals $-a_c$ and a_{N-S} equals zero. Finally, and most interestingly, when the car is at the point on the circle between N and E a_{E-W} equals $-a_c SinN$ and a_{N-S} equals $-a_c CosN$, as indicated on the figure on page 129.

Next, consider the velocity described in terms of the east-west and north-south lines, using similar symbols, V_{E-W} and V_{N-S}. When the car is at the N point, V_{E-W} equals $+V$ and V_{N-S} equals zero. When the car reaches the E point, V_{E-W} equals zero and V_{N-S} equals $-V$. The reason for using these two perpendicular directions goes back to the point made in chapter 2 under "Velocity." Changes in the north-south direction are independent of changes in the east-west direction and vice versa. Changes in V_{E-W} are dependent only on a_{E-W} and similarly for changes in V_{N-S}. Review the statements made to this point about acceleration and velocity of the car at different points on the circle. If they do not make sense, reread them or seek help. It is important that the discussion to this point be understood completely.

Recall from chapter 2 that the distance a car traveled in a straight line during a time T is equal to T multiplied by the car's average speed during that time interval; for example, if the average speed was five miles per fortnight and the time interval was one one-hundredth of a fortnight, the distance traveled was five one-hundredths of a mile. (This would be about 250 feet.) Alternatively, if the average speed was 40 miles per hour (64 km/hr) and the time was one-eighth of an hour, the distance traveled would be five miles (8 km). The distance traveled is the change in the car's position. The speed is the rate of change of the car's position. Therefore, the rule can also be stated as follows: The car's change in position in a time T equals T multiplied by the car's average rate of change of position during that time. The arithmetic relating position and speed through time is the same as the arithmetic relating speed and acceleration through time. Therefore, one can also state that as the car goes around the circle, its change in speed along the east-west line in a time T equals T multiplied by the average east-west acceleration of the car during that time. This can be stated in symbols as follows:

$$<\Delta V_{E\,W} = a_{E\text{-}W}>T$$

where $\Delta V_{E\text{-}W}$ is the change in $V_{E\text{-}W}$ during the time T and $<a_{E\text{-}W}>$ is the average value of $a_{E\text{-}W}$ during that time. To be specific, consider T to be the time interval during which the car travels from N to E as shown in the figure on page 128. During that interval, $V_{E\text{-}W}$ changes from $+V$ to zero. Therefore, $\Delta V_{E\text{-}W}$ equals $-V$. During that same time, $a_{E\text{-}W}$ changes from zero to $-a_C$. (Check that this is so!)

   If $a_{E\text{-}W}$ changed at a constant rate during the time that the car went from N to E, its average value, $<a_{E\text{-}W}>$, would simply be one-half the sum of its starting value and its final value, that is, $<a_{E\text{-}W}>$ would equal $-a_C/2$. Unfortunately for simplicity, this is not the case. That $a_{E\text{-}W}$ does not change at a constant rate with time as the car moves from N to E can be seen from its value when the car has gone half-way, that is, after time $T/2$ has elapsed. At the halfway point, N equals $45°$. Since $Sin\,45°$ equals 0.707, $a_{E\text{-}W}$ at that point equals $-0.707a_C$. With only half of the time T elapsed, more than 70 percent of the increase in $a_{E\text{-}W}$ from its value of zero at N to its value of $-a_C$ at E has occurred. This means that the average value of $a_{E\text{-}W}$, $<a_{E\text{-}W}>$, lies somewhere between $-a_C/2$ and $-a_C$.

   From the above, the average value of $a_{E\text{-}W}$ as the car goes from N to E can be written as

$$<a_{E\text{-}W}> = -ka_C \qquad \text{(continues)}$$

(continued)

where k is a positive number lying between one-half and one. The expression for the change in ΔV_{E-W} can now be written substituting for $<a_{E-W}>$ the expression $-ka_c$. This leads to following:

$$\Delta V_{E-W} = -ka_c T$$

T is the time required for the car to go from N to E—one-fourth the way around the circle. The time required for it to go all the way around the circle is equal to the distance around the circle divided by the speed of the car. (Recall the discussion in chapter 2. This is equivalent to the statement that a car going 45 miles per hour will go 90 miles in 90/45 hours.) As has been known since at least the time of Archimedes, the distance around a circle having a radius of R is $2\Pi R$, where Π is approximately 3.14. Thus, the time the car takes to complete one lap is $2\Pi R/V$, and the time T it takes to go one-fourth that distance is one-fourth of $2\Pi R/V$, namely $(\Pi R)/(2 V)$. This allows the equation for the change in V_{E-W} to be further refined so that it can be written as follows:

$$\Delta V_{E-W} = -ka_c(\Pi R)/(2\ V)$$

(continued from page 127)

CONFIRMATION OF UNIVERSAL GRAVITATION

Equation 4–1 is the expression for centripetal acceleration that Newton used in showing that the Moon was kept in its orbit by the same gravitational force that pulled the apple to the ground and that the ratio of the Moon's acceleration to that of the apple was equal to the square of the ratio of the respective distances of the apple and the Moon from the center of the Earth. This is worth discussing as a further example of centripetal forces.

Picture an apple orbiting the Earth at treetop level. It has a centripetal acceleration of V^2/R where V is its orbital speed and R is the radius of the Earth. With the apple having a mass M, Newton's second law shows

But it has been known all along what $\Delta V_{E\text{-}W}$ is, namely $-V$, since as the car moves from N to E, $V_{E\text{-}W}$ changes from $+V$ to zero. Thus,

$$-V = -ka_c(\Pi R)/(2\ V)$$

or, rearranging terms,

$$a_c = (2/k\Pi)(V^2/R)$$

This is extremely important since, even though k (known to lie somewhere between one-half and one) has not been evaluated, the dependence of the centripetal acceleration on V and R has been determined. If the speed is doubled while the radius of curvature is unchanged, the centripetal acceleration increases by a factor of 4. If the speed is held the same while the radius of curvature doubles, the centripetal acceleration is cut in half.

It turns out that k is equal to $2/\Pi$ (approximately 0.61). Substituting $k = 2/\Pi$ into the expression above for a_c yields the simple, elegant, and incredibly important expression:

$$a_c = V^2/R$$

4-1

that the centripetal force on the orbiting apple is MV^2/R. Where does that centripetal force come from? It is from the apple's weight, of course. What else is there? Since the apple's weight is Mg, equating that weight to the centripetal force leads to the following:

$$M(V^2/R) = Mg$$

Simplifying by dividing both sides by M leads to:

$$g = V^2/R$$

In short, the centripetal acceleration of an object of whatever mass (weight) orbiting near the surface of the Earth is g. The speed of the apple in orbit can be calculated from this by substituting for g and for R, which is 21,000,000 feet (6,400,000 m). From this, it is seen that V, the apple's speed in orbit, is 26,000 ft/sec, which is 17,000 miles per hour (27,400 km/hr). Compare this with the speeds of artificial Earth satellites.

As was known from the time of Newton and before, the Moon orbits the Earth in a near-circular orbit approximately every 27.3 days. The radius of the Moon's orbit, R_{Moon}, is known to be approximately 238,000 miles (383,000 km). Thus, the distance the Moon travels in every orbit is $2\pi R_{Moon} = 1,500,000$ miles (2,214,000 km). The distance traveled in the time available requires the speed of the Moon, V_{Moon}, to be approximately 2,300 miles per hour (3,700 km/hr). The centripetal acceleration of the Moon, g_{Moon}, therefore follows from this and is:

$$g_{Moon} = V_{Moon}^2/R_{Moon} = (2300)^2/238,000 = 22.2 \text{ miles/hr}^2 = 0.009 \text{ ft/sec}^2$$

The apple is about 4,000 miles (6,400 km) from the center of the Earth, and the Moon 238,000 miles (383,000 km). The ratio of these distances is 1/60, and the square of the ratio, $(1/60)^2$, equals 1/3,600. If one divides the value of the gravitational acceleration on Earth in the U.S. system, $g = 32 \text{ ft/sec}^2$, by 3,600, one obtains 0.009 ft/sec^2, the gravitational acceleration of the Moon expressed in U.S. units. (Do this in S.I.) When Newton first did the calculation, he did not yet have an accurate value for R_{Moon}, and his results did not verify his theory that the gravitational force fell off with the square of the distance from the center of the Earth. Before the end of his career, however, the correct value was available, and he was able to confirm quantitatively the correctness of his universal theory of gravitation.

There was a lot of arithmetic displayed in this section. It was to drive home the idea that one does not begin to understand something until one can describe it in numbers, that is, quantitatively. The other half of that thought is that when one obtains a good quantitative verification of one's theories, it is a very good feeling indeed and provides the confidence needed to carry on. For a careful accident reconstructionist who is very busy, this happens on a regular basis and is one of the rewards of this type of forensic work.

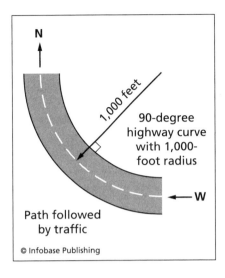

N

1,000 feet

90-degree
highway curve
with 1,000-
foot radius

◄— W

Path followed
by traffic

© Infobase Publishing

Sketch of a broad curve in a
highway, designed for a high
critical speed

CRITICAL-SPEED-SCUFF FORMULA

It has been shown that the centripetal acceleration of a car moving around a circular path is proportional to the square of the car's speed and inversely proportional to the radius of curvature, namely V^2/R. It was seen that when the circular path of an object is due to gravitational attraction—as with the Moon and the apple in the whimsical example cited above—the mass of the moving object dropped out of the expression, which is to say that mass did not appear in the final equation. This means that any object orbiting the Earth at the distance of the Moon will travel at the speed of the Moon. It turns out that something similar occurs with a vehicle following a curved path since the frictional force that keeps it following the curved path is proportional to the vehicle's weight and hence to its mass.

The figure on page 140 shows tire tracks made by a car's side-slipping tires. The figure on page 139 is a drawing of a car laying down critical-speed scuff marks. Although the radius of curvature of the path may vary slightly (or, sometimes, greatly), R will be taken as constant here. For a car of mass M to have this acceleration, the force F_C exerted on it must have the following form:

$$F_C = MV^2/R$$

The interesting development comes when one asks where that force comes from. Just as the tire/pavement friction provided the longitudinal force needed to decelerate a car when its driver applied the brakes, tire/pavement friction provides the centripetal force needed to make the car follow a circular path. Now, however, the tire/road interaction provides a lateral force, a sideways force on the car, in contrast with the longitudinal force it applied when the car was decelerating.

Normally, a car going around a curve in the road does not leave CSSMs. It is only when it is traveling at a speed that is too high for the sharpness of the curve that this happens. However, the force required to make the car follow a curved path is always given by the above expression, and it always comes from the tire/pavement friction force directed toward the center of curvature of the curve.

Just as was the case for the longitudinal tire/pavement force, there is a maximum lateral force the tire/pavement friction can produce. Think of a car with its front wheels straight and a bulldozer trying to push it sideways by exerting a force lined up with the car's center of mass. What is the maximum force that the bulldozer can apply before the car starts to slide sideways? With μ the coefficient of friction between tires and pavement, that maximum force, F_{Max}, will be μ multiplied by the car's weight, just as it was for the frictional force for the longitudinal skidding described in chapter 2.

It is not clear that the effective coefficient of friction for a tire sliding sideways is the same as it is when it is sliding forward. However, it is assumed to be the same. Knowing the maximum lateral force that the tire/road interaction can provide permits one to determine the maximum possible speed V_{max} with which a vehicle can go around a curve with a radius of curvature R. This follows since the maximum lateral frictional force will be equal to the maximum centripetal force available, F_{Cmax}. There is nowhere else for the centripetal force to come from. Therefore μMg is the maximum value that MV^2/R can take on. The maximum value of MV^2/R corresponds to the maximum value of V, namely V_{max}. Therefore, the maximum value of MV^2/R can be stated as MV_{max}^2/R. Equating the maximum centripetal force to MV_{max}^2/R, to this quantity, leads to:

$$MV_{max}^2/R = \mu Mg$$

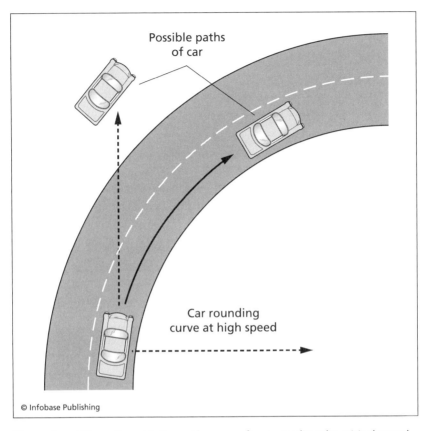

Possible paths
of car

Car rounding
curve at high speed

© Infobase Publishing

Illustration of the path *not* followed by a car after exceeding the critical speed
for a curve

Rearranging these terms, $V_{max,}$ the maximum speed with which a car
can go around a curve with radius of curvature R can be stated as the
following:

$$V_{max} = \sqrt{R\mu g}$$

or equivalently recalling the meaning of the superscript of ½:

$$V_{max} = (R\mu g)^{1/2}$$

(Equation 4–2)

Equation 4–2 is the *critical speed formula*. V_{max} is the *critical speed* for a curve of radius R when the tire/road coefficient of friction is μ. Just as with the skid-to-a-stop formula, it sometimes is written in a way that allows one to obtain V_{max} in miles per hour after substituting for R in feet. Using $g = 32.2$ ft/sec² and the conversion factor for going from ft/sec to miles per hour, Equation 4–2 can be written

$$V_{max} = 3.87\sqrt{\mu R}$$

(Equation 4–3)

Highway engineers use the critical-speed formula to design curves in roads. Starting with a knowledge of the speeds at which cars will be traveling on the road they determine the minimum radius of curvature for the road's curves. (Given the value of land, the goal is for the road not to take up more land than is necessary. Another consideration is to minimize the amount of earth and rock to be moved in the construction of the road. Minimizing the radius of curvature for a given direction change minimizes both the area needed for the curve and the amount of earth-moving that is needed.) The engineers' approach is to ensure that the critical speed for all the curves is considerably higher than the highest speeds expected on the new road. Sometimes, following a crash where a car ran off the road, there is a question as to whether the design engineers did a good job; for example, the figure on page 135 represents a highway curve with a radius of curvature of 1,000 feet (305 m) and a length of 1,570 feet (478 m). This curve will carry cars traversing it though a 90° change of direction, as can been seen. Traffic entering the curve heading west emerges from the curve heading north. There is no banking of the curve. Using Equation 4–2 and a μ of 0.8 show that the critical speed for the curve is 109 miles per hour (175 km/hr). This value is far higher than the speed limits of 65 or 70 miles per hour (105 km/hr or 113 km/hr) that prevail on most high-speed highways in the United States and Canada. It is in fact nearly 30 miles per hour higher than the highest posted U.S. speed limits: 80 miles per hour (130 km/hr), which prevail for some counties in western Texas.

In most of the United States and Canada, highways are occasionally snow-packed. This can reduce the tire/road coefficient of friction to 0.2 or lower. Show that with μ equal to 0.2, the critical speed for the curve

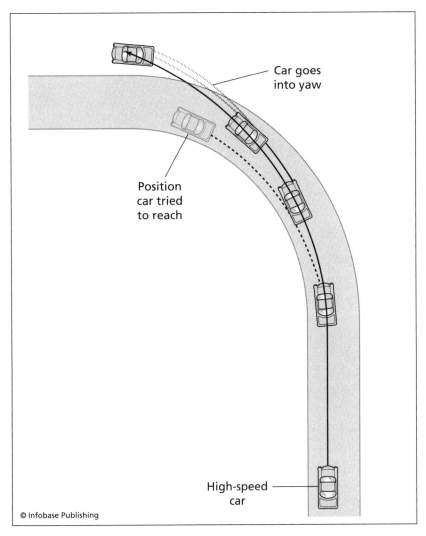

Illustration of the path followed by a car after exceeding the critical speed for the curve it was following, with the critical-speed scuff marks shown

shown in the figure on page 135 falls to 54.5 miles per hour (87.7 km/hr). On rarer occasions and primarily in the mid-southern United States, roads may become covered with wet ice, leading to a μ of 0.05 or lower. Show that under those conditions the critical speed would be cut by a further factor of two, to about 27 miles per hour (44 km/hr).

Crossover in cornering marks, indicating the place on the road where an inside tire making cornering marks crossed over the path followed by the front tire on the same side of the vehicle

© Infobase Publishing

Even on the Interstate Highway System in the United States, there are some terrains where traffic engineers do not have the luxury of designing curves with a radius of curvature of 1,000 feet (305 m). Show that if, instead of the curve depicted in the figure on page 135 mountainous terrain required that a road have a curve with a radius of curvature of only 100 feet (30.5 m), the critical speed for that curve when the road is dry will be only 35 miles per hour (56 km/hr).

Recall the girl and the merry-go-round. There is presumably a rotation rate for the merry-go-round that is so great that the girl cannot hold on. Her maximum grip is exceeded by the centripetal force needed to keep her going around in circles. When that happens, she will part ways with the merry-go-round and fly off in the direction she was headed when her grip was broken. Apply that reasoning to a car successfully traveling in a circle of radius R. The equivalent action to the merry-go-round increasing its rotation rate is for the car's driver to increase the car's speed. Eventually, the speed will exceed the critical speed for the radius of the path the car had been following. What happens then? In a sense, the car's tires will "break loose." If the car then behaved like the girl thrown off the merry-go-round when her hands broke loose, the car would go straight off the road, as shown in the figure on page 137. That is not what happens. Instead of the car shooting off the road in a straight line for having exceeded the critical speed, it just moves out to a larger radius of curvature and then continues around the curve. It is a self-adjusting reaction by the car. By shifting outward to a curve with a

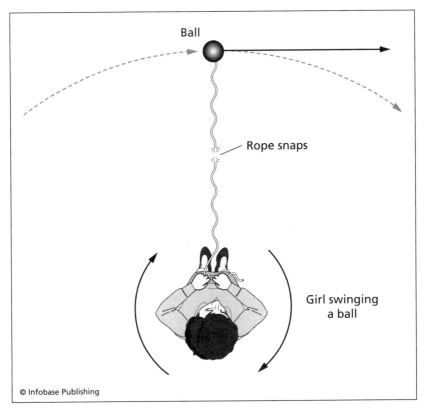

Ball

Rope snaps

Girl swinging
a ball

© Infobase Publishing

A different type of critical speed being exceeded, and the consequences

higher radius of curvature, it moves to a path for which its speed does not exceed the critical speed. (A crude analogy lies with a ball being swung in a circle by a child who is connected to the ball by an elastic rope. There will be a maximum speed corresponding to each length of the rope, and the rope will lengthen as the ball's speed is increased so that the radius of the circular orbit will be the right value for each speed, given the force the stretched rope can apply to the ball. This contrasts with what happens with a nonstretchable string when the required centripetal force exceeds the strength of the string, as shown in the figure on this page.

Picture again what happens to the car that is increasing its speed around a curved path. When the speed exceeds a certain level, the rear end of the car slips outward so that the rear tires go from tracking inside the front tires to tracking outside of them, as described earlier in the chapter. Often, the outward slip of the rear end takes place after cornering marks have started to appear, allowing one to see a crossover point where the mark from the outside rear tire crosses the mark from the outside front tire. (Normally, the marks made by the tires on the outside of the curve are darker than those made by the inside tires. This is the result of the weight shift associated with the vehicle's motion where weight is lifted off the inside tires and increased on the outside tires. This is referred to by the phrases *unloading* and *loading,* respectively.) The figure on page 140 shows such a crossover. This adjustment where a small rotation of the car about its yaw axis shifts the car's rear end outward orients the rear tires so that their lateral friction force is directed more nearly toward the center of rotation of the car's path; that is, it increases the centripetal force available from the rear tires.

All too often, of course, the increasing radius of curvature that the car seeks causes it to go off the road. Once that happens, the car often rolls over and, frequently, unrestrained occupants ejected. The highest risk factor for fatal injuries in a motor vehicle crash is being ejected.

APPLYING THE CRITICAL-SPEED FORMULA

More often than might be thought, an inspection of an accident scene will reveal cornering marks made by one or more of the accident vehicles before impact. The cornering marks are recognizable because of their lateral striations. In those cases where two or more cornering marks belonging to a set can be found, it is usually possible to get a good estimate of the speed of the vehicle leaving them by using the critical-speed formula. All that is needed is to measure the radius of curvature R of one of the marks selected as a critical-speed scuff mark and determine the tire/pavement coefficient of friction μ for that stretch of pavement. Since the curves are not perfect arcs, the radius will be measured at several points along the mark to get a feel for R. Normally, if the driver was not applying throttle as the marks were being created, R will decrease as one moves forward on the mark. This is because part of the frictional force generated by the side sliding tires is longitudinal and goes to decelerate the car. As the car slows down, with the steering wheel turned hard to one direction or the other, the available centripetal force pulls the car's trajectory into a tighter curve. The radius of curvature R should be found

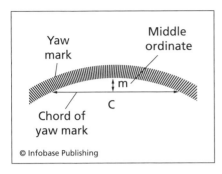

Yaw mark

Middle ordinate

↕ m

Chord of yaw mark

C

© Infobase Publishing

Illustrating one method of finding the radius of curvature of critical-speed scuff marks

to be constant or slowly decreasing along the mark if the coefficient of friction does not vary along the mark. Ideally, there should be marks from three of the vehicle's tires; however, two marks from the same side of the car will be sufficient. When a car starts to lay down cornering marks, it is usually the front outside tire that starts marking first, then the rear outside tire. Thus, when there are just two cornering marks to examine, it is usually the two outside tires that have made the marks. They should be treated as useful for the critical-speed formula only after the point where the rear tire has started tracking outside the front tire, that is, past the crossover point.

MEASURING THE RADIUS OF CURVATURE

There are several ways to measure the radius of curvature of these cornering marks. Most commonly, a tape measure is stretched between two points on the mark separated by at least 50 feet (15 m) and preferably 100 feet (30.5 m). Since the mark is taken to be an arc of a circle, the tape is a chord of that arc; the length of that chord will be designated C. At the middle point on the tape, one measures the distance to the mark. This distance is the middle ordinate of the arc. Call it m (See the figure). A little geometry shows that the radius of curvature R of the arc is given by the following expression:

$$R = C^2/8m + m/2$$

4–4

When one is dealing with critical-speed scuff marks, the value of the first term is always so great that the second term can be neglected. Typical numbers are C equal to 100 feet (30.5 m) and m equal to 1.25 feet

(0.4 m). Substituting these numbers into the expression for R yields the following:

$$R = 10,000/10 + 0.625 \text{ feet}$$

The radius of curvature of the mark in question can be stated to be 1,000 feet (305 m). That it would be absurd to work with $R = 1,000.625$ feet (304.9905 m) can be seen from recalling the purpose for which it is going to be used. It is going to be substituted into the critical-speed scuff formula, $V = (R\mu g)^{1/2}$. Given that neither μ nor g is going to be stated to better than two-digit precision, substituting a value of R with seven-figure precision would reveal that one did not know what one was doing.

In an alternative method for obtaining R, one begins by laying down a chord to define endpoints of an arc. Next, instead of measuring the middle ordinate, one uses a measuring wheel to determine the length S of the arc itself. Some straightforward geometry reveals that the following relationship holds between the measured quantities and R.

$$\sin(S/2R) = C/2R$$

One way to extract R from this equation, that is, to solve it for R, is to graph on the same axes the expressions on the left and right sides of the equation, taking R as the variable. The value of R at which the two lines intersect is the answer. The advantage of this method is that it avoids reliance on measurements of the middle ordinate, m. It is never possible to eliminate all error from physical measurements, and therefore the goal is to minimize the importance of the errors. Length measurements made on the roadway tend to have the same degree of uncertainty regardless of the magnitude of the length being measured. The middle ordinate is usually a small number, sometimes just a inch or so, meaning that its measurements have relatively large uncertainties. As can be seen from Equation 4–4 for R, a relatively large error in m will introduce a large error in R and, hence, in the speed calculated from the critical-speed formula, even though R only enters it as a square root.

The table on page 145 contains police measurements of points along a set of four critical-speed scuff marks.

As an exercise, plot these numbers on graph paper, and then measure the radius of curvature of the marks at various places along the marks.

X (feet)	Y(feet) Mark #1	Y(feet) Mark #2	Y(feet) Mark #3	Y(feet) Mark #4
0.0	17.25	16.80		
10.0	18.25	17.55		
20.0	19.08	18.23		
30.0	19.75	18.73	13.60	
40.0	20.10	18.81	13.95	
50.0	20.35	18.75	13.77	
60.0	20.32	18.43	13.55	
70.0	20.10	17.88	13.10	
80.0	19.55	17.20	12.19	
90.0	18.95	16.07	11.40	
100.0	18.02	14.75	10.15	
110.0	16.95	13.31	8.56	
120.0	15.60	11.52	6.82	
130.0	13.90	9.25	4.85	9.85
140.0	11.97	6.83	2.52	8.13
150.0	9.75	3.94	-0.09	6.05
160.0	7.20	0.82	-2.82	4.05
170.0	4.50	-2.58	-5.79	1.67
173.7			-6.91	
180.0	1.34			-1.10
181.5		-6.75		
183.8	0.00			
190.0	-2.11			
197.3				-6.33

Note: An array of data taken from a four-mark set of yaw marks. The value for X was measured along a straight line near the edge of the road. The value for Y for each X value listed was the distance from the straight reference line to the tire mark for that X value.

What conclusions can be drawn? What would be the effect on the conclusions if it turned out that the road had had an uneven coating of black
ice at the time the marks were created? The phrase *black ice* is used for
the thin layer of transparent ice that sometimes appears on roads. It is
actually frost and forms on subfreezing surfaces when the temperature of
the air falls below the dew point. Because it is transparent, drivers often
are not aware of it and therefore may rely on tire/pavement friction that
is not present. What would be the consequences for the driver of the car
leaving these marks if the police did not realize that there was a greatly
reduced tire/pavement coefficient of friction on the road when they were
made? What can be said about the trajectory of the car if the coefficient
of friction varied between 0.8 and 0.4 in some irregular fashion as it
lay down these marks? Finally, use the fact that the car that made these
marks had a wheelbase of 8.25 feet (2.5 m) and a track width in both
front and rear of 4.9 feet (1.5 m). If these terms are unfamiliar, look back
to the discussion of the investigation of the hit and-run in chapter 2.

A final comment relates to a subject that has been touched on lightly
so far and will be taken up in some detail in a later chapter: precision.
Thanks to calculators and computers, some investigators, either through
carelessness or ignorance, include far too many digits in reporting the
speeds that they have calculated. This seems to be particularly common for speeds obtained from the CSSM method. Consider the speed
indicated by a CSSM with a radius of curvature of 990 feet (302 m) on
a road presenting a tire/pavement coefficient of friction of 0.8. Substituting into the critical-speed scuff formula derived earlier, one would
obtain, in U.S. units:

$$V = (990 \times 0.8 \times 32)^{1/2} = (25,344)^{1/2}$$

So far, so good, though there might be some objection to displaying five-
digit precision given that the coefficient of friction is probably known to
only one-digit precision. Nevertheless, the real error takes place at the
next step when the investigator takes the square root and reports that:

$$V = 159.1979899 \text{ ft/sec}$$

just because his or her calculator provided that fine number. Although
it is rare that a speed with quite this many digits would be reported, it

is not uncommon to see four or five digits being used to report something that at best is not known to better than two digits. In other words, the speed calculated from the measurements described above should be reported as 160 ft/sec (49 m/s).

A KEY ASSUMPTION REVEALED

This chapter has presented the very important CSSM method for determining speed. An important step along the way was the derivation of the maximum speed V_{Max} with which a vehicle can follow a path with radius of curvature R when the tire/pavement coefficient of friction is µ, namely the critical-speed formula

$$V_{\text{Max}} = \sqrt{R\mu g}$$

The confession is that there was a giant step taken in concluding that any vehicle that produced curved marks with lateral striations was traveling at the maximum speed for that curve. This was equivalent to stating that all vehicles are able to round a given curve at the maximum theoretical speed for that radius of curvature, or, stated differently, it was equivalent to saying that whenever a vehicle rounding a curved path began to sideslip, it was traveling at the critical speed for that path. For this to be true, all the frictional force of all four of the vehicle's tires must be contributing to the centripetal force the vehicle's center of mass. In general, one cannot expect this to be the situation since the frictional force will be in the opposite direction in which the tire is sliding. For this reason, it seems to require a leap of faith to conclude that the car that created yaw marks with a radius of curvature R was traveling at the maximum speed possible for that value of R.

The essence of the CSSM method is the assumption that when a car creates yaw marks, it is traveling at the maximum possible speed consistent with the radius of curvature of its path. The method is, of course, testable. All one has to do is to create yaw marks with a car while it is traveling at a known rate of speed. This is usually done on a paved surface that provides a great deal of room on all sides and simply involves swerving hard with the car. If the swerve is sudden enough, measurable yaw marks will be created. The radius of curvature of each mark is then measured and substituted into the critical-speed formula so that the result can be compared with the known speed of the vehicle that left the marks. During the past 30 years, a great number of such tests have been done, using a variety of maneuvers. For reasons that are still not understood, the results from these tests support a broad use of the CSSM method. This is very important since the increasing fraction of vehicles that are equipped with antilock brakes will soon eliminate the skid-to-a-stop technique for finding speed. The CSSM method may become the only way in which tire marks can be used to estimate vehicle speed.

5

Murder Poorly Disguised as an Accident

The case featured in this chapter exemplifies how law and technology are enmeshed in the forensic enterprise and the fact that most criminals are too ignorant about physics to make their crimes resemble accidents successfully. It is presented here both to introduce several new disciplines used in the field of accident reconstruction and to give an idea of how accident reconstruction exposes such crudely disguised acts. The case is based on an actual tragic event, though with some identifying aspects changed. One of the criminal-law concepts which it illustrates is that a distinction exists between disproving an innocent explanation for an event and proving that the person who was shielded by the innocent explanation had committed a crime. This concept is related to the idea—honored more in some areas of the law than others—that proving an event to have been a crime requires more than establishing that no one has been able to provide a noncriminal explanation for the event. An additional object lesson from the story told in this chapter is that disaster can follow when forensic investigators fail to keep their minds open early in an investigation. As for accident reconstruction techniques, this chapter harkens back to the fall formula developed in chapter 3 while also introducing in a simple way the speed-from-crush approach to estimating vehicle impact speeds. Finally, since the case involved the consumption by fire of a car and its occupants, the subject of incendiary automobile fires is discussed, along with the production and the use of electric sparks in igniting such fires.

FIRE IN THE DITCH

On a cold December morning in 1983, James Michael awoke around 6:00 A.M. to a crackling sound coming from the hillside road that his house fronted. Leaping from bed, he saw flames shooting up from the other side of the road and discovered that they were coming from a late-model Saab 900. He saw the burning car on the embankment lining the road, with its front bumper nosed down into the narrow stream at the foot of the embankment. He noted that its headlights were still on, illuminating the snow lying in the darkness alongside the road. As he called 911, he noted that his outdoor thermometer read −4°F (−20°C). Within minutes, the police chief of Mr. Michael's small rural town arrived, followed by the volunteer fire department and, finally, a state trooper. The photo shows the country road leading up to and past the crash site. The arrow points to a landmark on the opposite side of the road from where the car was discovered.

Even before the flames were extinguished, the charred remains of two people could be seen inside the car, one near the steering wheel and the other lying atop some kind of support in the rear-seat area. In addition, a number of what appeared to be cinder blocks could be seen in the car's front interior in a jumbled pile and also behind what had been the front-seat backs.

The first responders determined from the license plate that the vehicle was registered to a local postal employee living a tenth of a mile uphill from the crash. She was known to the responders, as was her teenage son and her husband, a recent retiree from the state police with whom the trooper at the scene and by then the officer in charge was personally acquainted. The trooper walked with a local law-enforcement officers up to the home of the presumed victims. They found the woman's husband up and dressed but, to their surprise, he had no interest in accompanying them back down to the burning car. Instead, he ran to the garage, returning seconds later shouting angrily that his stepson had taken a bucket of

Looking down the road toward the crash site, which was on the left side *(New Hampshire State Police)*

gasoline that he had been told explicitly to leave at home. He said that the gasoline was being used to clean a carburetor that his stepson had brought home from his after-school job at an automobile repair shop. He added that his wife, upset at having to drive her son to his job site before taking him to school that morning, had peeled out as she left the driveway. Asked about the cinder blocks thought to have been seen in the car, he replied that the boy had loaded them onto the plywood platform in the rear of the car to improve the car's traction. The plywood, he said, was there to support his wife's mailbags while she made deliveries along her route.

In a casual conversation years after the event, the local police officer paraphrased what he remembered of the porch conversation, in particular what the trooper had said regarding what had happened, namely the following:

The gasoline pail must have been placed on the platform above the back seat. When the car accelerated violently, the pail would have slid around, probably causing the gasoline to slosh over. This would have led the son to climb in back to steady it. Because of the temperature, the car's windows would have been rolled up and its electric seat heaters operating. In that closed environment, the driver probably became woozy, which would explain her veering off the road. Or maybe she was turning around to help steady the gasoline and that caused her to lose control. At any event, when the car ran off the road and down the embankment, the cinder blocks flew forward, knocking out both occupants. That's why they did not attempt to get out of the car.

The crash would also have shorted out the seat heaters, igniting the gasoline. A really tragic accident and a warning not to transport open containers of gasoline in a car.

This paraphrasing accurately tracked the theory contained in the trooper's formal report which was filed a month after the 1983 event. Not contained in that report was any mention of a stain on the husband's pants that the police officer still recalled years later, commenting "The red stain on that guy's pants sure didn't look like paint to me, but I wasn't the officer in charge, and the Trooper accepted the paint explanation."

After the trooper announced his conclusions on the porch, he said that since there was no need for further investigation, the car and contents would be released as soon as the usual paperwork could be completed, and that is what happened. Within a few days of the fire, the human remains were cremated without an autopsy or even any examination by the medical examiner, and the car was compacted.

The sum total of the 1983 investigation consisted of eight photographs, five of the car at its postimpact rest position and three after it was removed to its temporary holding lot. Nevertheless, those photos were enough to destroy every aspect of the earlier theory of the event, a theory that had shielded the person on whom suspicion fairly or unfairly normally falls following a suspicious death, the victim's spouse.

In the late 1990s, the state police were approached by a middle-aged woman, Claudia Kaltenberg, claiming that her now-ex-boyfriend told her that he had murdered his wife and stepson with an ax in 1983 and staged a car crash and fire to cover it up. When the state police seemed to her to lack sufficient interest in what she had to say, she went to the attorney general (AG), the top law-enforcement official in the state. When she again sensed that she was rebuffed, she wrote to the FBI reporting a conspiracy extending throughout state government with the goal of covering up a terrible crime.

Contrary to Ms. Kaltenberg's impression, the AG's office had taken her very seriously and had immediately begun an investigation. The AG's detectives recognized in their first review of the file that the earlier investigation had been inadequate, an inadequacy they attributed to the investigating trooper's understandable sympathy for a friend who had just lost his wife and stepson.

Before reading past the sidebar on "Prejudice in Forensic Investigation," list the questions that should have been asked or otherwise investigated in the immediate aftermath of the fire in 1983. In making the list, use the facts and statements set out above and also the accident reconstruction and forensic science ideas described so far in this book.

Prejudice in Forensic Investigation

The most important detrimental prejudices in forensic investigations, in increasing seriousness, are: (1) preconceptions as to how a particular test will turn out; (2) the investigator's knowledge of how the hiring party hopes the investigation will turn out; (3) excess attachment to a theory of the case early in the investigation.

Preconception Pitfalls

Forensic investigations often require physical tests; this is especially true with accident reconstruction. As with any scientific work, it is important to avoid prejudging an experiment or, if this is impossible, to be aware of the risks of the preconception so as to avoid being influenced by it. Believing that one knows beforehand how a test will turn out can affect the test's validity in a number of ways, some of them blatant, some of them quite subtle. At its most blatant, the preconception can lead to skipping the experiment entirely and, instead, doing a dry lab. Doing a dry lab (dry labbing) is writing a report as if

(continues)

the experiment had been done, supplying the results that one is sure would have been obtained in the experiment. It is a rare student who has not done this at one time or another in a lab course with the risk of failing the course if discovered. When a forensic scientist does this, it is at the risk of going to jail. In contrast, one of the subtlest errors arising from a preconception of a test result is the instrument-tapping fallacy. Everyone tends to fall into this trap, including those who do not even think of themselves as making scientific measurements. In the version from which the name arises, it takes the form of tapping on an instrument when the instrument does not read what one expects, but not tapping otherwise. It may be that the instrument had a stuck indicator needle and that the tapping unstuck it, permitting it to move to the correct reading. (Sticking due to friction is common with the needles in mechanical barometers; they should always be tapped to obtain a correct value for the atmospheric pressure.) However, to avoid error, one must also tap the instrument when its initial reading is the one that is expected. In short, one always taps or one never taps. (The instrument-tapping fallacy can occur in many contexts, most of which do not involve an instrument to tap. One example is the tendency to redo calculations if one does not like the first answer while not doing so if the answer first calculated is the one expected. List two other contexts where the instrument-tapping fallacy can lead to error.)

Wish-to-Please Pitfalls
The danger of a forensic scientist being influenced, consciously or unconsciously, by the employing party's hopes pervades all aspects of a forensic investigation and not just in the performance of tests or experiments. An obvious way to avoid this danger is to keep the investigators ignorant of the employing party's identification, for example, whether it is the prosecutor or the defense attorney. However, though this can sometimes be readily done for individual tests requested by the investigator, this approach to blind testing is usually very difficult to manage for the entire investigation. Usually, the forensic investigators know the identification of the party who has hired them and, therefore, how that party hopes the investigation will turn out. (Though

most parties at a very early stage in an investigation may be simply interested in the truth, letting the chips fall where they may, once a prosecutor has decided to go forward, the emphasis will be on obtaining evidence to support the prosecution; the defense attorney has no choice but to strive for evidence that will create reasonable doubt of the defendant's guilt.) Since the forensic investigator must be seeking the truth and not be simply assisting one side or the other, he or she has always to be on guard against being swayed by considerations having nothing to do with science.

Early-Theory-Adoption Pitfalls

By adopting a theory early on, even the most honest and objective investigator can be led astray. Of all the sources of error, becoming married to a theory too early in one's work is probably the most common source of failed investigations. Perhaps because their experience leads them to quickly see patterns, police investigators tend to be most susceptible to this flaw, and the consequent narrowing of concentration to confirmatory evidence. This confirmation error leads to selecting tests that can confirm the favored theory to the exclusion of those that could contradict it. There is no better illustration of this pitfall than the case presented in this chapter. The first investigator decided almost immediately that he was looking at a tragic accident and not a deliberate act. His efforts, therefore, became directed from the outset not at learning what happened but at developing the answers necessary to support this theory. This he did by figuring out how to explain in a nonincriminating way (1) why the car veered off a relatively straight dry road into the ditch in the absence of other traffic only seconds after it had left its own driveway, (2) why neither victim exited the car after what was such a soft impact that the vehicle lights were still on, (3) why the younger victim was awkwardly positioned between the plywood platform and the ceiling rather than being in a front seat next to his mother, and (4) why the gasoline ignited. Once he heard about the gasoline and the cinder blocks, he looked no further than his own

(continues)

(continued)

imagination for evidence supporting his theory of the case. That he did this completely innocently and with no thought that he was covering up a crime exemplifies how powerfully the early adoption of a theory can distort a forensic investigation.

After pointing out the danger of adopting a theory of a case early in an investigation, it must be admitted that it is nearly impossible to avoid doing so. Indeed, without some model or models for what might have happened, it is difficult if not impossible to organize one's investigation. This is what makes it so important for the forensic investigator to reflect continually on whether the investigation has become too narrowly focused. The best safeguard is to devise tests or questions continually that have the capacity to disprove the favored theory.

THE INVESTIGATION

Specialists in forensic engineering science get called in at widely varying stages in an investigation. They, of course, prefer to be in at the start, while the physical evidence from the underlying event is still lying around (some would say "before the blood dries"). On other occasions, they are called in after the first scene investigation is complete and then work with law enforcement or defense in trying to complete the picture. The present case was somewhat unusual, though not unique, in that the event had occurred years before and had been subject to two extended investigations before the outside forensic specialists were invited in. This meant, among other things, a tremendously large file to assimilate before venturing to take any new steps.

Unasked Questions

After reviewing the file, which had grown quite lengthy by that time because of the initial legwork done by the AG's detectives, the forensic task force assembled by the AG pointed out that the following preliminary questions should have been asked immediately after the interview at the victims' residence was completed:

1. Did the 1982 Saab 900 have rear-wheel drive?

2. Were the Saab's rest position and frontal damage consistent with its having gone off the road at highway speeds?

3. Was it plausible that electric seat heaters ignited the gasoline? Were there any other ignition sources for the gasoline either inside or outside the occupant compartment?

4. How long would it take a fire that was ignited inside a closed Saab 900 to develop into the blaze discovered by the resident from across the road?

5. Was it plausible that neither occupant of the vehicle could have opened a door and jumped out after the impact?

Answers

As to the first question, most persons with even a minor knowledge of automobile history would have known that one of the characterizing features of Saab automobiles was their exclusive use of front wheel drive since the first one hit the streets in 1950, decades before most other manufacturers abandoned rear wheel drive. This question as to which end of the Saab housed the drive wheels was important, given the explanation offered the police officers in 1983 for the presence of the cinder blocks. It may have turned out that the man giving that explanation knew that it was only his stepson's ignorance that led him to add weight over the rear wheels of a front-wheel-drive car. However, failure to explore this question was characteristic of the 1983 investigation.

Why it would have been foolish to add weight in the back of a Saab to increase its traction and why, nevertheless, the average driver at the time might have thought it a reasonable thing to do are discussed in the sidebar on Vehicle Acceleration.

MURDER

By the time the full investigation got under way more than a decade after the deaths, the working theory of the case was that criminal activity had been behind the incident. More particularly, the theory was that the victims were already dead when they were placed in the car along with the bucket of gasoline and that the car had been placed at the edge of the road and the gasoline ignited before being pushed down the embankment. (Given the discussion of prejudice in forensic investigations, what, if any, bad effect might this working theory have had on the investigation?) This theory seemed to be supported by the relatively little frontal damage displayed in the photographs of the vehicle involved in the incident. Could the investigators' theory have minimized this damage in their eyes? Also, the difficulty of igniting gasoline and maintaining it burning under the conditions that supposedly prevailed in December 1983 further supported the investigators' belief that the fire was *incendiary,* that is, that it had been set, rather than being accidental.

First Crash Test

Two series of road and crash tests were carried out in the late 1990s using two 1982 Saab 900s in good condition which had been made available through the cooperation of Saab, Inc., and the assistance of a local Saab dealer. It is standard practice in many types of forensic investigation to make use of what is called an exemplar. In this case, each of the test vehicles was an exemplar of the vehicle involved in the 1983 crash and fire. Typically, one can obtain a great deal of information about an event from working with an undamaged version of a key object involved in the event.

Determining Where the Car Would Head by Itself

Could the car have rolled several hundred feet without a driver before crashing that morning in 1983? The question had first been raised by an anonymous report that actual tests had shown that this was not only possible but likely. In addition, the thought occurred to the later investigators that if the 1983 impact and fire had been a criminal act, the person responsible would have wanted to be some distance from the vehicle when it left the road. Even though the event had taken place early in the morning, it would have been impossible to be sure that no one would come along the road at just the time the car, already burning or not, was leaving the road. Because of these considerations, the first test done during the detailed investigation called for an exemplar vehicle to be permitted to roll, driverless, along the road from a starting location several hundred feet from the 1983 impact point.

(continues on page 164)

Vehicle Acceleration

In investigations of motor-vehicle crashes, one often needs to know how fast a particular vehicle could have accelerated during the seconds or minutes before the crash. This comes up, for example, when in the wake of an intersection collision a driver says that he or she was just starting up after stopping for a stop sign. If the accident reconstructionist has determined the car's speed at impact, knowledge of its acceleration rate may provide a test of the driver's truthfulness concerning from where it started. The exploration in chapter 2 of frictional forces in connection with learning how quickly a vehicle can stop provides the information needed to calculate maximum acceleration rates. As will be seen, the maximum acceleration rate is usually much lower than the maximum deceleration rate.

As has been said earlier, the word *acceleration* applies to both speeding up and slowing down, just as an elevator both elevates people and goods and lowers them. In short, any change in velocity is acceleration. Nevertheless, the practice in this book has been to use the nontechnical word *deceleration* for slowing down and to limit acceleration to refer to increasing speed. For example, when a car starts up from a stop sign, it will said to be accelerating, and when it brakes for the next stop sign, it will be said to be decelerating.

Pressing down on a vehicle's accelerator pedal causes the vehicle's throttle to open wider, allowing more fuel into its engine. This in turn causes more power to be sent to the drive wheels, which then increase the force with which the tires on those wheels push on the road. It should be a check on one's understanding of Newton's third law of motion to see whether one understands why the car accelerates because that force on the pavement points to the rear of the vehicle. In any event, this is what happens. The car speeds up, and by knowing the weight of the vehicle, the acceleration desired, and Newton's second law of motion, one can determine the force that is needed.

(continues)

(continued)

Say that a 3,200-pound (14,200-N) vehicle is to be accelerated at a rate of 0.33g. What is the force required at the point where the rubber meets the road? One starts with the second law,

$$F = MA$$

The vehicle has a mass M of 100 slugs (1,460 kg). Stated in U.S. units, then, the force is 100A, and one just needs to substitute for A the 0.33g in U.S. units to reach the needed force F. (In S.I., the relationship becomes 1460A with 0.33g to be stated in m/sec².) The answer is +1,056 pounds (4,697 N). Defining the forward direction as positive, each of the drive wheels must cause a force of –528 pounds (–2,348 N) to be exerted on the pavement. (Note the sign, and remember the third law.)

What if one wanted to accelerate at 2g or 10g? Could one just proceed as above to solve for F? Well, yes, but calculating the necessary force and supplying it are two distinct tasks. There is a limit to the force that even the most powerful engine on the road or racetrack can produce at the drive wheels. An even more important limitation is the maximum force that the drive wheels can cause their tires to apply to the pavement before those tires break away and the wheels start spinning.

From chapter 2, the maximum frictional force that can be produced between tire and road is μW_T, where W_T is the weight supported by tire, that is, the force with which the tire is pressed down against the pavement, and μ is the tire/pavement coefficient of friction. The example of the 3,200-pound (14,200-N) vehicle needing to accelerate at 0.33g will be continued so as to explore the meaning of the friction limitation. The vehicle will be taken to be an empty rear-wheel-drive pickup truck, for which the weight split between the front and rear axles is typically about 70–30. This split means that W_T is about 15 percent of the total weight, W, which has been given as 3,200 pounds (14,200 N). Thus, W_T is 480 pounds (2,130 N), and the maximum frictional force available at each tire is 480μ.

On dry pavement, μ is usually close to 0.8, for which the maximum tire/pavement force available is 385 pounds (1,700 N). Therefore, when the pickup's engine tries to produce a force of −528 pounds (−2,348 N) at the tire/pavement interface, the rear tires will break away. In short, trying to make the truck accelerate at 0.33g will cause the drive wheels to spin and, generally, make a lot of noise and sometimes smoke. This does not mean that there will be no acceleration. A vehicle peeling out is accelerating even as its drive wheels are spinning and the tires are squealing and deteriorating.

What is the acceleration for the pickup truck as it peels out? As always, Newton's second law holds, and the acceleration will equal F'/M, where F' is the total force exerted against the pavement by the two spinning drive wheels. But that will equal twice the force of each spinning tire against the road, namely the maximum frictional force just calculated, 385 pounds (1,700 N). Therefore, F' equals 770 pounds (3,400 N) and will accelerate the 100-slug pickup at 7.7 ft/sec^2, which is about 0.24g.

But wait: Two important factors were left out. One is the difference between static and sliding friction, as already revealed in the chapter 2 sidebar on "Static Versus Sliding Friction and Antilock Braking." Until now, since the interest was on skidding to a stop, the emphasis was on sliding friction. Most people have found that when trying to slide something heavy across the floor that more force is required to get it started than is required to keep it sliding. Another way of stating this is to say that the static coefficient of friction is higher than the sliding coefficient, one of the factors arguing for antilock brakes, as stated in chapter 2.

The statement that the tire/pavement value for μ is usually approximately 0.8 is referring to the sliding coefficient. When the sliding value for μ at the tire/pavement interface is 0.8, the static value is normally 0.85 to 0.90. It is clear that the condition for tire breakaway has to be recalculated. This can be done with little additional effort. If μ equals

(continues)

(continued)

0.9, the maximum frictional force for the pickup truck example will be higher by a factor of 9/8 from that found above. This makes it 433 pounds (1,930 N) at each tire, still not quite enough to cause the car to accelerate at 0.33g. However, applying the second factor ignored above may be enough to meet the threshold.

The other factor was weight shift. As most people know from observation, when a car accelerates rapidly, its front end rises and its rear end sinks. This reflects the weight-shift caused by the acceleration. The weight on the front tires is reduced, and the weight on the rear ones is increased. Up to a point, the higher the acceleration rate, the greater is this shift.

For the 3,200-pound (14,200-N) pickup how much weight shift has to occur to permit the 0.33g acceleration when the static value for μ is 0.9? In other words, how much does that 70–30 split have to change to increase the maximum available friction force from 433 pounds (1,910 N) to 528 pounds (2,350 N)? Show that a shift to 63–37 will do it. (Hint: There is a short way to do this and a longer way.)

Consider now that the pickup truck is stopped on a snowy road, such that the static coefficient of friction is reduced to only 0.25. Show that with no weight shift the maximum force producible by the drive wheels is 240 pounds (1,068 N). If the driver carefully applies power to the drive wheels so as to produce the maximum possible force at each wheel without slipping (120 pounds), the vehicle will accelerate forward at 2.4 ft/sec^2, which is only 0.075g. (Are these the correct values?) The no-weight-shift assumption is a good one at the lower acceleration levels.

Actually, the slippery surface presents an even worse situation than the above numbers indicate, and it is because of the slipping differential. At one time or another, most people have with puzzlement watched the drive wheels of a car stuck in the snow. As its driver tries to get free, the drive wheel in the snow spins like crazy, whining, while the one on dry pavement just sits there doing nothing. Many of these memories, at least the earliest, are of one's childhood as the hoped for ride to school became progressively more unlikely. Although it must seem like an incredibly bad arrangement to send the power to the tire that has no traction while ignoring the one that could easily move the car forward if it only had a little power, it is just the adverse effect of a needed feature. At the meeting point of the drive wheel axles and the shaft that provides power to those axles is the differential gear. The differential gear is designed to permit different rotation rates for the two axles. But for this benefit, life-shortening stress would be placed on the vehicle's mechanical linkage and tires every time the vehicle went around a curve. (In what way does it do this? Hint: When a car goes around a curve, the path followed by the wheel on the outside of the curve is longer than the path followed by inside one.) Many modern cars and most trucks provide the opportunity to lock the differential gear. This is of great benefit whenever one of the drive wheels encounters significantly less frictional force than the other. In addition to encounters with snow and mud, large vehicles can occasionally have one drive tire lifted entirely off the pavement during some maneuvers. At any event, the driver who locks the differential when to do so is helpful must remember to release the lock once the vehicle is on a dry surface.

When the tire on one of the drive wheels breaks loose and starts spinning, essentially all of the engine power will go to that wheel. Although this usually does not happen on dry pavement, it is of course common on slippery surfaces, as mentioned. On dry surfaces, it is common for both tires to break lose at once and spin. When just one of the tires breaks loose, most if not all of the engine power goes to that drive wheel, and the vehicle's acceleration drops accordingly. In the example just described, the force accelerating the vehicle would fall from 240 pounds (1,068 N) to less than half of that. Show that for a sliding coefficient of friction of 0.20, the force accelerating the vehicle falls to 96 pounds (427 N) and that the forward acceleration of the vehicle falls to

(continues)

(continued)

slightly less than one ft/sec^2. At that acceleration, how long would it take to reach 10 miles per hour?

What of the situation of the pickup truck on the snowy road if its owner previously placed 200 pounds (890 N) of bagged cement in the bed directly over the rear axle. How much will this action increase the acceleration possible without a tire breaking loose and spinning?

The shift to front-wheel drive that has taken place in the car population during the past 30 years has greatly benefited those people who have to drive on slippery surfaces. It even improves the acceleration possible on dry pavement for vehicles with sufficiently powerful engines. It is true that the weight over the drive wheels now decreases rather than increases when the vehicle is accelerated. However, that drawback is more than made up for by the greater drive-wheel weight in the first place. As a final thought on the subject, consider the situation of a rear-engine car with front-wheel drive. Are there any?

(continued from page 158)

In preparation for the driverless tests, one of the exemplar vehicles was equipped with an accelerometer similar to the one described in the chapter 2 discussion of coefficient-of-friction measurement. It would measure and record the deceleration impulse when the car went off the road and crashed. Other instruments included a speed radar mounted in the middle of the road just past the 1983 crash site so that the exemplar's speed could be monitored.

Recognizing the uncertainty in the outcome of this test, the investigators placed a John Deere front-end loader on the road with the exemplar, making it available to redirect the exemplar, should it start to leave the road too soon. It turned out that this was a wise precaution since, in all the runs carried out, the exemplar never went far before heading for the shoulder and requiring assistance from the John Deer equipment. The conclusion drawn from these experiments was that it was highly unlikely that a 1982 Saab 900 (or any automobile) would roll down the road without a driver for hundreds of feet before it ran off the road.

Impact

On the final run, the test vehicle was herded so that it remained on the road, picking up speed, until it had almost reached the impact site, at which point it was allowed permitted to roll on freely by itself. The result was that it ran off the road at 20 miles per hour (32 km/hr) at almost exactly the 1983 impact point.

The photos show the exemplar vehicle's rest position at the bottom of the embankment, taken from different perspectives. As can be seen, its front bumper came to rest on the far side of the stream even as its rear end remained hung up on the embankment. This contrasted with the 1983 incident, in which the vehicle appeared not to have been "airborne" for any part of the journey. The meaning of this difference is made clear by the sidebar on "Fall Formula" in chapter 3, strongly suggesting that at 20 miles per hour (32 km/hr) the exemplar was going significantly faster when it left the road than the vehicle was that crashed and burned in 1983.

View of an exemplar vehicle at rest after a staged crash at 20 miles per hour (32 km/hr) at the site of the 1983 crash *(Courtesy of the author)*

View from a different angle of the scene shown in the figure on page 165 *(Courtesy of the author)*

The first photo on page 167 shows the front-end damage to the exemplar vehicle while it was still in its rest position, and the second photo shows that damage with the vehicle on a level surface. Comparisons of this damage with that sustained by the vehicle in the 1983 impact provide further evidence that in 1983 the vehicle went off the road at a speed much lower than 20 miles per hour (32 km/hr). Is this a legitimate conclusion? What information is necessary to conclude from the relative damage that the speed was much lower, as opposed to simply lower?

The original theory was that the Saab was traveling at highway speeds when it left the road. Given that normal highway speed on this road would be somewhere between 30 and 50 miles per hour (48 and 80 km/hr), can the earlier theory be tested without doing runs at those speeds? This question and related points are discussed in the sidebar on Forensic Reenactments.

IGNITION TESTS

It will be recalled that the abbreviated investigation in 1983 had started with the conclusion that the event was an accident and then developed the theories to support that conclusion. One of the required theories had to explain how the gasoline ignition was accidental. The electric seat heaters, a relatively new feature at the time, were seized on as the explanation.

A close-up of the front end of the exemplar vehicle at its rest position, showing the damage inflicted on it by the impact *(Courtesy of the author)*

Another view of the frontal damage on the exemplar involved in the 20 miles per hour (32-km/hr) impact, after the vehicle had been hauled away from its postimpact rest position to a storage facility *(Courtesy of the author)*

Most accident reconstructionists know that in the absence of an open flame or an energetic electrical spark, it is very difficult to ignite gasoline.

Contrary to appearances and general belief, only material in gaseous form (that is, in the form of gas, which is also called vapor) burns. Solids and liquids do not burn. When liquid gasoline is set ablaze, it is gasoline vapor directly above the liquid that creates the flame. Burning, also called combustion, is a chemical reaction in which oxygen rapidly combines with vapor from the material being burned. Combustion of gasoline can occur only when the mixture of gasoline vapor and oxygen falls within a fairly narrow range. If there is either too low or too high a concentration of gasoline vapor in the air, no combustion can take place. The presence of a combustible mixture is a good example of a necessary but not sufficient condition. Necessary for combustion, a combustible mixture will not ignite unless it comes into the presence of an energetic spark, a flame, or a very high temperature.

Everyone knows that if paper is placed on a sufficiently hot stove, it will catch fire (ignite). What is happening is that hot gases are driven out of the paper into the air where they ignite. At that point, the original source of high temperature is no longer needed because the burning gases from the paper maintain the paper's surface hot enough to cause the continued emission of gases to burn. The same thing happens with a liquid. If gasoline is placed on a surface that is sufficiently hot and the vapor that evaporates forms the right mixture with the surrounding oxygen, the gasoline with ignite. The key to the relatively safe use of gasoline with automobiles is that, normally, no surface associated with the automobile engine is hot enough to ignite gasoline that falls on it. This includes the exhaust pipe and the catalytic converter.

Hot Surfaces

The catalytic converter, a part of the exhaust system, is normally the hottest exposed surface of modern cars, including 1982 Saabs. In the interest of completeness in the search for potential ignition sources for the gasoline spilled in the crash, the investigation measured the temperature of the exposed housing of the catalytic converter on one of the exemplar vehicles. A temperature-sensing element (a thermocouple) was held against the device while the vehicle's engine was running.

Forensic Reenactments

Sometimes, a forensic investigation calls for the staging of an event that either reenacts an earlier event or tests a theory as to how an earlier event occurred. Contrary to what might at first be thought, it is rarely necessary to have every element of the reenactment the same as those of the earlier event. The elements that need to be the same depend on the information sought from the reenactment. For example, an experiment showing that a pedestrian in the roadway in daylight could be seen from a point 500 feet (150 m) away would be worthless for addressing the question as to whether the pedestrian could be seen from that point at night, and a judge would exclude from evidence the findings of the daylight test; on the other hand, if it was found that the pedestrian could not be seen from that point during daylight hours, it is most likely that the results of that experiment would be admitted in court. As can be seen, the circumstances under which a positive finding was obtained must meet many more conditions than a test with a negative finding if the results are to be admitted into evidence. Continuing with the visibility (conspicuity) example, assume that it was found that a pedestrian could be seen from a distance of 500 feet (150 m) at nighttime at the same hour as an accident under investigation took place. Such affirmative evidence could still be attacked and possibly excluded from evidence if (1) the exemplar pedestrian was not more or less the same size as the victim, (2) the exemplar pedestrian was not wearing the same type of clothes as the victim, especially if the exemplar was wearing lighter clothes, (3) the meteorological conditions were different on the two nights, (4) the presence and/or phase of the Moon was different on the two nights, and so forth. This is so even before one brings up the question of how the distance at which a moving observer can perceive an object is affected by whether or not the observer expected the object to be there.

As a practical matter, it essentially is impossible to emulate every single condition of an earlier event when one is doing the reenactment. Recognizing that an adversary in court who wishes to exclude the facts

(continues)

(continued)

shown by one's reenactment will argue that it did not correspond to the original conditions, it is crucial that one reason through the differences that do exist so as to overcome such arguments. This is equivalent to convincing a judge that the differences noted are irrelevant to the results. In the Saab case, the suspicion was that rather than leaving the road at a speed of 40 miles per hour (64 km/hr) in 1983, the vehicle was simply allowed to roll off the embankment. Therefore, it was unnecessary to do a reenactment at 40 miles per hour. If the crash at 20 miles per hour (32 km/hr) showed crush damage significantly greater than that seen in the 1983 photographs, that would be strong evidence that the impact occurred at less than 20 miles per hour (32 km/hr). The same is true if the distance traveled by the exemplar car while "airborne" at 20 miles per hour (32 km/hr) was greater than that traveled in 1983. On the other hand, had the test at 20 miles per hour (32 km/hr) resulted in crush damage and/or airborne distance less than was shown in the 1983 photographs, then the hypothesis that the car in 1983 had simply rolled down the embankment would have been invalidated.

Sometimes, one does not have all of the conditions that may have been relevant to an earlier event. Nevertheless, it is still often worth doing tests directed at such an event. The gasoline-ignition test in the Saab case was an example of this. Although it was not possible to prove definitively that the gasoline could not have ignited without criminal intervention in 1983, it was possible to cast strong doubt on that possibility.

Rather than simply allow the engine to idle, the throttle was opened to the point where it was operating at 2,500 rpm. Doing the measurements with the vehicle at rest was a conservative approach, since this led to higher temperatures than would exist, when the car's motion would cause a stream of air to flow across the converter, carrying heat away.

Twelve minutes after starting the engine and causing it to run at 2,500 rpm, the temperature at the surface of the catalytic converter had risen to 130°C (266°F) and seemed to be leveling off. At that point, the throttle was opened further, and the engine speed increased to 3,000 rpm. After five minutes at this engine speed, the temperature leveled off at 250°C (482°F). Although this temperature was approaching the range where it might cause ignition of liquid gasoline, it was achieved under conditions far different from those that prevailed that morning in 1983. In addition to the cooling air stream that would have blown across the underside of the vehicle that morning, the engine that day was reportedly operating for only a short time before the crash. At 40 miles per hour (64 km/hr), the car would have traveled the 500 feet (150 m) from the victims' house to the crash site in less than 10 seconds.

Another factor lessening the likelihood that a hot catalytic converter surface could have served as the ignition source was its location and orientation—underneath the center of the vehicle and facing downward. Given the tightness of the Saab occupant compartment, it essentially would have been impossible for gasoline spilled in that compartment to have leaked out and come into contact with the catalytic converter.

Spark Test

Even if somehow the gentle impact that had occurred in 1983 had disrupted the wiring to the seat heaters, it appeared very doubtful that any sparking that resulted would have had sufficient energy to ignite the gasoline vapor in the occupant compartment. The energy requirement relates to the spark having to heat the air/vapor mixture to its ignition temperature, that is, to the point where combustion is triggered.

Ignition seemed unlikely even with an energetic spark, given the near-zero chance of a combustible mixture being present in the closed occupant compartment. To examine this question, investigators arranged to introduce an energetic spark along with gasoline into the exemplar vehicle. One-and-a-half-gallons (5.7 L) of gasoline in a bucket was placed in the vehicle to simulate the report from 1983. For the spark, they chose an automobile sparkplug powered by an automobile battery connected to the sparkplug through an automobile *induction coil*. This was a combination known to ignite gasoline mixtures, it being the means of triggering combustion within automobile-engine cylinders. The spark plug

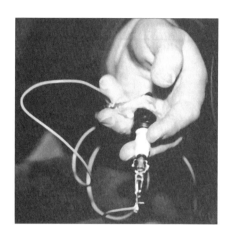

Spark plug mounted in exemplar vehicle *(Courtesy of the author)*

was taped to the front interior of the exemplar vehicle in such a way that the spark gap was exposed to the atmosphere within the car, as shown in the photo. Wires connected it to a fully charged 12 volt automobile battery through the induction coil. By opening and closing the contact with the coil, the investigators could apply a pulse of several thousand volts to the spark-plug gap, causing a spark to occur. The sidebar on "Spark Plugs and Induction" explains how this worked.

In addition to outfitting the exemplar vehicle with the spark plug, a blasting cap that could be detonated from outside the car was taped between the two front seats. The car's rear area had been modified in the same way that the postal worker's car had been—by placing a plywood platform in place of the backseats. The pail of gasoline was placed atop the platform. Then, with the engine running, the headlights lit, and the seat heaters turned on, the car's doors were closed with its windows rolled up. Thus arranged, the exemplar was poised on the lip of the embankment, its heading directed at the rest position of the car in 1983. The air temperature was low, but not quite as cold as that day in 1983.

With the exemplar as described above, the investigators triggered the spark by opening and closing the connection to the coil. The spark provided its own confirmation, audibly and visibly (through reflected light). Significantly, although no one expected ignition, let alone an explosion, everyone stood about 100 feet (30 m) back from the car during the first sparking. After no ignition occurred with the first spark, the investigators triggered about 25 more sparks with the car sitting above the embankment, with similar null results. Then the car was permitted

Introducing flaming rag into interior of exemplar *(Courtesy of the author)*

to roll down the embankment and crash at the bottom. That caused the gasoline to spill and indeed to splash throughout the interior of the occupant compartment. It was visible running down the windows after the car came to rest, with its engine still running and its headlights lit.

Within a minute of the crash, the spark plug was again triggered, producing the same audible signal. The same results occurred—no ignition—and this continued to be the situation as 10 more sparks were triggered. At that point, the blasting cap was detonated, also with no ignition. The conclusion was that a combustible mixture of gasoline did not exist within the car and therefore had not existed during the colder day in 1983.

After the sparking phase, the burn test moved on to attempts to ignite the gasoline with a flame. To that end, one of the firefighters in attendance opened a door, thrust a burning rag (on the end of a stick) into the car, and closed the door. The instant the rag entered the occupant compartment, the gasoline ignited with a whoosh. However, once the door was closed the flames died back to invisibility. Opening the door reinvigorated them, but the same deadening effect on the burn occurred

(continues on page 176)

Spark Plugs and Induction

One of the more interesting early "modern" discoveries about electricity played a key role during the first 100 years of internal combustion engines in automobiles. It is electrical induction, a phenomenon that lies at the heart of the connection between electricity and magnetism. For more than 3,000 years, there had been no hint that electricity, which for most of that period was limited to what is now called static electricity, had anything to do with magnetism. The modern era for electricity began with work in the 18th century by the first American physicist, Benjamin Franklin (1706–98). It is surprising that few Americans realize that, long before his activities in connection with the American Revolution, Franklin was famous throughout the scientific world for his electrical experiments and the conclusions that he had drawn from them. Building on Franklin's work elucidating and cataloguing the nature of static electricity, Luigi Galvani (1737–98) and Alessandro Volta (1745–1827) in Italy investigated the production and nature of electrical current, discovered by Franklin to consist of moving charges. Although imperfect, there is a reasonable analogy between the flow of electrical charges and the flow of liquids. Just as water flows from a hill into a valley, electric charges flow from a region of high voltage to a region of low voltage. By connecting one end of a wire to the high-voltage side of a battery and the other to the low-voltage side, charges were permitted to flow as current (a word that itself was probably drawn from the analogies spun by Franklin).

The massive step forward that revealed the connection between electricity and magnetism was taken in 1819 by Hans Christian Oersted (1770–1851) of Denmark. Initially by accident, he found that a magnetized pivotable needle (in effect, a navigational compass) placed near a wire deflected whenever the wire carried current, the direction of deflection depending on the direction of the current. Since the operation of the compass depends on its needle being magnetized and thus sensitive to the magnetic field of the Earth, Oersted correctly concluded that the moving charges in the wire created a magnetic field that was far stronger than the Earth's. Using the compass as a probe he was able to map out this current-induced magnetic field.

The next surprise that linked electricity with magnetism was the observation that just as the presence of an electric current set up a magnetic field, electric current could be created by moving a closed loop of wire through a magnetic field. One says that the magnetic field induces a current in the loop moving through it. The faster the loop was moved, the higher the induced current. The same effect could be obtained without moving the loop at all but just by changing the strength of the magnetic field in which the loop resided. If the loop was not quite complete so that a current could not pass along the wire, it was found that moving it through the magnetic field caused a voltage to appear between the wire's two ends. It was also found that however the magnetic field through the loop was changed in strength, the voltage appeared, and that the faster the magnetic field changed, the larger was the induced voltage.

Finally, the two effects linking magnetic fields on the one hand and electric current or voltage on the other were combined. Two wire loops were placed in close proximity to one another and one of them was connected across a battery resulting in a current in that loop. Because of the current in one loop wire, a magnetic field was created and the second loop was in that field. Then, when the current in the first loop was halted by disconnecting it from the battery, the magnetic field across the second loop changed abruptly, causing a current to be generated in the second loop. If the second loop is not closed on itself there will be, instead of an induced current, an induced voltage across the ends of the second wire. When instead of a single loop the second wire has many coils, the voltage across its ends can be very high, much higher than the voltage used to generate the current through the first loop. This, in short, is the basis of electric transformers used, for example, to convert the 13,000-volt power carried past city residences on distribution wires down to the 110 or 220 volts used within the residences. The device referred to generically as "the coil" contained in automobiles for more than 100 years uses this principle. When the

(continues)

(continued)

current generated in the first coil by the automobile battery (for many years standardized at 12 volts) is switched off, the falling magnetic field generates a very high voltage in the second coil. It is this voltage that, applied at precisely the correct time, causes a spark across one of the spark plugs, thereby detonating the gasoline-air mixture in the chamber associated with that spark plug. When one speaks of the timing in an internal combustion engine, this is ultimately that to which one is referring.

(continues on page 173)

as soon as the door was closed. Finally, so as to simulate the concluding events in 1983, the firefighter broke one of the windows, permitting the gasoline and other contents of the vehicle to burn. The fire was allowed to burn for about 15 minutes and then extinguished. To simulate the appearance of the vehicle in 1983 after its fire had been extinguished, a hole was introduced by an ax into the hood of the exemplar vehicle.

It was concluded that, even with a direct ignition of the gasoline, the fire would not have advanced to a rapid, continuing burn with the doors and windows closed. The conclusion compelled was that on the day the victims were burned there must have been an opening in the occupant compartment allowing oxygen to enter, thereby maintaining a combustion mixture.

SECOND CRASH TEST

As mentioned in connection with the ignition tests, the exemplar vehicle was permitted to roll down the embankment from a starting start to the position in which the vehicle had been found in 1983. The impact was observed to be gentle, one likely to have been incapable of causing injury to vehicle occupants, regardless of whether or not they were restrained by seat belts. It would not have been severe enough to trigger air bags,

The exemplar car in its rest position after being permitted to roll down the embankment and before it had been burned *(Courtesy of the author)*

Another view of the exemplar car, now burning *(Courtesy of the author)*

Damage to the exemplar car, shown after it was burned and removed from it impact position *(Courtesy of the author)*

A second view of the damage to the exemplar car that had simply rolled down the embankment to impact *(Courtesy of the author)*

had the vehicle been so equipped. The engine continued to run after impact and the headlights remained lit. The nose of the vehicle ended up on the near side of the stream. The two photos on page 177 show the car in its rest position prior to being burned and during the burn. The photos on page 178 show the impact damage to the front end of that car after it had been removed to a storage location following the burn. In extinguishing the blaze, one of the firefighters assisting the investigation had used an ax to make a hole in the hood more or less as had been done in 1983.

RESULTS AND CONCLUSIONS

The conclusion was that the vehicle found burning in 1983 had simply rolled down the embankment after having been at rest prior to that. Its speed at impact was therefore only that gained from that short roll, probably 5 miles per hour (8 km/hr). The further conclusion was that there was an accelerant contributing to the fire in 1983, that it had been ignited deliberately, and that a source of outside air—probably from an

Damage to the car in 1983 *(New Hampshire State Police)*

Another view of the damage photographed in 1983 *(New Hampshire State Police)*

The car at its rest position at the bottom of the embankment in 1983 *(New Hampshire State Police)*

A second view of the rest position in 1983 *(New Hampshire State Police)*

open window—ensured the continuity of the burn. At one point, the possibility that there had been no gasoline involved was considered and dismissed. In spite of the fact that the interiors of modern cars, in particular the plastic content, once commenced can support very hot fires, the length of time that such fires take to be underway argued in favor of an accelerant. This also fitted the report of the victims' family member.

The photos on page 167 show the damage that would have occurred to the vehicle in 1983 had it left the road while traveling even as slowly as 20 miles per hour (32 km/hr). The other photos on pages 165 and 166 show the distance that such a speed would have carried a 20-mile-per-hour (32-km/hr) vehicle from the road edge during its fall. The photographs shown in those four figures are to be compared with the four photos on pages 179 and 180 which show the postimpact damage and the rest position respectively of the vehicle involved in the 1983 incident. From this comparison, it was and is easy to conclude that the victims' car did not veer off the road and down the embankment in spite of the account provided to (and accepted by) the investigating officers in 1983.

Similarly, from comparing the 1983 photographs with the photographs of the postimpact rest position and damage to the second exemplar vehicle, it is easy to conclude that the victims' vehicle rolled down the embankment to impact from a standing start just as did that exemplar.

LIMITATIONS OF CONCLUSIONS

Though the facile 1983 explanation built around a belief that the incident was an accident was demolished, it did not follow that the person shielded by that explanation could be arrested for murder. It is true that if the 1983 work had been done properly, its results would have led to that person being closely scrutinized and possibly to the discovery of evidence sufficient to support his arrest and conviction. That evidence, if it ever existed, did not exist nearly two decades later. Similarly, it would be impossible to find at that point evidence that the tragedy was a murder-suicide involving only the two victims, to mention one theory not contradicted by the physical evidence. What about the statement reported by Ms. Kaltenberg? Even assuming that her ex-boyfriend (who was indeed the husband and stepfather, respectively, of the victims) said what she reported, such a statement is not enough to support an arrest, let alone a criminal conviction. People say strange untrue things every day. To see this, one need go no further than the accounts of persons convicted of crimes that they were later proven not to have committed, convicted in part on the basis of their having confessed!

6

Subway Stop

It is important to get a feeling for the awkward form in which information needed by the forensic investigator is often delivered. This chapter makes use of a train accident to show how the first step in a forensic accident investigation is often the untangling of apparently unintelligible test data. This particular example also brings up the precision with which physical measurements can be stated legitimately and the error that is made in using overly precise numbers to describe such measurements. Also, the fact that this accident occurred at night permits the subject of perception time to be revisited to explore what it means to say that a hazard entered one's field of vision.

With its first line having opened to the public in 1904, the New York City subway system is the world's oldest motorized under-the-street transportation system. Millions use it every day to move from one point to another within the 322 square miles (834 km²) that make up New York City. In view of the number of riders, the number of trains, and the high speeds that the trains must travel, the modern system has a remarkably low accident rate. That those few accidents that do occur are rarely caused by faulty equipment or operator error is a tribute to the care with which the New York Transit Authority (NYTA) runs the system. Essentially, all the personal injury accidents are of the type labeled man-under events that arise from a person on the tracks who is impaired in some way. Usually, the person has decided to lie, sit, or walk on the tracks. In the aftermath of some of these man-under events, the NYTA is sued, based on the claim that the train should have stopped before striking the person on its tracks. Unless there is an assertion that defective brakes or other equipment lengthened the train's stopping distance, the claim in the lawsuit is that the operator committed the tort of negligence. The elements of this tort are listed in the chapter 1 discussion of the U.S. legal system. The key one, of course, is that the defendant or its agent was negligent. In a negligence action against the NYTA based on a man-under event, the allegation is usually that the operator negligently failed to apply the emergency brakes at the point they should have been applied.

One might ask how a train operator can be blamed. It is common knowledge wherever trains run that if one stands on an active railroad track, one will sooner or later be killed, given the distance that trains require to come to a halt. Unlike automobile drivers, who are usually required to avoid running over a person standing in the path of their vehicles, train operators generally are neither required nor expected to be able to do so. Operators of subway trains form a partial exception to this rule, for their trains differ from cross-country passenger and freight trains in a way that places more responsibility on their operators. Since subway trains must travel at high speed between closely spaced stations, they are designed to both accelerate and decelerate more rapidly than inter-city trains. Apart from their not having the option of swerving to avoid something in their path, operators of subway trains are therefore treated surprisingly like automobile operators when assessing operator negligence in the wake of an accident.

As in all cases sounding in technical issues, a party contemplating bringing a lawsuit against the NYTA is well advised first to hire a forensic expert to examine its claims. If and when a suit is filed, the NYTA, as defendant, will hire its own forensic expert. The discussion that follows is based on one such case.

Photograph of station *(Courtesy of the author)*

MAN ON THE TRACKS

The tracks of the New York City subway system are elevated above city streets for much of their mileage outside the borough of Manhattan. One rainy night shortly before midnight, while entering a station located on such a track in the borough of Brooklyn, a 10-car train ran over a man lying partway onto the tracks. Although he survived, he lost both legs. They were amputated during emergency surgery the night of the accident. Some months later, he sued the NYTA, claiming that the train should have halted before it reached him.

The train was well into the station when it struck the man, though short of where it would have normally stopped. The photo shows a view of this station during daylight hours, with a train approaching. The figure contains a sketch of the layout immediately after the accident, showing the train next to the platform where it stopped. The north end of the platform, on the left of the sketch, is the zero-point for the other positions identified.

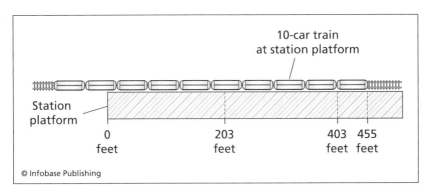

Sketch of accident scene

Once the case was in suit, the NYTA hired a mechanical engineer and a physicist, among others, to investigate the claim. Since the injured man was found not far from where the front of the train would have come to rest during its normal stop at the station, the negligence claim was not dismissible on its face. The physics of the situation had to be looked at in detail.

Presuming no defect in the station lighting or in the train, there were, broadly speaking, three possible outcomes to the forensic investigation:

(a) The operator of the train was not negligent.

(b) The operator of the train may have been negligent, but the negligence made no difference.

(c) The operator of the train was negligent, and the accident would not have occurred otherwise.

THE INVESTIGATION

What form could negligence by the woman operating the train have taken in this case? It was pretty much limited to her not having applied the emergency brake as soon she should have. She would also have been negligent if she were exceeding the 30 miles per hour (48 km/hr) speed limit set for that particular stretch of tracks. She reported was traveling at 25 miles per hour (40 km/hr) as she approached the station, as well as when she spotted the man on the tracks. She said that she first saw him when he was 200 feet (61 m) in front of the train, her account being the basis for that detail in the figure on page 185. The investigators were also provided the following information:

1. The front of the train stopped 455 feet (139 m) into the station, that is, 455 feet south of the north end of the platform.

2. The man was found on the tracks between the train's first and second cars, 403 feet (123 m) south of the north end of the platform.

3. Including the power unit, the train consisted of 10 cars, each
   50 feet (15 m) long.

Since the position of the train and the position of the man immediately after the accident were measured without haste, those values can
be taken as reliable. Also, the specifications of the train are a matter of
verifiable public record. The figure on page 185 reflects the investigators'
interpretation of the operator's statement as to when she first saw the
man. However, in addition to having the uncertain reliability attaching
to an eyewitness statement, the statement is somewhat ambiguous on its
face. Does it refer to the operator's position when she first perceived a
man to be on the tracks, her position when she perceived that *something*
was on the tracks, or when the hazard first entered her field of vision?
The fact that well into the investigation the investigators did not even
know the meaning the operator herself placed on her words reflects
one of the problems in being an outside investigator for a large entity,
be it a private corporation or a government agency. The problem is lack
of direct, firsthand, access to information, which tends to have to pass
through several hands before reaching the investigator. The same is true
going the other direction, as questions from the investigator are passed
back to the person who may be able to answer them.

Of course, having the operator interpret her words would not address
the question of reliability that, in addition to everything else, is tied up
with the way in which she perceived events as they were happening. The
perception process is such that the operator would not have been able
to know immediately following the accident and far less able to give a
sensible answer months or years later regarding the sequence by which
she became aware of the man on the track and consequently where her
train was when she first realized the need to stop it.

FIELD OF VISION

The phrase *entered her field of vision* was used above, as it has been a
number of times already in this book. Until now, that phrase in its various forms has not been defined; it might have seemed, therefore, that its
meaning was clear on its face to everyone. Those encountering it in connection with a discussion of motor-vehicle collisions probably took it to

mean the first moment that an unobstructed straight line existed between the hazard and the driver's eyes, namely, the moment at which a line of sight first existed between the driver's eyes and the hazard. In the earlier examples, this was exactly what was meant. However, it can be seen that in general this definition will not serve. Consider a truck driver, riding high and looking straight ahead down a South Dakota road that goes on for miles without the slightest bend. He is westbound at 70 miles per hour (113 km/hr), and it is 10 o'clock A.M. on a sunny plains morning. The Sun is behind him, shining on, among other things, a buffalo sleeping crosswise on the road 10 miles (16 km) ahead. A straight line can be drawn from the trucker's eyes and the buffalo pelt. Can it be said that the hazard of colliding with a two-ton, potentially angry, bison has entered the driver's field of vision? Probably not. Consider the same situation, with the animal standing only 700 feet (210 m) away but in the middle of a cloudy night. Given the reach of the truck's headlights, it is still unlikely that the hazard has entered his field of vision, even though a straight line could be drawn between his eyes and the beast's eyes. A definition of the phrase that may have general applicability is as follows:

> A hazard first enters the field of vision of a vehicle operator approaching the hazard at the first position on the road that the operator, were the vehicle at rest, could have eventually perceived that hazard.

Defined in this way, it can be seen that it is the first moment that visual information about the hazard, though perhaps extremely minimal, could enter the driver's eye-brain system. This has obvious applicability to the discussion of perception-reaction time back in chapter 2, at which point the ease or difficulty with respect to which an object in the driver's line of sight could be perceived was not dealt with. The ease or difficulty depends, first of all, on how well the hazard stands out from its background, that is, how conspicuous the hazard is. In accident reconstruction and elsewhere, the term used is *conspicuity*. Generally, the greater an object's conspicuity, the shorter the time required to perceive its presence. The sidebar on "Conspicuity" discusses some of the elements that establish conspicuity.

Returning to the information provided by the train operator, it should be noted that even her statement about speed is open to question. Unlike airplanes, cars, and many cross-country trains, many of the NYTA subway

(continues on page 196)

Conspicuity

One often hears statements such as "The driver could have seen the pedestrian from a distance of 300 feet." Even apart from the uncertainty as to what "seen" means, the statement is usually wrong in a number of ways.

By saying that it is possible to see an object from a certain point most people usually mean that, standing at that point, one can eventually perceive in a general way from that point what the object is. Getting back to the language used earlier, this would then be the point at which the object can be said to have entered the field of vision of an approaching driver.

Consider what must be known to establish the maximum distance from which an object can be seen in the sense given above. For starters, it means much more than that there is no visual obstruction between the object and the point in question. We can see the Moon at a distance of 238,000 miles (383,000 km), but we cannot see a basketball 2 feet away in the absence of light, and in the absence of shadows, we cannot see anything that reflects the same color and intensity of light as its background.

The readiness with which an object can be seen is referred to as its *conspicuity*. Conspicuity is an objective quantity; it does not depend on how good the eyesight of an observer is, though it relates directly to whether an observer with a given level of eyesight is able to see the object. What it does depend on are the object's light-reflecting property relative to that of its background and the light incident on both. Because conspicuity is usually of the greatest importance under low-light conditions, it is under such conditions that most of this discussion will be conducted. A nighttime vehicle operator views the surrounding world including that part of it lying in front of his or her vehicle by means of artificial light, usually reflected light that originated from the headlights of the driver's own vehicle. The important point about the available light is not that it is not sunlight (apart from that fraction arriving by way of the Moon), but that it is far less intense than the

(continues)

(continued)

light available during even a cloudy day. Reflection of light is specular or diffuse, as determined by the reflecting surface. Light undergoing specular reflection acts like a rubber ball bouncing off a flat surface. The reflected light is confined to a narrow range of directions and therefore can be nearly as bright at the incident light. However, apart from the compound specular reflection from retroreflecting surfaces, only diffuse reflection is of interest here. In diffuse reflection the incident light is reflected (scattered) in all directions, with the result that, in any particular direction, the intensity of the reflected light is far less than that of the incident light.

A retroreflector is a special type of reflector, constructed to reflect light back in the direction from which it came with but a small amount of spreading. (By sketching two or more specularly reflecting surfaces connected to one another show how to make a retroreflector.) Modern highway signs and tape strips placed on large trucks and, increasingly, on the clothes of pedestrians and bicycles, have retroreflecting surfaces. All light falling on such surfaces, regardless of direction, is reflected back in the direction from which it came. Light incident on a retroreflector from vehicle headlights is sent directly back to the headlights, its slight spread allowing it to reach the operator's eyes. This greatly increases the efficiency of the headlights in picking out the object bearing the retroreflectors. This enhanced efficiency is reaffirmed continually when vehicle operators encounter pedestrians and cyclists bearing retroreflecting strips at night. It is usually those strips alone and not the persons wearing them that are picked up in the headlights and therefore are seen by the operator. Pedestrians struck by cars and trucks at night are rarely wearing retroreflecting tape. The postaccident analysis of their conspicuity nearly always involves a comparison of the reflectance of their diffuse-reflecting clothing with that of the background.

The conspicuity of an object depends on (1) the reflectance of the object, (2) the reflectance of the background, and (3) the level of light incident on both. The combination of conspicuity and distance

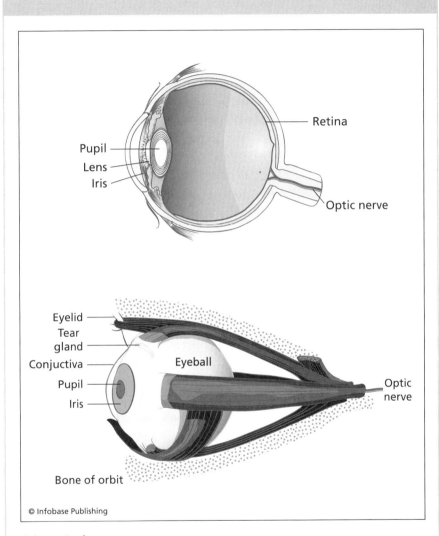

© Infobase Publishing

Schematic of eye

determine how likely it is that an object will seize the attention of a vehicle operator. When the light level is low, as it always is at night, aspects of the eye-brain system not discussed in the chapter 2 sidebar on "Perception-Reaction Time" and which are usually irrelevant during the daytime take on key importance. Therefore, while there will

(continues)

(continued)

be some overlap with the earlier perception-reaction discussion, the present one will go more deeply into the details of the eye.

The three major eye components involved in sight are the pupil/iris, the lens, and the retina, as shown schematically in the figure. When a person looks in the direction of an object, the light reflected from that object in the direction of the person passes through the lens, which focuses it so that an image of the object forms on the retina. By a feedback mechanism governed by the level of the light falling on the retina, the iris (the colored portion of the eye) varies the size of the pupil. In chapter 2, the role of the retina was described only briefly, how it contains millions of light-sensing elements and from each one sends a signal to the brain, with the brain then comparing the received pattern with its past experience to induce in the person the impression that he or she is seeing something. The present discussion is more concerned with how those sensing cells in the retina operate.

Each light-sensing cell in the retina is either a *rod* or a *cone,* to use the names given them long ago, based on their appearance under a microscope. Each type of cell, when activated by a sufficient light level, sends an electrical signal to the brain, all as discussed in the sidebar on "Perception-Reaction Time" in chapter 2. The light level needed for this is much higher for the cones than it is for the rods. This is the same as saying that the rods are much more sensitive to light than the cones. That color vision requires the cones to be activated explains why one does not see colors in low light. It is the rods that provide nighttime vision, and the signals that they produce are only of value to the brain in generating shades of gray.

The development of the human eye-brain system was rooted in and influenced by hundreds of millions of years of interactions between animals and their surroundings. Perhaps because of the lack of situations where light level changed abruptly during those eons and more particularly since the creature's survival did not depend on immediate accommodation to such abrupt changes, nighttime vision is seriously handicapped in dealing with rapid shifts in light level. To begin with, pupil-size adjustment in response to changes in light level is rather slow, requiring up to several seconds to be accomplished fully. Even though much of the adjustment normally takes place within one second, that can be a significant amount of time for the nighttime driver whose car is traveling 100 feet per second (30 m/s) and repeatedly encountering oncoming vehicles using the high beams (bright lights) on their headlights. Usually even more important is the fact that the sensitivity of the rod cells, that is, the amount of light they demand before sending a signal to the brain, depends on the level in the cells of the chemical compound rhodopsin. The more rhodopsin, the lower is the rod's threshold light level, the less light required for the rod to send a voltage signal to the brain. Just as with pupil size, there is a light-level-based feedback mechanism that determines rhodopsin level in the rods. Unfortunately, the rhodopsin level responds even more slowly than pupil size. Though most of the change takes place in the first 20 seconds or so, full response of the rhodopsin level to a light-level change can take up to several minutes. The slow pace at which the rhodopsin level changes is clear to persons moving from a brightly light sidewalk into a restaurant with particularly low light levels since vision accommodation tracks very closely to rhodopsin level under those conditions. As a result, the restaurant may appear too dark even to read the menu for several minutes, during which the surroundings gradually become more discernable. The opposite effect, also rhodopsin related, occurs when one moves from a dark place to a brightly lit one. The effect can be stunning if not blinding and the impulse is to shield one's eyes—typically by partially closing the lids or squinting—until the rhodopsin bleaching has occurred. Most people observe these effects—especially the need to shield one's eyes on moving from darkness into light—to be more pronounced in the younger years. This age dependence for the most part arises from the gradual obscuring of the lens that comes with age and the reduced range of light levels reaching the eyes. As the obscuring of the lens becomes worse, usually as the result of the clouding called cataracts, the level of light reaching the

(continues)

(continued)

retina even during daylight may fall below the cones' threshold level, depriving the person of color vision. Because this loss occurs so gradually, most people do not recognize it has happened, and it is only when they have the cataracts removed that they realize it. The muted grays of the hospital carpet observed on the way into the area of treatment turn out to be brilliantly colored on the way out.

There is yet another complication associated with changes in light level, especially if the changes are large enough to cause the cones either to cease or to commence taking part in the seeing process. As the cones enter or exit the process, there is a transient burst of activity in that part of the brain connected with vision. As a result, objects that otherwise would be visible may be missed during this period. Stated differently, during this shift, an object may need to have greater conspicuity to grab the attention of the observer than it would need under steady illumination.

The problems just noted that arise because of a change in light level will certainly affect the vehicle operator as oncoming headlights sweep past. More subtly but nonetheless real, momentary vision reduction also occurs when the operator shifts his or her gaze from the instrument panel to the highway or track ahead. Indeed, momentary vision reduction occurs whenever the operator switches his or her gaze between objects reflecting different levels of light, and the difference in reflected light between two different objects is generally more pronounced at night than during the day. Contrast plays an immense role in determining nighttime conspicuity. This is due in large part to the fact that color does not contribute to conspicuity at night. Also, shadows play a much smaller role. To be seen at night, objects must appear brighter or darker than their background; however, usually, the more reflectance an object has, the more likely it can be seen. A figure clad in dark clothes has very low reflectance compared with the same figure wearing light-colored clothing (even though the color itself cannot be distinguished) and for this reason is less likely to contrast with the typical nighttime backgrounds for people on or near a roadway. Typical reflectance levels for a darkly clad person are 0.03 to 0.05 (meaning that only 3 to 5 percent of the light falling on the person is reflected). The fraction of incident light from, for example, headlights, streetlights, or platform lights, that such a person reflects can be the same as the fraction reflected by the person's background. Pine trees have typical reflectance in the range of 0.02 to 0.08 and asphalt 0.06 to 0.13. To repeat, it is the difference between the reflectance of an object and the reflectance from the object's background that establishes the object's the conspicuity for a given light level. In effect, when one talks of contrast in this context, one is referring to the difference in reflectance.

Even with a very low reflectance difference, an object of interest will eventually be distinguishable from its background as the light level reaching the eye increases or, equivalently, as the eye becomes more light-sensitive because of pupil-size increase and rhodopsin production.

A final point needs to be addressed, and that is the way that a hazard can seize a vehicle operator's attention. For most of the discussion above and in the sidebar on "Perception-Reaction Time," it has been implicit that the vehicle operator was looking in the direction of the object when a line of sight was first established between the object and his or her eyes. In contrast, on most occasions, the hazard will call attention to itself when the observer is not looking in its direction. When it is stated that one's gaze is directed at an object, what is meant is that the eye has the object focused on that part of the retina known as the fovea. It is the fovea, with its high density of sensors, which can provide detailed information to the brain concerning the image focused on it. It provides foveal vision in contrast with the rest of the retina, which is involved in peripheral vision. Most of the objects focused on one's retina at any instant are detected, to the degree to which they are, by peripheral vision. The brain is alert, however, for items in the peripheral vision that may prove important and, when it senses such items or even the suggestion of such items, immediately causes the direction of gaze to shift slightly so as to bring their images onto the fovea for closer scrutiny. Nevertheless, the item has to be close enough and to have sufficient conspicuity to alert the brain to effect this shift in gaze.

(continues)

(continued)

The investigator who is not knowledgeable about how the eye-brain system operates and, in particular, about the respective roles of foveal and peripheral vision can be severely misled regarding what a vehicle operator should have seen and can therefore severely mislead others, including juries. Such an investigator, aware of what the hazard had been and where it had been, sets out to determine the point from which the vehicle operator "should first have seen the hazard" and approaches the accident site with his or her gaze directed at the spot where the hazard had been. This ensures that the foveal vision of the investigator will be engaged at the farthest possible point. As a result, the investigator will usually see the object at a distance far greater than a vehicle operator behaving in a normal fashion would have. In the real world, the eyes of a vehicle operator are constantly shifting—to the instrument panel, to the road ahead, to the rearview and side-view mirrors, to lights and informational signs along the roadway, and so forth. It would be only by coincidence that that driver's foveal vision would be directed toward the hazard at the very instant that the object first could have entered his or her field of vision. Normally, it will be some seconds later, when the driver is much closer that the hazard, focused on the nonfoveal part of the retina, will cause his or her gaze to snap to the direction needed for it to be focused on the fovea. Therefore, in most instances, a hazard can be said to enter a driver's field of vision at the point where its image in the peripheral vision is strong enough to make the driver examine it with foveal vision.

(continued from page 187)

trains were not equipped with a speed-recording device. In fact, this particular train did not even have a speedometer. The operator's speed estimate had to be based on her experience. Needless to say, there would have been an incentive for her to underestimate the train's speed approaching the station that night if it was in excess of the speed limit.

STOPPING A TRAIN

In contrast to the question of when the operator should have seen the man, it was straightforward to determine the distance this particular train required to stop once its brakes were applied. As are all modern trains and large trucks, the subway train was equipped with air brakes, a breakthrough advance when invented by George Westinghouse (1846–1914) in the 19th century. He solved the problem at a time when purely mechanical brakes were the standard means of stopping a train, the problem being how to apply all the brakes at once in a long string of cars. Given the momentum of the railroad cars trailing the locomotive and the relatively low coefficient of friction between wheels and track, locomotive brakes alone could do essentially nothing toward halting a train. Westinghouse introduced the two brake features that continue to be in use to this day. First, he departed from the approach then being followed, that of somehow mechanically linking the brakes on all the cars so that they could all be operated from a lever in the locomotive, and went to air pressure instead. By connecting air lines from car to car and using air pressure to activate the brakes on a signal from the locomotive, he solved the problem of activating the brakes throughout the train with essentially no delay. Also, by designing the system so that the brakes were activated not by an increase in pressure but by a drop in pressure, he produced a safety feature that was especially important in the days before dependable high-pressure hosing was available. Instead of the train losing its brakes when a hose ruptured or another defect caused a loss of pressure, the loss of pressure itself caused the brakes to be applied and the train to stop. This has continued to be the design used, not only with train brakes but also with those on most semitrailer trucks. An additional safety feature carried down to us from the railroads' original adoption of the Westinghouse brake system is the deadman switch (sometimes called simply the deadman), a device that takes many forms but in essence requires a continuous affirmative act by the operator to prevent the brakes from being activated. This idea has appeared in many other contexts. Probably the most familiar for most people is that of the power lawnmower equipped with a deadman's switch aimed at preventing the user from sticking a hand into the blade while it is rotating. Within a fraction of a second of the lawnmower handle being released, a braking mechanism halts the blade's motion.

On the subway train involved in the man-under accident being discussed, the operator had to maintain positive pressure on the throttle grip to prevent the brakes from activating. For nonemergency stopping, the operator would reduce the air pressure in the brake line slowly, causing a gradual application of the brakes in each car. In the subway trains operated by the NYTA, the air-brake system was augmented by electricity. To cause an emergency stop, the operator completely releases the throttle grip and manually shifts the brake lever to its maximum braking position. This has the effect of immediately dumping air from the brakes in the lead car and causing electrical signals to be sent to the independent air brakes in all the other cars.

Even when the emergency stopping procedure is followed, it is in the nature of air brakes for there to be a short lag between operator action and actual braking, a lag that does not occur with hydraulic brakes, the system used in automobiles. In this particular subway train, a delay of about one-half second occurs between the instant the operator applies the brakes and the instant that the brakes in the lead car are fully activated. Then there is an additional lag of about a quarter second between the activation of the lead-car brakes and those of the following cars. This three-quarters of a second has to be added to the perception-reaction time of the operator by an investigator needing to determine the point at which full braking took hold.

Once the train brakes are applied, the distance and time required to stop is determined in exactly the same way as was used in chapter 2 for the car skidding to a stop. As with the car, once the braking has reached a maximum, the deceleration essentially is constant until the train has stopped. Just as for the car, the stopping distance S is determined by the speed V at the start of maximum braking and the deceleration rate. In the case of the car, the deceleration was expressed as $g\mu$, with g, as usual, standing for the acceleration due to gravity (32 feet/sec^2 in the U.S. system and 9.8 m/sec^2 in S.I.) and μ the coefficient of friction between the sliding tires and pavement, even when not all of the tires were skidding. Thus, stopping distance was given by the expression:

$$S = V^2/(2g\mu)$$

For cars, the effective coefficient of sliding friction between tires and dry pavement is typically about 0.8, meaning that the deceleration would be 0.8*g*. The coefficient of friction between the steel wheels and steel tracks is much lower, being on the order of 0.2, about what one would expect for a car on a snowy road. One can see that from a given speed a train will require at least four times the distance to stop as a car on dry pavement. For example, an automobile traveling 40 miles per hour (64 km/hr) at the start of maximum braking typically will stop in about 66 feet (20 m). In contrast, the shortest distance within which a train traveling that speed can stop will be 264 feet (80.5 m), and that is under ideal conditions. As mentioned already, subway trains are designed for rapid acceleration and rapid braking and come much closer to this ideal than do intercity trains. In fact, long freight trains will take far greater distances to stop, hence the comment above about the inevitability of being run over if one stands long enough on tracks frequented by trains. Unlike the practice with brake design for cars, it was long the goal on trains that wheel lock-up is to be avoided, even under emergency braking. Although there has recently been a lot of attention given to introducing antilock braking on trains, the vast majority of the trains in operation are not so equipped. As a consequence and in contrast with cars, the accident reconstructionist cannot presume that train deceleration under maximum braking can be described by the tire/track coefficient of friction. In other words, the deceleration can be expected to be even worse than the 0.2 value above implies. For this reason, it is very important to do stopping tests with the train involved in any accident being investigated.

TEST STOPS AND FUZZY DATA

The forensic investigators for the defense requested that stopping tests be made using the train involved in the accident and that they be done at the station where the accident occurred. The NYTA did the requested tests and reported the results in the form of a data table produced by the recording device with which the train had been equipped temporarily. In the accompanying excerpt from that table, the first column gives a series of positions for the train, stated in terms of the distance in feet remaining until the train came to a full stop. The second column was described to the investigators as stating the speed of the train at the different positions. The outside investigators found these numbers to be confusing and contradictory.

When forensic investigators have to deal with test results obtained by someone else and then transmitted through a series of stages within a large organization, it sometimes becomes a major part of the investigation to determine the meaning of the transmitted data. In addition to the measurements not being exactly what the investigator would have chosen to make, the raw measurements have often already been analyzed, and instead of the actual measurements, the investigator receives the results of the analysis without even a clear statement as to what the basic measurements were. The first step in trying to understand the data, then, consists of figuring out what was measured and what was done with the results to produce the numbers given to the investigator.

Distance (ft)	Speed (miles per hour)
206.7	30.2
203.8	29.8
200.9	29.8
197.9	29.4
195.0	29.4
192.1	29.0
189.2	28.6
186.3	28.6
183.4	28.6
180.5	28.2
177.6	28.2
174.7	27.8
171.7	27.4
168.8	27.5
165.9	27.5
163.0	27.1
160.1	27.1
157.2	26.4

In the present case, it developed that the recording device consisted of a clock and a method of recording the time for each completion of a rotation by a test wheel. The actual measurement then consisted of noting the clock reading each time a wheel rotation was completed. Regrettably, it was not these clock readings that were provided but rather the sequence of train positions associated with the completion of each wheel rotation and a speed value identified with each point. Both of these numbers were calculated by internal circuitry of the measuring device. Just a glance at the excerpt in the table shows that a number of problems had to be resolved before going any further.

Given the nature of the measurements, one would expect that, regardless of the speed of the train, the intervals between adjacent cumulative distances should be constant—and equal to the circumference of the test wheel. It is universally true that the center of a wheel advances a distance equal to the circumference of the wheel each time that the wheel makes one complete rotation. However, from the data table provided, it appeared that although most of the distance increments are 2.9 feet (0.88 m), there is an occasional interval of 3.0 feet (0.91 m). Of more concern were the speed entries, which indicated that the speed changed either not at all between successive locations or by 0.4 miles per hour (0.64 km/hr).

As stated above, forensic investigators have to confront problems like this frequently. What do the numbers mean? Often, though not always, finding the answer to this question can transform apparently nonsensical figures into something useful. If the answer cannot be found, or if the answer does not help, the tests that generated the numbers have to be redone, usually at a high cost in time and money.

One additional piece of information regarding the braking test was provided, namely the circumference C of the test wheel: 2.911 feet (0.8872 m). The precision of that number, which should raise some eyebrows, will be dealt with in the sidebar on "Precision, Rounding, and Truncating."

At any event, if the circumference of the test wheel was as stated, the train will have moved through a distance of 2.911 feet (0.8872 m) each time the wheel made a complete rotation with a blip of some sort being generated at the completion of each rotation. The time interval T between the successive blips—that is, the time it took the wheel to make a rotation—is all that is needed to calculate the average speed *V* of the train during that rotation. In other words, with the train moving a distance 2.911 feet during a time *T,* the average speed for that particular 2.911 feet of travel would be 2.911/*T.* With *T* expressed in seconds, *V* will be in feet/sec. For example, if the time between successive blips was found to be a tenth of a second, the average speed for that tenth of a second would be 29.11 feet/sec (8.872 m/s). That was apparently the source of the speeds entered in the second column of the table. The actual times, either for one revolution or cumulatively, were not provided with the table.

Having received the information needed to understand the workings of the device that produced the braking data, the investigators realized that the distance figures were actually rounded-off values, which explained why the apparent distance increment varied between 2.9 and 3.0 feet. It was a rounding effect. The sidebar on "Precision, Rounding, and Truncating" explains this and more. It should be of particular value for those wondering how the circumference of the wheel could be known so precisely that it could be stated to be 2.911 feet.

UNFUZZING THE DATA

Knowing that the position increment built into the recording device was 2.911 feet explained why the position given in the table on page 200 sometimes changed by 2.9 feet and sometimes by 3.0 feet. The actual position (the cumulative change due to the repeated rotations of the reference wheel multiplied by the stated circumference of the wheel) was rounded off prior to the printout being made. In short, the recording device kept track of the cumulative distance to the nearest thousandth of a foot, taking the wheel circumference to be 2.911 feet, but then rounded off the result to the nearest tenth of a foot. The accompanying table on page 208 illustrates this by listing the actual position as defined compared with the rounded-off cumulative distances.

A more serious problem was presented by the reported speeds. They seemed to have been rounded off in a strange way since the increment between successive speed values was usually either 0.0 miles per hour or 0.4 miles per hour. If one attempts to calculate the acceleration implied by these values, one obtains a very strange sequence indeed. Recall that

(continues on page 206)

Precision, Rounding, and Truncating

Any person who thinks quantitatively about the world and has had some experience with measuring things should be startled to see the circumference of a train wheel given as 2.911 feet (0.8872 m). Given the nature of such a wheel, this is an extremely precise value for the circumference. As a general practice, it helps to work with comparisons when trying to appreciate extremely small (as in this case) or extremely large values for physical quantities. For example, in considering the likely reliability of a wheel circumference given to the nearest thousandth of a foot (0.0002 m), one can find with little effort that this distance increment is twice the diameter of the average human hair. The circumference has been stated to within a precision of two hairs.

How would the circumference of that wheel have been measured? There are two straightforward ways to do this. One is to measure the diameter of the wheel and multiply it by Π. The other is to roll the wheel along the track for one complete rotation and measure how far forward its center moves during that rotation. These methods, by the way, have been used for thousands of years. As pointed out elsewhere, the value of Π was known to within a precision of 0.01, meaning that Π could be stated with confidence to be 3.14 ± 0.01, by 400 B.C.E. (It is now known to thousands of significant digits, though that has not much bearing on ordinary designs and construction, for which 3.14159 is more than sufficient.) Distances between ancient cities were measured in basically the same way as the distance traveled by the subway train in its braking test was measured, a count being made of the number of rotations made by a wheel of known circumference, sometimes as a chariot on which the wheel was mounted traveled between the cities. Eratosthenes of Cyrene (296–194 B.C.E.) was said to have relied on this method as part of his determination of the circumference of the Earth 2,200 years ago, a determination closer to the correct value than the circumference used by Christopher Columbus (1451–1506) in planning his voyage of 1492.

(continues)

(continued)

Is it reasonable to believe that one can measure the distance rolled by the train wheel to within a thousandth of a foot? It is not. It also appears to be even more difficult to measure the diameter of the wheel to within a few ten-thousandths of a foot, the precision necessary if that is way the circumference was determined. Furthermore, even if by some heroic means this precision in the circumference could be obtained, it would soon become incorrect simply from wearing away of the rotating wheel.

Eratosthenes of Cyrene (296–194 B.C.E.) *(Ancient Art and Architecture Collection Ltd./The Bridgeman Art Library)*

From where could the degree of precision stated for the circumference being unreasonable have come? Frequently, persons not sensitive to the meaning of their result perform an arithmetic operation on a legitimate statement of their measurement and neglect to round off their answer. In that case, the appearance of high precision comes from arithmetic. For example, if one measures the diameter of a wheel with a tape measure and then multiplies the number obtained by Π, which even cheap calculators will give to 10 significant figures as 3.141592654, far more digits can appear in the final answer than were present in the measured number.

Departing from the specific example of the railroad wheel, consider a measurement showing the diameter of a wheel to be 5.25 inches (0.133 m). If the physical measurement could not be made more precisely than to within the closest one-sixteenth inch, the measurement would legitimately be stated as 5.250 ± 0.062 inches (0.133 ± 0.0016 m). This would serve as a reminder of the limitation on the precision. If, however, one forgot about the ± 0.062 inches when multiplying the measured 5.25 inches by Π, one could end up with a number for the circumference of 16.49336143 inches (0.4178318229 m). One who did not know better might knock a few of the digits off in the interest of fitting the number better on the page and state that the circumference of the wheel was 16.49336 inches (0.4178318 m). Such a statement would be a display of ignorance potentially fatal to the credibility of a forensic investigator. There are two approaches to ensuring that one does not overstate precision in this example. One is to recall that the underlying measurement was good to no more than three significant digits (often called significant figures) leading one to round off the result for the circumference to 16.5 inches (0.419 m). Alternatively, one can do the circumference calculation more carefully, carrying along the uncertainty in the diameter measurement and stating that C = (5.25 ± 0.062)Π, obtaining 16.49336143 ± 0.194778745 inches. It can immediately be seen that if the result has an uncertainty greater than 0.19 inches, it does not make sense to express it out to eight decimal places. In fact, one should not express it out to more than two decimal places. So the credible value for the circumference is 16.49 ± 0.19 inches (0.4188 ± 0.0048 m). In fact, since the uncertainty is nearly 0.2 inches, it does not make sense to express the result to the nearest hundredth of an inch. The proper statement is 16.5 ± 0.2 inches (0.419 ± 0.005 m). So, both approaches lead to the same modesty in stating the measured circumference. (Given the high precision with which Π is reliably known—that is, with which the relation between the diameter and circumference of a circle is known—it is legitimate to say that one had measured the circumference of a circle once one had measured its diameter.) However, by carrying along the uncertainty, one is given a better idea of the reliability of the end result. No matter how one approaches the problem, it is essential to keep in mind the conservative rule of thumb that the number of digits in the final answer should be no more than the number of digits in the least precise measurement entering the calculation.

(continues)

(continued)

Another example of an arithmetic operation leading to an over-statement of precision is simple division. The fact that one is able to measure a length to within one-third of an inch does not mean that one can make the measurement to within 0.333333333 . . . inch.

An amusing injection of false precision repeatedly shows up wherever units are converted from the S.I. ("the metric system") to the U.S. system or vice versa. For example, a rule that private planes cannot fly lower than 500 feet over a city can show up after conversion as a rule placing the minimum altitude at 152 m. Also a half-ton truck may appear, after applying the S.I. conversion, as a 4,448-N truck or, worse, a 453.9-kg truck. (Why is this worse?) Maybe a 100-meter dash becomes a 109.4-yard dash. This conversion-produced preciseness is particularly startling when, as often occurs, only the converted number and not the original is printed.

Rounding-Off Rules

In rounding off a number, one starts by dropping off successive digits starting from the right. As each digit is dropped, the next digit to the left is increased by one if the dropped digit was greater than five, and is left unchanged if the dropped digit was less than five. By convention, if the digit being dropped is equal to 5, then the next digit to the left is increased by one if it is odd, but left unchanged if it was even. Thus, 5.86 rounded off to two significant digits is 5.9, and 5.96 rounded off is 6.0. However, 5.84 rounded off is 5.8. Furthermore, 5.55 rounded off is 5.6, but 5.65 rounded off is also 5.6.

(continued from page 202)

acceleration is the change in speed divided by the time over which the change takes place. How is the acceleration to be obtained from data like those from the table on page 200? If one is told that the average speed for one rotation of the wheel is, for example, 29.0 miles per hour (42.6 fps) and that the wheel has a circumference of 2.911 feet, one can

Sometimes, instead of being rounded off, numbers are just chopped off; they are said to have been truncated. Usually this occurs because of the way a computer is programmed to report numbers; it is rarely desirable since truncation frequently changes the value of the number. Thus, truncating the number 5.86 to two significant digits yields 5.8. Depending on the magnitude of the digit dropped by truncating, the result can be the same or different from the result of rounding. (Describe why this is so.) As can be seen, truncating can cause the loss of information that rounding retains.

Remember the lesson urged by this discussion: A telltale indication that the author of a forensic report does not have an adequate grasp of his or her subject matter is the appearance in the report of overly precise values for physical quantities. For reasons described in this sidebar, excessively precise numbers are characterized by an excessive number of digits. An example would be a statement that the coefficient of friction μ between automobile tires and a stretch of pavement was measured to be 0.8437 based on a finding that a force of 27 pounds was required to pull a 32-pound drag sled across the pavement. Since neither the force nor the weight was known to more than two significant figures, the most precise statement possible for μ would be 0.84. However, because of the roughness with which measurements are made with drag sleds, it is probably misleading to state the measured μ to more than a single figure, namely 0.8. In conclusion, physical quantities described with unreasonable precision should always put the reader on alert for other errors.

obtain the time measurement. Since V equals D/T, T therefore equals D/V. When 2.911 and 42.6, respectively, are substituted for D and V, the result for T is 0.0683 seconds. (Confirm this calculation.) This is the time measurement that was the basic measurement made by the device, as opposed to 29.0 miles per hour which is a value calculated by the device. By doing this calculation, with, for example, a spreadsheet for every one of the data entries, it is possible to calculate for the entire run the cumulative time measured from the start of the run and produce a table displaying the important variables. The following table is a portion of such a table produced by the investigators in this manner. Just the data for the two seconds near the start of braking are included. The braking began 40.13 seconds into the run. Each of the time readings in this column corresponds to the completion of one turn of the train wheel. The corresponding number in the second column is the speed calculated for the most recent rotation by the device mounted on the train; that is, it comes from the same source as the speed column that excerpted the table of the data has provided the investigator. With a cumulative time and a value for speed corresponding to the time, it is straightforward to calculate the average acceleration ("deceleration") during each turn of the wheel. These accelerations are displayed in the third column in ft/sec² and in the fourth column as a multiple of g. It is in the acceleration values that the mischief created by the strange way in which the calculated speed was presented becomes apparent. This is shown graphically in the figure on page 209 where the acceleration values of column three of the table have been plotted against the time shown in column one. If the acceleration were really occurring as depicted in the chart, the ride would be a jerky one indeed. As a matter of fact, *jerk* is defined as the change in acceleration over time, just as *acceleration* is defined as the change in speed over time. One

Distance (feet)					
True	Rounded	True	Rounded	True	Rounded
2.911	2.9	26.199	26.2	49.487	49.5
5.822	5.8	29.110	29.1	52.398	52.4
8.733	8.7	32.021	32.0	55.309	55.3
11.644	11.6	34.932	34.9	58.220	58.2
14.555	14.6	37.843	37.8	61.131	61.1
17.466	17.5	40.754	40.8	64.042	64.0
20.377	20.4	43.665	43.7	66.953	67.0
23.288	23.3	46.576	46.6	69.864	69.9

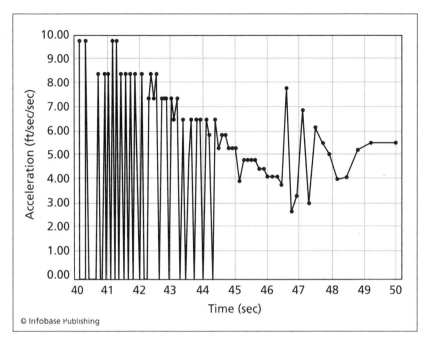

The erratic accelerations implied by data as presented

learns early on in one's automobile-driving career to release the brake the instant before one's car comes to a complete halt. Failure to do this leads to a sizeable jerk the instant the car stops moving because in a very short interval (a fraction of a second), the car's deceleration goes from a constant –0.3g or so to zero. The jerk is the change in acceleration divided by that fraction of a second. (What are the units of jerk?)

The apparent discontinuity of the acceleration of the train during braking was an artifact of the manner in which the data were presented in the printout sent to the investigator. By smoothing the data, a truer representation could be obtained of what was really happening during the braking. A graph of the speed and acceleration once the smoothing has been done is on page 211. This smoothing did not create a distortion of what was measured in terms of deceleration but rather extracted from the imperfect presentation of data the speed and acceleration that were actually associated with the braking test. (An even more realistic presentation would have a smooth curve connecting the individual points.)

Time (sec)	Speed (miles per hour)	Acceleration (ft/sec/sec)	Acceleration (g)
40.13	32.2		
40.19	31.8	9.78	0.30
40.25	31.8	0.00	0.00
40.32	31.8	0.00	0.00
40.38	31.8	0.00	0.00
40.44	31.4	9.78	0.30
40.50	31.4	0.00	0.00
40.57	31.4	0.00	0.00
40.63	31.4	0.00	0.00
40.69	31.4	0.00	0.00
40.76	31.0	8.38	0.26
40.82	31.0	0.00	0.00
40.88	31.0	0.00	0.00
40.95	30.6	8.38	0.26
41.01	30.6	0.00	0.00
41.08	30.2	8.38	0.26
41.15	30.2	0.00	0.00
41.21	29.8	9.78	0.30
41.28	29.8	0.00	0.00
41.34	29.4	9.78	0.30
41.41	29.4	0.00	0.00
41.48	29.0	8.38	0.26
41.55	29.0	0.00	0.00
41.62	28.6	8.38	0.26
41.69	28.6	0.00	0.00
41.76	28.2	8.38	0.26
41.83	28.2	0.00	0.00
41.90	27.8	8.83	0.26
41.97	27.5	6.29	0.20
42.04	27.5	0.00	0.00

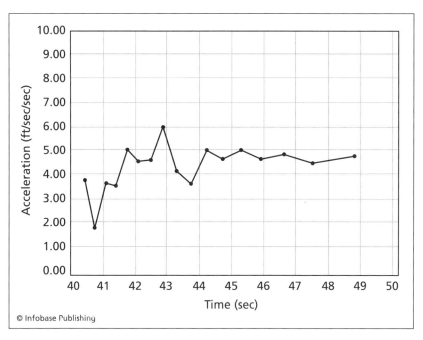

Graph of speed and acceleration after smoothing

The most important conclusion to be drawn from the stopping data was that the train required 270 feet (82.3 m) to come to a halt when the emergency brake was applied at a speed of 32.4 miles per hour (52.1 km/hr). This included the distance traveled during the less than full braking that occurred during the 1.5 seconds that passed after the brakes were applied (by releasing the deadman switch and moving the brake lever to full stop) before maximum braking commenced. (Compare this with the three-fourths second theoretical time mention earlier.) From the point that maximum braking commenced until the train stopped, the train traveled 200 feet (61.0 m). During the 70 feet (21 m) after the brake lever was applied but prior to full braking, the train slowed from a speed of 32.4 miles per hour (52.1 km/hr) to 29.8 miles per hour (48.0 km/hr) due to a combination of rolling resistance and partial braking. (Rolling resistance refers to the slowing that would occur while the train was coasting with no braking and no throttle applied.) From the relationship between coefficient of friction and stopping distance, show that with 200 feet (61.0 m) required to stop from a speed of about 30 miles per hour (48 km/hr), the effective coefficient of friction was about 0.15.

TIME-DISTANCE ANALYSIS

It will be seen in what follows that the time-distance analysis for the man-under event was exactly the same as carried out in chapter 2 in determining whether the hit-and-run driver would have been able to stop without hitting the girl had he or she been traveling at 40 miles per hour (64 km/hr) instead of at 55 miles per hour (88 km/hr). Thus, the first step was to determine how long it would have taken the train to stop from a speed of 25 miles per hour (40 km/hr), the speed the operator stated she was traveling.

The reasonable assumption was made that the fraction of the total kinetic energy lost during the period between brake-lever application and the moment that full braking commenced would be the same starting at 25 miles per hour (40 km/hr) as it was for the test speed of 32.4 miles per hour (52.0 km/hr). During the test, the train speed fell from 32.4 miles per hour (52.0 km/hr) to 29 miles per hour (47 km/hr) between the application of the brakes and the moment that full braking commenced. The fractional change in kinetic energy is easy to calculate and does not require using the mass of the train or converting from miles per hour to feet per second. Because the kinetic energy is proportional to the square of the speed, the fractional change is $(32.4^2 - 29^2)/(32.4)^2$, namely 0.20. The train lost 20 percent of its initial speed during the transition period. When a train traveling at 25 miles per hour (40 km/hr) loses 20 percent of its kinetic energy, its speed falls to 22.4 miles per hour (36.0 km/hr). (Show that this is so.)

Assuming that the deceleration rate is constant during the transition period, the average speed during that period will be approximately 23.7 miles per hour (38.1 km/hr). At an average speed of 23.7 miles per hour for 1.5 seconds, the train will travel 52 feet (15.8 m). To obtain the additional distance traveled by the train under full braking, the deceleration rate of 0.15g observed with full braking during the test was used. The result was that the train would slow under maximum braking from a speed of 22.4 miles per hour (36.0 km/hr) to a halt in a distance of 113 feet (34.4 m). Adding the two distances 52 feet and 113 feet leads to the conclusion that the train traveling into that station at 25 miles per hour (40 km/hr) would come to a complete stop in 165 feet (50.3 m) following the application of emergency braking.

The next step in the analysis is to allow for the operator's perception-reaction time. Because of the simple choice that confronted her once she had perceived something on the tracks in front of her train, her reaction time can be taken to be very short. Instead of the rule-of-thumb reaction time of 0.75 seconds commonly used for highway accidents, the reaction time in this case is probably as short as 0.25 seconds. If the accident had occurred during daylight hours, it would be reasonable to assign the operator a very short perception time as well, given the limited nature of the hazards that train operators encounter. However, because of reduced lighting conditions, the perception time is difficult to estimate. Recall that perception begins when the hazard enters the field of vision of the operator, something that occurs in this case only when the operator is close enough to the man on the tracks that—were she simply sitting in the train and looking down the tracks—she would have been able to see him. That, in turn, depends on how much illumination the station lights cast on the tracks and the resulting contrast between the man and the background. The headlights on the train reportedly provided lighting only for 100 feet (30 m) in front of the train. However, visits to the station under lighting conditions approximating those of the night of the accident showed that a person with dark clothes lying on the tracks at the position of the injured man could be seen from a distance of more than 300 feet by a person standing in the train operator's booth on a train that was not moving. Therefore, it was conservatively concluded that a train operator whose gaze was directed down the track as the train entered the station, would have had the hazard enter his or her field of vision at a distance of 300 feet (91 m).

Whenever one arrives at a point where the needed input data is soft, one must seek another approach, preferably one that can rely on solid information. In this case, the solid relevant information includes the rest positions of the train and of the man. The assumption is made that the man on the tracks was not moved significantly by the train's passing over his legs.

As shown in the figure on page 185, the front of the train came to a halt 455 feet (139 m) into the station and 52 feet (16 m) past the man. If it entered the station traveling 25 miles per hour (40 km/hr), as the operator reported, one need only go back 165 feet (50.3 m) from the rest position to find where the emergency brake was applied. This would be when the train (meaning the front of the power unit) was 290 feet (88.4 m) into the station, that is, 165 feet north of its rest position 455 feet into the station. That would place it 113 feet north of the man on the tracks when the emergency brake went on. As a trial value for the operator's perception time, 1.0 second was selected, making total perception-reaction time 1.25 sec. During that 1.25 seconds time, the train at 25 miles per hour (36.7 fps) would have traveled 46 feet (14 m). Adding this travel distance, which would have occurred during the perception-reaction time, to the travel distance that would have occurred after the emergency brake was applied yields 211 feet (64.3 m). This is the distance the train would have traveled between the moment the hazard entered the operator's and the moment that the train came to a stop—for an initial speed of 25 miles per hour (40 km/hr) and a perception-reaction time of 1.25 seconds. Under those circumstances, the hazard would have entered the operator's field of vision when the train was 244 feet (74.4 m) into the station, from which position the man on the tracks would have been 159 feet (48.5 m) ahead of the train. The figure below illustrates the results

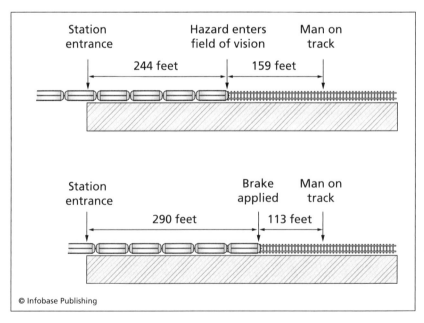

© Infobase Publishing

Position of the train at key points, calculated for a train speed of 25 miles per hour (40 km/hr)

of the calculations for the conditions of speed and perception-reaction time as just stated.

What conclusions, if any can be drawn from the calculation just completed for the hypothetical initial speed of 25 miles per hour (40 km/hr) and perception-reaction time of 1.25 seconds? The most obvious and perhaps least significant is that it places the train 40 feet (12 m) closer to the man when the hazard first entered the operators' eyes than the operator stated the distance to be when she first saw the man. The more important conclusion is that if the hazard did not enter her eyes until she was just 158 feet (48 m) short of running over him, she must not have been looking down the track as she entered the station, given the visibility studies showing that a dark-clothed man on the tracks at that point would enter the field of vision of an operator of an approaching train from a distance of more than 300 feet (90 m). It bears repeating that this is not the distance from which the operator of an approaching train "should have seen" the man but rather the distance from which the hazard could have entered the operator's field of vision, thus starting the perception-reaction process. "Could have," since the operator has to be looking in that direction for this to happen.

THE OPERATOR'S WAY OUT

A greater distance can be calculated for the point at which the hazard first entered the operator's eyes the night of the accident by either increasing her perception-reaction time or increasing her speed (or both, of course). For example, increasing her perception time by one second will increase by 37 feet (11 m) the distance traveled at 25 miles per hour (40 km/hr) during the perception-reaction time. That would place her that much farther away when the hazard would have first entered her field of vision, namely at a distance of 195 feet (59.4 m) from the man on the tracks. While that is suggestively close to the 200 feet (61.0 m) that she gave for the distance at which she first saw him, that is a misleading coincidence. (Why?) At any event, given the visibility that prevailed the night of the accident, that is still closer than the point at which the hazard could have entered her field of vision.

Next, leaving her perception-reaction time at 1.25 seconds, the calculation was redone for an initial speed of 32.4 miles per hour (52.1 km/hr), the speed used for the stopping test. It was found that at that speed, the train required 270 feet (82.3 m) to come to a full stop from the point at which the brakes were applied by action of the operator. The distance traveled at 32.4 miles per hour (52.1 km/hr) during a perception-reaction time of 1.25 seconds is 59.4 feet (18.1 m). Adding that to the stopping distance once the brakes are applied at that speed yields 329 feet (100 m). The speed limit during the approach to the station was 30 miles per hour (48 km/hr). Do the calculation for that speed; that is, determine the distance between the operator and the hazard when the hazard first could have entered her field of vision. Also determine where she would have been at the end of her perception period, that is, the point at which it can be said that she first saw the hazard.

CONCLUDING COMMENTS

The discussion above included a lot of what can only be called arithmetic. It was included for two reasons: One was to show how much of forensic analysis, even by physicists and engineers, involves mathematics at a level no higher than what should be learned in elementary school, and the other was to show the requirement that the world be treated quantitatively when people's lives and livelihoods are to be affected by one's conclusions. So what was concluded here? Was the train operator negligent? The answer is that this was one of the many accidents for which it is not possible to prove that the defendant was negligent, nor to prove the opposite. It was shown that by accepting a reasonable value for the perception-reaction time, it would have been possible for the accident to occur even with the train operator looking straight down the tracks as she entered the station at the speed limit or a bit higher. It was shown to be unlikely that she was both exercising proper care by looking down the tracks and traveling at the 25 miles per hour (40 km/hr) she reported. Given that she regularly has to estimate her train's speed with a precision of better than plus or minus 5 miles per hour (8 km/hr) through visual clues alone (that is, without a speedometer), some retraining might have been in order. However, that underestimate of the speed did not constitute negligence. (Why?)

In spite of the investigation providing a defense for the operator and therefore her employer, the question was close enough that one would expect the case to go to trial unless a settlement could be reached by the parties. At trial, the plaintiffs' attorneys would need an expert witness to support their allegation of negligence. Is the question close enough for an honest expert in the engineering sciences to support that allegation? What holes can you see, if any, in the argument that would probably be used by the defense attorney in trying the case?

CANDOR IN ANALYSIS

In describing the accident and the forensic analysis of it in this chapter, one had a luxury not usually available when doing the analysis in preparation for testifying as an expert witness at trial, the luxury of candor. The adversarial legal system employed in the United States, Canada, and throughout much, though not all, of the world, pressures participants to hold their cards fairly close to their chest. This does not mean necessarily that they are dishonest or trying to get away with something; rather, it means that candor in writing reports or speaking can provide the opposing party, who can use the phrases out of context or imbue them with more or different meanings than intended, with ammunition that can be used at trial. Fortunately, there is a new mechanism available to judges in the United States whereby the experts on opposing sides can be used to sort out among themselves what the real issues are in a dispute. One way in which this approach has been implemented is for the experts on each side to submit to the judge the names of several experts in their field whom they trust to make an honest, disinterested analysis of the case. Presuming that there is overlap between the two lists submitted, the judge then appoints one of the persons recommended by both sides to carry out the task. Obviously, this approach will work only when each side believes that the facts strongly support at least part of its theory of the case and when the experts who have been hired are honest. Usually, the two elements go together. When a party realizes that it does not have a leg to stand on but still wishes to go forward, the expert it needs to support its case is usually incompetent or dishonest.

It is one of the frustrations of the legal system that it is difficult to determine whether a person arguing in support of a nonsensical theory really believes the theory because of incompetence or is a dishonest person lending his or her credentials in support of the party paying him or her. Most recently, a new approach has been suggested for ensuring that persons being offered as experts are making arguments that are competent. This approach, which appears to have particular applicability in the forensic engineering sciences, requires that the proposed expert prepare a detailed written report stating the facts of the case and his or her analysis of them, in short the type of report that an engineer working in industry or that engineering and science students produce in the university. This report would be submitted to the opposing party early in the litigation process, and that party would have the right to ask the judge to send the report out for what is called peer review. Peer review is nearly universally accepted as part of the process of publishing papers in the professional literature. The editor of a peer-reviewed journal, on receiving a manuscript for publication, sends it out to two or three experts in the field that the manuscript discusses. The reports of the referees are then used in making the decision as to whether to accept the manuscript for publication. This is a system that has been in place for more than 100 years. It has its critics and it has some shortcomings. However, it has been suggested that it, or something similar to it, could prevent or greatly reduce bogus technical theories from keeping alive litigation that without the support of those theories would quickly wither away. This and other measures are examples of the statements in the introduction and chapter 1 about continuing efforts to improve the fairness of trials.

The Grounding of the
Merchant Vessel *Tamano*

Throughout most of American history, shipwrecks constituted most of the serious accidents of transit (transportation). U.S. coastal waters contain remnants from thousands of ships sunk over the centuries, the vast majority of which have disappeared from memory. Many of these wrecks took human life, sometimes in great number, such as the mid-19th century wreck of the *Lady Elgin,* which carried 450 passengers to the bottom of Lake Michigan; most were firefighters and their families returning to Milwaukee after an outing in Chicago. Another was the SS *City of Portland* (Maine), lost with all hands on Thanksgiving Day 1898 en route to Portland after leaving Boston harbor in a blizzard of ice. So great a blow was that sinking that for decades people in its home city characterized past events by whether it had occurred before or after "the Portland went down." Unlike those two disasters, differing from many others only in the total number of deaths, a sinking not likely to be forgotten is that of the RMS *Titanic* in April 1912. In the North Atlantic just a few hundred miles from the North American coast on its very first voyage, the RMS *Titanic* sank along with more than 1,500 of her passengers and crew after its starboard (right) hull was opened by an encounter with an iceberg. An iceberg bearing a swath of red paint and thought to have been the one struck by the *Titanic* was photographed at least once in the 24 hours after the tragedy. Survivors estimated that the mountain of ice that doomed their ship, the iceberg to which they had remained in close proximity for hours while awaiting rescue, reached above them by 50 to 100 feet (15 to 30 m) and covered an area 200 to 400 feet (61 to 122 m) by 100 to 200 feet (30 to 61 m). Review the discussion in chapter 1 of Archimedes' principle, and then explain what it means to say something like "That's just the tip of the iceberg," or "Only 10 percent of an iceberg is above the surface." Does this mean necessarily that an iceberg that sticks out of the ocean 100 feet (91 m) will only float in water that is at least 900 feet (275 m) deep? Using the densities of ice and seawater, estimate the total volume of the iceberg described by the survivors from the RMS *Titanic*. Should the density used be that of freshwater ice or saltwater ice? How much and what kind of difference does it make? After estimating its volume, calculate the iceberg's mass and then its weight, expressing the answers in both U.S. units and in S.I.

Even those wrecks not causing injury or death always cause economic loss, measured in amounts up to the billions of dollars in such cases as the *Exxon Valdez* in Williams's Sound, Alaska, at the end of the 20th century. Even before the *Exxon Valdez,* it had been recognized that if environmental damage is not included in the total, the total loss could be very much underestimated. Especially with respect to shipping accidents, it is now seen that short- and long-term environmental damage can be as important as the traditionally recognized forms of loss.

The 450 square miles (1,170 km²) of Casco Bay in the State of Maine have seen a great number of shipwrecks during the nearly 500 years that have passed since the first European vessel entered it. Although the foundering of the *Hesperus* on the reef of Norman's Woe did not take place there, the poem memorializing it may owe its creation to the fact that its author, Henry Longfellow (1807–82), was formed by his childhood and early manhood on its shores.

This chapter addresses the 1972 collision between the oil tanker N/V *Tamano* and Soldiers' Ledge, 40 feet (12 m) below the surface of low tide and lying along one of the marine passageways into the Port of Portland on Casco Bay. Early on the morning of July 22, the *Tamano,* proceeding under its own power in calm seas, was slowly advancing along a narrow channel—a gut—between two of the islands forming the outer perimeter of the port. This particular gut was part of Hussey Sound. Though not the usual path for large ships entering the port, this gut was the most direct approach to the power generating station that was the *Tamano*'s first destination on its arrival in the United States with Bunker C fuel oil from Venezuela. Because Bunker C congeals at temperatures below 55°F (12.8°C), heaters were operating throughout the many separate tanks the ship contained.

As the *Tamano* was passing into Hussey Sound, the tide was ebbing with two hours to go until the next low tide. The tidal current of about one and a half knots (0.77 m/s) was flowing against the motion of the *Tamano*. The tidal range in that area on the day of the accident was 8.4 feet (2.6 m), somewhat less than the 10-foot (3-m) average range for Casco Bay. Though narrow, the Hussey Sound gut was deep. With one notable exception, it was significantly deeper even at low tide than the 44 feet (13 m) drawn by the *Tamano* as it entered port that morning. The ship had an overall length of 810 feet (247 m), an overall breadth (beam) of 128 feet (39 m), and a top deck 14 feet (4.3 m) above the waterline. Show that it was displacing approximately 3,520,000 cubic feet (99,700 m³) of water. With a density of 64 pounds per cubic foot (10,000 N/m³), this volume of water weighs about 225 million pounds (a billion newtons). How much did the *Tamano* weigh?

The navigational channel through the gut was marked by buoys placed and maintained by the U.S. Coast Guard for the purpose of guiding ship traffic. In fact, they had just recently been removed for servicing and reinstalled a few days earlier. Shortly before 1:30 A.M., the *Tamano* collided with Navigational Buoy No. 6, an important marker since its purpose was to divert traffic away from Soldier Ledge. Soldier Ledge was a granite mass that, prior to World War II, had reached to within 30 feet (9.1 m) of the surface at low tide. Because of the U.S. Navy operations in the area in during the war—Hussey Sound had been home to the North Atlantic Fleet—the ledge had been dynamited so that its highest point was reduced to the present 40 feet (12 m) below the surface at average low tide. This was enough to clear all the vessels of the World War II era.

Both on the night of the collision and during the legal proceedings that followed, there were disputes as to where on the ship Buoy No. 6 had

The *Tamano* surrounded by spilled
oil *(UPI/CORBIS)*

hit. The seaman on duty at the bow of the vessel that night estimated that
he had seen the impact occur a full 39 feet (11.9 m) inboard from the
ship's starboard limit. This would mean that to avoid the buoy, he would
have had to be more than 39 feet (11.7 m) further to port (left). There
was testimony by witnesses that the buoy, after the first contact, had
scraped along the hull, making a final impact toward the aft extremity
of the ship. The harbor pilot responsible for guiding the ship recorded
that Buoy No. 6 passed the middle of the ship at 1:20 A.M.

Within seconds of the collision with Buoy No. 6, a piercing whistle
began to emanate from the forward tank on the starboard side, a chilling
sound under the circumstances. It meant that oil was flowing out of the
ship and into the waters of Casco Bay. A tank had been ruptured.

Rather than drop anchor in the narrow channel, the harbor pilot
brought the vessel to its normal anchorage area in Hussey Sound. With
the ship anchored, its crew members turned their attention to the
problem. With the whistle continuing to sound, they began to transfer
oil from the ruptured tank into one of the intact tanks in the center of
the vessel, using a sump pump that drew liquid from near the bottom
of the tank. As long as oil was flowing out the bottom, there was no
danger that the pump would pull in seawater. When, after two more
hours, the whistling stopped, the pumping was halted, though it was
the prevailing opinion that the rupture had occurred close to the water

The oil from the *Tamano* washing up on Long Island, Maine *(UPI/CORBIS)*

line, as a result of the collision with the buoy. Proceeding on the basis of that theory, the crew then shifted to drawing oil from the other tanks forward of the center of the vessel so as to raise the bow and presumably the damaged section of starboard hull. In retrospect, this action was seen to have caused more oil to flow from the ruptured tank into the bay. Why?

After another four and a half hours, during which the bow was lifted four feet (1.2 m), no sign of a leak in the starboard hull was seen. At that point, a commercial diver in a dry suit was sent down in the oily waters to explore. He found oil congealed on the starboard side and especially on the bottom of the hull to a thickness of 6 inches (0.15 m) or more. The Bunker C fuel oil gelled up at temperatures well above the seawater temperature, which was approximately 50°F (10°C) that mid-summer night. The tank heaters normally maintained the oil at 136°F (58°C) to ensure that it would flow readily when it needed to be discharged into land-based containers. This also enabled it to flow readily into the cold seawater, and once out of the tank, it quickly clumped together into a jellylike substance, part of it adhering to the hull and the rest floating to the surface.

In addition to the gelled oil coating the bottom of the vessel, the diver found a jagged 20-foot (6.1-m) gash in the bottom of the forward starboard tank, a gash varying in width from 6 inches to a foot (0.15 m to 0.3 m). It had not been Buoy No. 6 but rather Soldier Ledge that had ripped open the tank, letting its contents spill into the bay. As the *Tamano* moved through the gut drawing 44 feet (13.4 m), for 20 feet (6.1 m) of that passage the bottom of its forward starboard tank was dragged across a granite mass that was less than 44 feet (13.4 m) below the surface and perhaps as little as 40 feet (12.2 m). In the language of mariners, the *Tamano* had grounded, though without its crew being aware of it at the time. The photo on page 222 shows the *Tamano* surrounded by oil, with a boom deployed near the vessel in an attempt to contain the spilled oil. By the time the boom was put in place, it was too late, at least for the oil that gushed out during the first hours after the rupture occurred. This is reflected in the photograph on page 223 showing some of the spilled 100,000 gallons (380,000 L) washed up on one of the islands of Casco Bay.

ARCHIMEDES' EQUILIBRIUM

Before the rupture, the oil in the forward starboard tank was 55.7 feet (17.0 m) deep. Although, after the rupture, approximately 15 square feet (1.39 m²) of the bottom of the tank was open to the sea and air could flow into the top of the tank to replace the oil flowing out (generating a whistling sound), not all of the oil flowed out. Why not? Also, how much remained?

First, the answer to the second question. At 3:30 A.M. on the morning of the grounding, the depth of liquid in the ruptured tank after the whistling stopped was measured to be 46.6 feet (14.2 m) deep, 9.1 feet (2.8 m) lower than before the rupture. Then, the transfer of weight from front to rear was carried out. When that concluded, the depth of liquid in the ruptured tank was 44.6 feet (13.6 m). The draft (that is, the depth of the ship in the water) at the location of the ruptured starboard tank was then 40.6 feet (12.4 m), nearly 4 feet (1.2 m) less than it had been at the time of the rupture.

To complete the answer to the questions posed above, one has to return to a variation of Archimedes' principle while taking account of Newton's first law. It also helps to review the material of the sidebar on "Pressure."

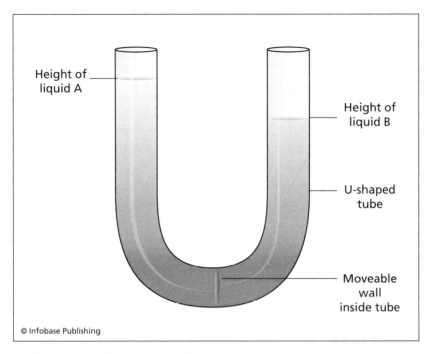

Height of liquid A

Height of liquid B

U-shaped tube

Moveable wall inside tube

© Infobase Publishing

An illustration of the balancing of liquid columns

The figure shows a U-shaped tube with liquids on the two sides. At the bottom of the U is a disk separating the liquids. That disk is free to slide in either direction. If the disk remains at the bottom without moving, it must be that the force exerted by the column on the right side of the disk is equal in magnitude to that exerted by the column on the left side of the disk. Since the columns are different in height, the conclusion is that the liquid in the higher column must be of lower density (weight per volume). When one actually does the experiment, one finds that it is not necessary to have the disk present. The columns act the same way without it.

Moving now to the ship with the ruptured tank, the claim is that the water just outside the tank is like the bottom of a column of ocean water 44 feet high, and the oil in the tank is like the other column in the drawing on page 238. Seawater at 55°F (12°C) has a density close to 64.1 pounds per cubic foot (10,000 newtons per cubic meter), and the Bunker C fuel oil at 136°F (58°C) had a density of approximately 58.7 pounds

(continues on page 228)

Pressure and Hydrostatics

Hydrostatics is the study of static fluids, that is, fluids, that do not flow, usually as the result of a balancing of forces. Some may have trouble thinking of all the water surrounding the *Tamano* as somehow being the equivalent, at the bottom of the front starboard tank, of a simple column of water 40.6 feet (12.4 m) high. It helps to modify the model so as to think in terms of pressure rather than force. Pressure is just force per unit area; for example, near sea level, the atmosphere exerts a force of approximately 14.7 pounds on every square inch (101,000 N/m^2) of the surface of the Earth. One says that the pressure is 14.7 pounds per square inch. The thing about a fluid such as air or water is that the same pressure is exerted in all directions at a given point within the volume of the fluid. Thus, the atmosphere will exert at the same pressure on all four sides of a cube. If the cube is open to the air, like a cube-shaped box with a hole in it, the pressure (and force) on both surfaces of all six sides is the same, and so the net force is zero. However, once the cube is closed and the air is pumped out of it, the atmospheric pressure will crush the cube unless it is made of a material able to withstand the resulting crushing force.

Seawater acts the same. At every point 40 feet (12 m) below the surface of the ocean, the pressure in all directions is the same. In terms of pounds per square feet, it will be equal to the weight of a column of water one square foot (0.09 m^2) in area and 40 feet (12 m) high. Such a column will have a volume of 40 cubic feet (1.13 m^3). Given the density of seawater, 64.1 pounds per cubic feet (10,100 n/m^3), that column will weigh about 2,560 pounds (11,400 N). This means that at that depth, the water pressure will be 2,560 pounds per square foot (122,600 N/m^2). To get a feeling for this, compare with it with the 14.7 pounds per square inch atmospheric pressure. One can convert this seawater pressure to pounds per square inch by dividing by the number of square inches in a square foot, 144, obtaining a pressure of 17.8 pounds per square inch (123,000 N/m^2).

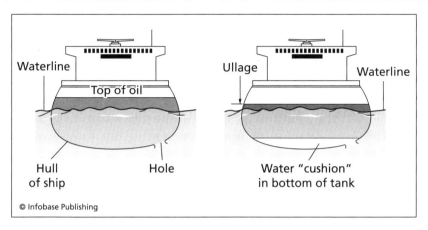

Waterline

Top of oil

Hull of ship

Hole

Ullage

Waterline

Water "cushion" in bottom of tank

© Infobase Publishing

Two oil-containing hulls, one with a hole in the bottom, presented to illustrate why a water cushion arises under the lighter-than-water oil when the depth of oil is reduced by pumping.

As long as the water pressure on the bottom of the ruptured tank is equal to the pressure of the oil in the tank, neither water nor oil will flow past the hole in the tank. The oil will not move out and the water will not move in. What is the height of a one square-foot column of the oil weighing 2,560 pounds? It is 2,560 pounds/ft² divided by 58.7 pounds/ft³ (the density of the oil). The result is 43.6 feet (13.3 m). (Check that the dimensions work out.) Thus, if the bottom of the tank is 40 feet (12 m) below the surface and, before the rupture, the oil was more than 43.6 feet (13.3 m) in depth, the oil flows out the hole only until the depth of the oil is reduced to 43.6 feet (13.3 m). On the other hand, if the oil was originally less than 43.6 feet (13.3 m), not only will oil not flow out, but water will flow in. Describe what will happen if the oil depth was 40 feet (12 m) exactly and the draft of the vessel at that point was 40 feet (12 m) exactly. In particular, describe quantitatively the contents of the tank once the flow has come to a halt and the liquid is in equilibrium. Why might one say that this creates a water cushion?

(continued from page 225)

per cubic foot (9,220 newtons per cubic meter). Therefore, the 40.6-foot (12.4-m) column of water will support a column of Bunker C that is 40.6 × (64.1/58.7) = 44.3 feet (13.5 m) high.

CREATING A WATER CUSHION

With the situation at equilibrium, the crew attempted to remove oil from the top of the ruptured tank. What effect would that have? Removing oil from the top will reduce the pressure of the oil against the water interface at the rupture. Since this pressure had been balancing the pressure of the water trying to get in, the result will be that water will enter the bottom of the tank until equilibrium is reestablished. What does equilibrium mean? It means that the downward pressure of the oil at the oil/water interface equals the upward pressure of the water. Now the weight of the water layer plus the weight of the oil counters the pressure of the water "trying" to enter at the rupture. For example, if the bottom of the tank is 40 feet (12 m) below the surface and, as a result of pumping the oil out the top, one foot of water enters the tank, the pressure at the top of that one-foot layer will be equivalent to 39 feet (11.9 m) of water. Since the weight of the oil per square foot (or per square meter) is somewhat more than nine-tenths the weight of the sea water per square foot (or per square meter), the height of the oil supported by the water pressure will always be about 1.1 times the equivalent depth of the water under the oil. A corollary of this is that the water layer increases by one foot in thickness for every 1.1 feet of oil that is removed from the top. If all of the oil is removed, the water inside the tank will be level with the surface of the ocean outside the tank.

How is the depth of oil in the tanks of an oil tanker measured? The amount of engine oil in an automobile or truck is measured by running a dip stick to the bottom of the reservoir, then removing it, and noting the level on the stick to which the oil adheres. The stick is marked with lines identified as "full," "add," and the like. Using this method for an oil tanker would require a mighty long dipstick, in excess of 60 feet (18.3 m) in the case of the *Tamano*. Then, after inserting this giant dipstick, one would have to have some place to lay it down to look at the point the oil had reached on it. Instead of doing this, an open tube is lowered into the tank. Since the audio characteristics of the tube (the way it sounds when one puts his or her ear to the opening at the top) change abruptly when the lower end of the tube is closed by reaching the liquid surface, it is straightforward to measure the distance between the top of the liquid and the top of the tank. This distance is called the ullage. Since the bottom of the tank is always the same distance from the top, knowing the ullage is tantamount to knowing the depth of liquid in the tank.

FUEL DELIVERY

The next step in handling the damaged vessel was to pump liquid from the ruptured tank into a small vessel (called a lighter) alongside the *Tamano*. After many hours of pumping, the crew decided that an adequate water cushion existed so that there would be no concern if the oil in the intact tanks was off-loaded and converged to its destination, the power station. Therefore, this was done. The quantity of oil removed from those tanks for this purpose caused the ship to rise eight feet (2.4 m). The effect this had on the oil in the ruptured tank underlay a large part of the controversy over damages and negligence that was involved in the later litigation.

The fishermen and home owners of Casco Bay alleged that the off-loading that caused the ship to rise in the water also led to a great deal more oil gushing out of the ruptured tank. They said that it was obvious that this had happened to anyone observing the *Tamano* during the off-loading, as much more oil and clumps of oil appeared in the water at that time. They sued those responsible for the off-loading, alleging negligence. (That is, the lawsuit was for the tort of negligence.)

The defendants in the lawsuit responded that because the oil had been pumped from the ruptured tank for a total of 13 hours, there was more than an adequate water cushion under the oil in the tank. In other words, they said that although the liquid in the ruptured tank flowed out the hole at the bottom of the tank as the ship rose in the water, that was all just seawater and that the oil that was still in that tank was riding atop the water cushion and never reached the bottom of the tank during the operation. As for the additional oil that appeared in the Casco Bay waters around the *Tamano,* that was just the oil that had come out previously and congealed on the bottom. During the offloading, it had shaken loose and, being lighter than the water, had risen to the surface. But the major argument lay in the volume of liquid pumped out of that tank in the attempt to create a water cushion.

The plaintiffs in the action had the burden of convincing the judge that, during the off-loading process, oil had poured into the bay in addition to that spilled already. If they could not explain why there was no water cushion or an insufficient water cushion in spite of all those hours of pumping from the ruptured tank, it would be very difficult to convince anyone that there was additional oil spilled. What they did have was an entry the first mate had made in his log book showing that the ullage in the ruptured tank at the end of the 13 hours of pumping from the tank was identical to the ullage before that pumping commenced.

What would be the significance of the first mate's ullage reading? Could it be described as a smoking gun? How could it be possible that the ullage was the same in the ruptured tank after 13 hours of pumping during which liquid clearly was being taken from the tank?

After spending the time necessary to provide thoughtful answers to the questions posed, it should be interesting to read the decisions of the judges at the various levels in the federal judicial system that dealt with this case in the middle 1970s. One of the aspects of interest is the detailed discussion of navigational principles that the trial judge used in his ruling. Enhancing the interest is the fact that the judge at the appeals court, in reversing the trial judge, severely criticized the trial judge for not in fact knowing essential aspects of navigation, aspects that underlay the events leading up to the collision of the M/V *Tamano* with Soldier Ledge.

8

Crane Collapse

A cme Inc. had borrowed the old crane owned by Jamaica, Inc., yearly for 34 years before it killed one of Acme's workers. Every time that the lights fronting the top of Acme's building façade needed to be replaced, Acme borrowed the crane, the only one nearby that had a boom sufficiently long to reach the 45-foot (13.7-m) level of the light fixtures. During the 34 years that this borrowing had continued, many crane-safety provisions had been enacted by the public and private agencies concerned with industrial safety. In addition, crane manufacturers themselves had introduced additional safety features, many of them directed at automatically limiting the crane operator's freedom to place the boom. This marked a systematic departure from the old approach in which it was left up to the operator to know and avoid the boom positions that would cause the crane to tip over. Because the Jamaica crane lacked the benefit of the later safety features, the theories put forth immediately after the accident all assumed that the operator had been at fault and that he had put the boom into a position that caused the collapse. Supporting this line of reasoning was the lack of experience the Acme employee had with crane operation. Supporting this theory from Jamaica's point of view was the fact that it would exonerate Jamaica of responsibility. For purposes of this chapter, the theory of collapse has the advantage of allowing the introduction of a very important concept: the force moment. As it turned out, the accident had quite a different explanation, one that requires an elementary understanding of hydraulic systems as well as of force moments.

The photo below shows a typical crane of the type involved in the accident under discussion. It is equipped with an articulated boom. The boom is the working part of the crane. In systems such as the one involved in the accident discussed here, the boom supports a bucket that allows a worker to be moved to the point, usually some distance above the ground, where work needs to be carried out. In this type of crane, the boom can ascend from a nested (stowed) position to an extended (deployed) position, the position of the bucket depending on the direction and angle of the boom's lower segment and the angle the upper segment makes with the lower segment. Something described as articulated has at least one moveable joint. The elbow joint is what makes the human arm articulated. A crane with an articulated boom has a great deal of flexibility since the orientations of the two segments can be varied semi-independently of one another. The accompanying photo and the figure on page 233 show several possible configurations for such a boom, which is mounted on a base that can be rotated horizontally with respect to the vehicle supporting it. The usefulness of a crane such as this lies in its ability to place its bucket close to a wide range of locations without

A truck crane with articulated boom *(Courtesy of the author)*

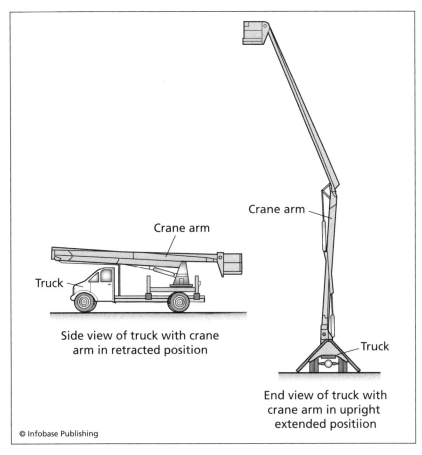

Crane arm

Crane arm

Truck

Side view of truck with crane
arm in retracted position

Truck

End view of truck with
crane arm in upright
extended positiion

© Infobase Publishing

An illustration that demonstrates the range of movement of the truck crane's
extendable arm

the truck being moved. These locations can be in any direction from the
truck and at a range of distances and elevations with respect to the center
of the truck. Most cranes of this type have two sets of operating controls:
One set is at the rear of the truck; the other is in the bucket. In that way,
the worker in the bucket can make the fine adjustments necessary to put
the bucket in exactly the position needed to do the work.

It turns out, for reasons discussed in the sidebar on "Force Moments
and Stability," that more than just the length of the boom limits the range
of positions in which the operator may place the bucket. Some of the
positions that are physically reachable will cause the crane to overturn.

An outrigger in its fully stowed position *(Courtesy of the author)*

To increase the range of safe positions beyond what it would be otherwise, the Jamaica crane was equipped with outriggers. Outriggers provide four legs, four ground contacts that take over from the truck's four tires. By being placed further out from the midline of the truck, these legs create a wider base with which to support the boom. The photo above shows right-side outriggers in their mostly retracted (stowed) positions, while the following photo shows the right front outrigger in its fully extended (deployed) position.

Many types of equipment are provided with outriggers to increase stability during use while permitting the equipment to have a relatively narrow width as it is being transported over public highways. Some outriggers are deployed and locked in place by hand. The ones on the crane involved in the accident used a hydraulic system for this purpose, as well as for stowing the outriggers when they were no longer needed. The sidebar on "Hydraulics" explains some of the features of hydraulic systems.

THE CRANE COLLAPSES

In preparation for changing the bulbs, two workers familiarized themselves with the crane. This included deploying the outriggers from the truck body and seeing that the bucket could be successfully maneuvered using the controls on the truck. They then broke for lunch, returning an hour later, at which time one of the two men got into the bucket. Using the

An outrigger in its fully extended position *(Courtesy of the author)*

controls in the bucket, he lifted himself up on the way to the point where he had to do the bulb changing. Shortly after the bucket had reached the necessary height, the man standing near the truck shouted a warning, as the right outriggers lifted off the pavement. Unfortunately, nothing could be done by that point, and the crane rotated counterclockwise faster and faster, slamming the bucket against the pavement at a greater speed than that with which the man would have hit the pavement had he jumped from the bucket at its full height. (How could this be, given that all weights fall at the same acceleration under the force of gravity?) Although he had no external injuries, he died within minutes. His aorta had ruptured because of the inertial forces on it due to the impact deceleration.

For days in the aftermath of the accident, an army of investigators— some representing Acme, some representing Jamaica, some representing their respective insurance companies, some representing OSHA, and some representing the police—crawled over the fallen crane, taking hundreds of photographs. Since cranes of this type, when they tip over, usually do so because of the boom position, a great deal of effort was put into determining where the bucket would have been before it fell. This involved measuring the orientation of the base on which the boom was mounted, the angle that the lower boom made with the base, and the angle that the upper boom made with the lower boom. Lots of geometry was done and arguments broke out over whether it showed the boom had been in a dangerous position.

(continues on page 240)

Force Moments and Stability

Chapters 2 and 3 introduced the concept of force in connection with Newton's laws of motion, with emphasis placed on cars and other objects being accelerated by forces. Forces also play a key role, of course, even when nothing is being accelerated or even moved. The force the floor exerts on the furniture resting on it is what prevents the furniture from falling into the basement. It does this by balancing the gravitational force pulling down on the furniture. By Newton's third law, as discussed in chapter 3, the force with which the floor must push up on a 100-pound (445-N) person so that the person is supported by the floor is exactly 100 pounds (445 N). This is also the force with which the floor of an elevator moving up at a constant speed must push upward on the same person—recall that a net force of zero on an object does not ensure that the object is at rest but merely that it is not accelerated. The person on the elevator moving at a constant speed is not accelerated. The person is being pulled downward by a gravitational force of 100 pounds (445 N); therefore, the elevator must be pushing the opposite direction on the person with the same force. What provides that pushing force, the extra upward force of 100 pounds (445 N) when the person steps onto the elevator? The cable supporting the elevator compartment certainly feels it. With the person in the elevator, the tension in the cable is 100 pounds (445 N) greater than it was previously. Changing the picture a bit, imagine a young woman pulling roots out of the ground, the kind with two ends sticking in the ground and a loop extending above the surface. From her weightlifting experience at the gym, she estimates that on average she has to pull up with a force of 35 pounds (156 N) to rip each root out. Her hands hurting, she thinks about the teeter-totter (see saw) from her school days and moves her small bike rack near to the roots needing removal. Then, she places a 6-foot (1.8-m) two-by-four across the bar at the top of the bike rack so that 2 feet (0.6 m) stick out on the root side. After attaching a hook to that end of the board and sliding it under a root, she pushes down on the other end of the board. As she had expected, she found that the uprooting was accomplished with a force much less than 35 pounds (156 N). What had changed?

The answer is known intuitively by anyone who can balance a person twice his weight by choosing the right positions for the two of them on a teeter-totter board. To move from an intuitive knowledge to one where the explanation can be put into words, it is useful to define the term *force moment*. The accompanying figure shows

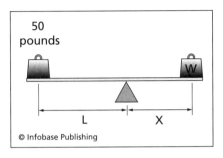

© Infobase Publishing

Illustration of force moments

an object weighing 50 pounds (222 N) on a board at a distance L from the fulcrum about which the board tips. If the angle defining the tip of the board is not changing, then the force moment on the board is zero relative to the fulcrum. This is something like Newton's first law that states an object with zero force on it is either at rest or moving at constant velocity. It will be found that to be correct, the first law must be stated in terms of the center of mass of the object since it is possible for there to be zero net force on an object and yet for the force moment on it to be nonzero. In such a situation the rotation of the object will be accelerating even though the center of mass is at rest or moving with a constant velocity.

Superficially, force moments play a role in angular motion similar to that played by forces in linear motion. In the example shown in the figure, the 50-pound (222-N) weight exerts a counterclockwise force moment of 50L about the pivot point. The force moment is equal to the force multiplied by the distance L, which is called the moment arm. On the other side of the pivot point, at a distance Y, is an object of weight W on the board. It exerts a clockwise force moment of WX about the pivot point. The condition for the board to be balanced, for it not to rotate about the pivot point, is that these two oppositely directed force moments cancel each other out. The condition then is that WX equal 50L. If W is 25 pounds (111 N), X must be twice as long as L;

(continues)

(continued)

that is, W must be twice as far from the pivot point as the 50-pound (222-N) weight. One says that W must have twice the moment arm as the 50-pound (222-N) weight if the teeter-totter is to balance.

Force moments determine whether a structure is stable or it is on the verge of tipping over. Force-moment considerations combined with the shape of a structure determine the long-term stability of the structure. Thinking about structure and force moments allows one to say why a pencil lying on the floor is quite stable. It also allows one to say why, although a pencil that is flat on one end can be stood upright on that end, it is not very stable in that position, and why it is essentially impossible to balance the pencil on its pointed end. (In the former case, the flat end is such a tiny base that the slightest tipping of the pencil will result in an unbalanced force moment. In the second example, the base presented by the point is far smaller.)

The accompanying figure shows a simplified diagram of a crane, with the boom extending out to the left side of the truck supporting it. The tires on the left side of the truck form a pivot line for the rig. (Actually, the pivot line in this case is determined by the left edges of the left tires.) The weight of the boom, for force moment purposes, acts as if it were all located at the boom's center of mass, as shown. Similarly, the entire weight of the truck acts as though it were centered at the truck's center of mass. The boom exerts a counterclockwise force moment about the pivot line, and the farther out to the left the boom extends, the greater the magnitude of that force moment. Counteracting that force moment about the pivot line is the clockwise force moment exerted by the truck weight. Whereas the clockwise force moment remains constant, the counterclockwise one changes every time the distance of the boom to the left of the truck changes. In particular, the further out the boom moves, the greater the counterclockwise force moment. To obtain the greatest use from the crane, it is given a long boom that is capable of reaching up very high. However, the consequence of this is that it is then

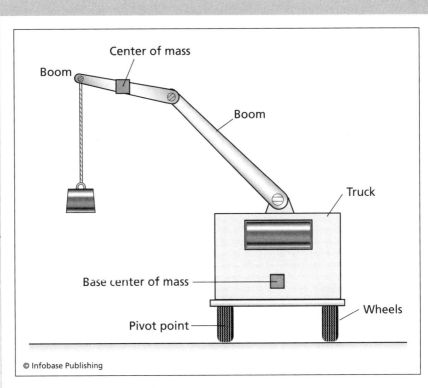

Sketch of crane with articulated boom

possible to place the bucket at a horizontal distance from the truck that results in the boom's force moment being greater than that of the truck. When that happens, the truck tips over to the left. It can be seen from the drawing that the greater the truck's track width, the further out the boom can be moved without the truck tipping. Stated differently, the greater the track width, the broader the range of safe motion for the boom. The addition of outriggers provides in effect a widening of the track width. By establishing the pivot point farther from the centerline of the truck, the outriggers provide a benefit in both directions: an increase in the moment arm of the truck's weight and, a reduction in the boom's moment arm.

(continued from page 235)

Eventually, one of the investigators pointed out that the right-front outrigger was partially retracted. There was some effort to dismiss the significance of this finding, along the line of its having being pushed up into its housing by the force of the crash. It was pointed out that there was no telltale pool of hydraulic fluid on the pavement such as would suggest a failure of the hydraulic system, with which the boom and outriggers were controlled. That this last point was irrelevant can be seen from the sidebar on "Hydraulics" and its subsequent material.

THE SOLUTION

There can be failures of hydraulic system components without any external leakage of fluid; for example, the figure on page 239 is a simple schematic of how the hydraulic fluid is used to deploy and stow each of the outriggers on the crane. The outrigger foot is at the end of a rod that extends from a cylinder. Inside the cylinder, the rod is connected to a piston, which is able to move up or down within the cylinder while maintaining a pressure seal at the walls of the cylinder by means of a *gasket*. There is a valve in the hydraulic circuit identified as a switch and manipulated by a joystick. The operator, by moving the joystick in one direction will allow high pressure fluid to enter the part of the cylinder above the piston while permitting fluid to exit the lower part of the cylinder. In this way, the piston and hence the outrigger is forced downward. Once the outrigger is fully deployed, the valve controlled by the joystick is allowed to return to its center position (not shown). This locks the fluid into the upper part of the cylinder, permitting the foot of the outrigger to support whatever force is imposed on it through the operation of the crane boom—as long as the gasket between the outer edge of the piston and the cylinder's inner wall does not permit any fluid to leak past.

Similarly, when the outrigger is going to be retracted and stowed to allow the crane to be transported over the highway, the joystick is pushed in the other direction, forcing high-pressure fluid into the lower part of the cylinder while allowing it to escape from the upper part. When the piston has reached the top of the cylinder, the valve is allowed to return to its center position, locking into place the fluid in the lower cylinder.

(continues on page 242)

Hydraulics

There are a number of methods by which mechanical systems are controlled whenever the need exists to move components that are so distant from the point of control that their movement by simple mechanical linkage is impractical. In chapter 6, in the discussion of trains, one such method was described in connection with air brakes used on trains and large trucks. Air pressure is used in other applications as well, giving rise to what are often called pneumatic controls. Although pneumatic controls have many advantages, they have two major disadvantages, both connected to the fact that air (or any gas) is compressible. This means that when one increases the pressure at the control point, it takes some time for the pressure to build up at the point where the work must be done, whether to apply brakes or some other function. This was the explanation for the lag time in the application of air brakes after the train operator moved the brake lever. Also as a consequence of the compressibility, if the vessel containing the high-pressure air ruptures, the expanding air can do a great deal of damage as well as cause injuries to those nearby. Both problems are avoided with hydraulic controls, which use incompressible liquid—hydraulic fluid—to transmit force from the control point to the various places where work needs to be done. (Strictly speaking, it should be called hydraulic liquid since the word *fluid* refers to both liquids and gases.) In addition, hydraulic systems have an advantage whenever a machine needs to remain in a certain configuration for an extended period of time. It is done by introducing the appropriate volume of hydraulic fluid into a chamber to achieve the desired configuration and then closing the chamber. As long as there is no leak in the chamber, the hydraulic fluid will resist whatever force is exerted against the element in question. In contrast, if air is introduced into the chamber for this purpose and the chamber then closed, when the force being resisted increases, the air will compress, permitting the element to move and so changing the configuration. Another benefit arising from the incompressibility of the hydraulic fluid is that the hydraulic circuit

(continues)

(continued)

can be used to move machinery elements very smoothly and by tightly controlled distances. One refers to *metering* the hydraulic fluid, as it is shifted from one part of the system to another, to be described below.

The basic operation of a hydraulic system requires something to circulate the hydraulic fluid and to develop sufficient pressure for the fluid to exert the force needed to move the various parts that are controlled by the system. Where the fluid travels depends on the hydraulic circuit, which in turn depends on a system of tubes (usually made of metal) and valves. Braking of most motor vehicles apart from trains and heavy trucks is done with hydraulic systems. In their simplest form, the vehicle operator depressing a brake pedal generates the pressure in the hydraulic brake system that applies the brakes at each wheel. In vehicles that have power brakes of one type or another, there is a separate pump to maintain hydraulic pressure and the depression of the brake pedal simply permits pressurized hydraulic fluid to enter the lines running to the individual brakes at each wheel. Because a leak in the brake lines can lead to an abrupt failure of the brakes, modern vehicles have dual hydraulic systems so that even if the brakes to two wheels fail because of a leak or rupture in a brake line, the other two will continue to have braking available. When this occurs, it is usually obvious where the leak or rupture was because of the oily hydraulic fluid that appears either on the metal brake line or elsewhere. This contrasts with the work that must be done to locate an air leak, for example, in a tire.

Most hydraulic systems used with heavy machinery depend on a pump that constantly maintains hydraulic pressure. The pressurized hydraulic fluid is then drawn on in a manner determined by the operator through opening and closing valves within the circuit.

(continued from page 240)

Just as the locking-in during the deployment operation ensured that the piston would not retract regardless of whatever upward force was placed on the outrigger foot (as long as the gasket did not leak), with the fluid

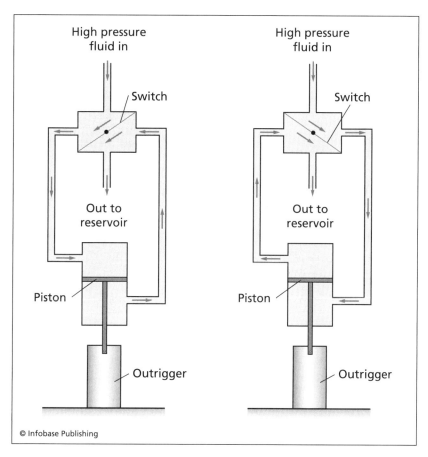

High pressure fluid in

Switch

Out to reservoir

Piston

Outrigger

High pressure fluid in

Switch

Out to reservoir

Piston

Outrigger

© Infobase Publishing

The hydraulic circuit associated with the outriggers

locked into the lower half of the cylinder after the piston is pushed to its upper limit, the outrigger will remain stowed regardless of whatever downward force is exerted against the outrigger foot. Of course, one does not expect this force to be any greater than the outrigger weight.

As mentioned above, in the wake of the accident while the crane was still lying partially on its side, the right-front outrigger was found to be partially retracted. In the follow-up investigation, employees of the company that owned the crane mentioned that whenever the crane sat around unused for any period of time, the right front outrigger drooped, even though it had been completely stowed not long before. With this revelation, most of the investigators concluded that the problem of the collapse had been solved. The right front outrigger unit had a leaky internal gasket

A drooping outrigger *(Courtesy of the author)*

that permitted the piston to move upward in response to a force on its associated outrigger foot. With that outrigger not supporting the weight it was called to support, the moment arm of the boom when extended to the left of the truck was increased, and the moment arm associated with the truck's weight decreased. The result was that the crane went from a stable structure with the force moment of the boom canceled out by the weight of the truck to a structure that was tipping over to the left.

The investigators for the family of the dead worker nailed down their theory for the collapse by mounting a strain gauge on the truck near the suspected outrigger, as shown in the photo on page 245. The outrigger was then deployed to the point where the truck was lifted a short distance, enough to take some of the weight off its springs but not enough to lift the tires off the pavement. Then the hydraulic valve was centered so that the fluid was in principle locked into the upper chamber under pressure. The strain gauge revealed that even without the stress of an extended boom, the outrigger continually crept upward. Claims filed in the aftermath of the tragedy were then resolved based upon the conclusion that faulty maintenance of the crane by Jamaica had led to the dangerous condition that killed the Acme worker.

WORKERS' COMPENSATION

Although there was no question but that the family of the unfortunate man killed by the crane should be compensated, the question of the responsibility of a company that, like a bad neighbor who borrows a tool for 34 years without acquiring his or her own or finding a means of doing without, was left unresolved. The explanation for that lack of resolution lies in a legal doctrine forming part of statutory law in all

Measurements with a strain gauge   *(Courtesy of the author)*

the states of the United States. For many years up to the early part of the 20th century, if a worker was injured or killed on the job, his or her employer did not have to pay compensation unless it could be shown that the employer's negligence caused the injury or death. Because of the burden that this placed on the workers, there was essentially never an instance where compensation was provided. To correct this situation, which to many seemed harsh, especially given the long hours and subsistence wages of many workers, legislation (originally labeled *workman's compensation,* or some variant of that) was enacted by the various states as well as, for the small fraction of employees on the federal payroll, by the federal government. Long since referred to as Workers' Compensation, these laws provide that a worker who was injured for any reason while on the job shall receive compensation and assistance in returning to the workforce. The employer pays for this compensation and assistance through mandatory insurance premiums. In exchange for receiving compensation for on-the-job injuries without having to prove his or her employer negligent, the worker is barred from suing the employer at all in connection with on-the-job injuries. Although this results in some obvious injustice, as for example, when the injury has resulted from the operation of a machine from which the employer has removed safety features to speed up production, the societal decision to date has been that the benefits of the present system outweigh any unfairness.

9

Scaffolding Collapse

The introduction asserted that, more than other forensic scientists, investigators in the forensic engineering sciences can be at a loss as to how to start and what to do when called in on a case. This is because of the breadth of analytical methods they might be expected to bring to bear on problem. The event analyzed in this chapter is an example of the phenomenon of the investigator not knowing quite where to start, even whether he or she has a contribution to make. The facts were known and the question to be addressed was known, but it was unclear from where the answer was to come and if it could be obtained. Along the way to figuring out how to find the answer and then finding it, the investigator had to explore questions traditionally categorized, respectively, as meteorology, fluid dynamics (the science of how gases and liquids flow), strength of materials, and mechanical engineering.

THE ACCIDENT

On a hot summer afternoon, two men were painting the exterior surface of a large gas-storage tank while standing on a platform supported 50

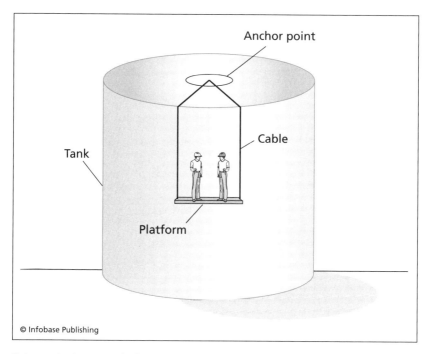

Anchor point

Cable

Tank

Platform

© Infobase Publishing

Schematic showing platform suspended on the side of the tank by two cables attached to the top of the tank

feet (15 m) above the ground by two steel cables. The tank was 150 feet (46 m) in diameter and 110 feet (34 m) in height at its outside wall. The platform was 32 feet (9.8 m) long by one-and-a-half feet (0.5 m) wide and, including the painters and their supplies, weighed 1,500 pounds (6,700 N). The arrangement for suspending the platform from the top of the tank is shown schematically in the figure above.

Just after 4:00 P.M., the area was struck by a sudden squall. It lasted less than a minute, but when the gusty, shifting wind had died down, the platform and the men lay on the ground, one dead, the other seriously injured. The photo on page 248 shows the collapsed platform and some of its associated rigging, including tangles of cable, as they lay on the ground the day of the accident. The immediate cause of the collapse was the failure of both the steel cables, which had parted just where they passed over the outer edge of the tank's roof, at the metal lip joining the roof to the walls.

The platform and associated rigging after the collapse *(OSHA)*

WRONGFUL-DEATH CLAIM AND RESPONSE

The family of the man who was killed in the accident brought a wrong-ful-death action (see chapter 1) against the company that had rigged the cables that had supported the platform. They claimed that the rigging was improperly done and in such a way that permitted the cables to come into contact with and bend around the edge of the tank roof and that this both weakened the cables through abrasion and exerted bend-ing stresses to the cables while they were under load. The key element of their claim was that but for the weakening that one or both of these effects caused in the cables, the cables would not have parted under the stress caused by the wind.

The defendant responded that the forces applied to the cables because of the wind were so great or potentially so great that the collapse would have occurred regardless of the nature of the rigging, regardless of any weakening that might have existed. In other words, the defendant was saying that even with the cables at full strength and rigged properly, the wind gusts were so strong that the cables would have parted. Given the wind strength observed at the site (and recorded wind speeds of up to 55 miles per hour [88 km/hr] at a nearby National Weather Service center), this defense had a certain plausibility.

THE FACTS

The basic facts underlying whatever analysis that was to be undertaken include both those specific to the configuration and components of the rigging and those common and relating to all engineering designs. In major part, they consist of the following several issues.

Rigging Design

The tank's roof sloped upward toward its center from where it met the vertical wall. The upper ends of the cables were attached at the center at a fixation point, from where each ran outward, passing over a wheel mounted a few feet back from the perimeter. The wheel was to keep the ropes from coming into contact with the edge of the tank and also to provide them a larger radius of curvature as they changed direction from basically horizontal to vertical on their way down to the platform. With the painters at the height they were operating just before the collapse, approximately 125 feet (38 m) of cable ran from the fixation point to each end of the platform.

The Cables

Each of the two cables had a diameter of five-sixteenths of an inch (0.0079 m) and was characterized by the nomenclature 6x19 IWRC (Independent Wire Rope Core with six bundles of 19 steel strands, each braided around the solid steel core). The photo on page 250 shows a typical such cable. Cables like these, commonly referred to as wire ropes, are in broad industrial use. Because of the role they fulfill, serious injury or death can easily be the result when they fail. To increase the likelihood that the proper selection of wire rope is made for each task, their specifications are made readily available. In the aftermath of their failure, investigators can quickly gain the information needed to begin their analysis. Five sixteenth-of-an-inch 6 × 19 IWRC wire ropes are specified to not fail under tension (that is, when they are being pulled) until a force in excess of 9,000 pounds (40,000 N) is applied. As long as the wire ropes in this case were subject only to tensile forces, they should have been able to support a total weight of at least 18,000 pounds (80,000 N). Stated more generally, they should have been able to withstand a downward force of at least 18,000 pounds (80,000 N). The photo shows the broken strands of one of the failed cables.

Photograph of the strands at one cable failure point *(Courtesy of the author)*

Safety Factors

Because of variables that cannot be completely controlled or even known, a rope will always be designed to be stronger than its specified strength. This is a type of safety factor. Safety factors are used in the design of all structures intended to bear loads. For example, a crane that is going to be specified as capable of supporting 50,000 pounds (222,000 N) may be designed to have a theoretical bearing capacity of 250,000 pounds (1,110,000 N). One would say that a safety factor of five was built into the design.

THE PLAINTIFFS' BURDEN

To support their claim that the rigging was improper under industry and/or OSHA standards in such a way and that it had caused a weakening of the cables, the plaintiffs brought in a scaffolding specialist. To evaluate and, they hoped, to counter the defense claim that any cable weakening was irrelevant since the cables would have broken regardless, they brought in a forensic engineering scientist, explained the case to her, showed the evidence to her, and waited. The defense argument, which she was expected to address, can be stated in its form most difficult to grapple with as follows:

> Even if the scaffolding was rigged wrong, which we do not admit, and even if that wrong rigging weakened the wire ropes so that they broke under a load of less than 9,000 pounds (40,000 N) each, the outcome would not have been changed if the ropes had their full strength the day of the big wind. The ropes would simply have broken that day under a greater load.

This defense could be refuted only by showing that under the conditions that prevailed at the time of the accident, it was more likely than not that at no time could a force in excess of 18,000 pounds (80,000 N) have been placed on the pair of wire ropes. Fortunately for the plaintiffs, the defense provided a framework within which the problem could be approached and the defense theory be attacked. It did this by supporting its theory with a statement by the survivor. He had said that immediately before the collapse, the wind had lifted the platform two feet (0.6 m) straight up before letting it drop and that as the platform dropped, pulling the cables taut, the cables snapped. The defense pointed to this sequence as one that would have or could have placed a force on the cables that exceeded the 18,000-pound (80,000-N) threshold.

ANALYSIS

Rather than dealing only with the mechanism touted by the defense as the reason any weakening of the cables was irrelevant, the engineering expert for the plaintiffs took a broad approach. This is always the best policy for a plaintiff since, having the burden of going forward, the plaintiff must be prepared to deal with modified defense theories put forward late in the process.

Recapitulating, the defense theory was that because of the force that the wind applied to the cables, or could have applied to the cables, any compromise in the cable strength was irrelevant. Responding to this general statement made it necessary to consider the different modes by which the wind squall could have applied extra force to the cables and then to calculate the maximum reasonable force that could have been applied by each mode. This meant listing all the ways that the wind could have applied a pulling force on the cables and then calculating the maximum force for each of these ways. Given the reason for carrying out this analysis, it is crucial to ensure that any simplifying assumptions made along the way are such as to increase the calculated force magnitude. The use of simplified models in doing calculations and the justification for doing so was discussed in the sidebar on "Forensic Reenactments" in chapter 5. In the present matter that discussion leads to the conclusion that, if, after introducing simplifications that increase the calculated force, it is found that the calculated force falls below the threshold, simplifying assumptions the problem has been solved without the need to carry out the much more complicated calculations required in the absence of the simplifying assumptions.

Listing the Ways

Therefore, what are the ways in which a strong squally wind blowing against the tank and painters' platform could have increased the tension in the cables supporting the platform? Before listing the mechanisms, one must decide what wind speed to use in calculating the force for the various mechanisms. Wind direction is not a consideration since, in keeping with the proper approach to these types of things, the wind will be assumed to blow on the platform from the direction that maximizes the tension in the cables. The figure below shows a top-down schematic view of the tank exposed to a horizontal wind. Regardless of the wind direction, there would be two regions of the tank where the wind was blowing approximately parallel (tangent) to the tank walls. In addition, there would be a portion that is in the lee, with the tank blocking the wind. Directly opposite the center of the lee portion on the *windward* side, the wind is headed directly toward the tank wall, rather like the winter wind blowing directly against the windows on a house. Since that

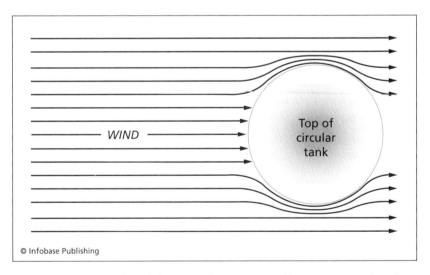

© Infobase Publishing

A schematic sketch of wind direction changes caused by a storage tank in the wind's path, from a point above the tank

stream of air cannot blow through the tank wall, it divides into a portion that circles the tank to the right, a portion that circles the tank to the left, a portion that is diverted upward, and a portion that is diverted downward.

With respect to the wind speed, why not just use the maximum value recorded at the nearby weather station, 55 miles per hour (88 km/hr)? That would not be appropriate since it is known that wind can vary significantly over very short distances. Although the weather station could have been at the point of maximum wind that day, it could just as easily experienced the lowest winds from the squall. Also, could the tank have increased the speed in its immediate vicinity? Probably not, since there were no other buildings nearby. However, because of the common experience of walking past tall buildings in a windy city, a jury might believe that it did increase the speed. Since the purpose of the study was to see whether it was even slightly possible that the wind could have applied forces to the cables greater than their normal breaking strength, one wants to be sure to overestimate the wind speed rather than to underestimate it. Therefore, using the speed measured at the National Weather Service as a reference, a wind speed at the tank of nearly twice that was used, namely 100 miles per hour (160 km/hr). In the context of this calculations, both the assumption regarding speed and that regarding wind direction can be said to be conservative, meaning that they support the argument of the adverse party.

THE WAYS THE WIND CAN BLOW

The plaintiffs' engineering expert listed the ways in which the sudden high wind could have increased the tension in the cables, as follows:

1. A downward gust against the upper surface of the platform suddenly increases the effective weight that the cables have to support;

2. An upward wind gust against the bottom surface of the platform lifts it up momentarily, after which it drops and, on pulling the cables taut, exerts a downward force much greater than the platform weight; and

3. The Bernoulli effect acts directly to pull down on the platform.

The Bernoulli effect? Most people first hear of the Bernoulli effect when they ask why airplanes stay up in the sky. The reference is the principle credited to the Dutch/Swiss scientist-mathematician Daniel Bernoulli (1700–82). It will be identified and described at the end of the sidebar on "The Force of Wind."

PUTTING IN NUMBERS

In keeping with the philosophy stated on page 251 of introducing sim-plifications as long as they increase the value of the calculated force, therefore, the value of q in the expressions for wind pressure was set to its maximum value of two so that Equation 9–3 gives the pressure p as $0.011V_{mph}^2$. Similarly, the platform was treated as if it were a solid surface rather that the open grillwork that it was, which greatly simplifies the calculation while boosting the value of the calculated total force. The platform was 32 feet (9.8 m) long and one-and-a-half feet (0.46 m) deep, giving it an area of 48 ft^2, which the forensic engineer approximated as 50 ft^2 (4.6 m^2). With the two painters and their equipment, it weighed about 1,500 pounds (6,700 N) and was supported by the two cables (wire ropes) as described above and as suggested in the drawing on page 247. For the wind to snap the two cables when the cables were at their full strength and not exposed to bending stresses, the wind would have had to have increased the downward force on the platform by at least 16,500 pounds (73,400 N). (Why?)

The most effective way in which the wind could have increased the downward force directly would have been by blowing straight down on the platform—as described on page 253. Because of the motiva-tion for the calculation by the plaintiff's expert, it was not necessary to go into detail about how likely it would have been to have a uniform down-draft at full wind speed. It can be said that because of the close proximity of the tank wall to the platform, it was possible that such a wind occurred. Taking the speed for such a wind to be 100 miles per hour (160 km/hr), Equation 9–3 for the pressure due to such a gust takes on the form:

$$p = 0.011 \times (100)^2 = 110 \text{ pounds/ft}^2 \ (5,270 \text{ N/m}^2)$$

(continues on page 260)

The Force of Wind

It is said that the force of the wind against a window is proportional to the square of the wind speed. Similarly, it is said that on a calm day, the resistance of air to a moving car is proportional to the square of the car's speed, that is, that it increases as the square of the speed in each case. All other things being equal, this means that the rate of fuel use by a car going 80 miles per hour (130 km/hr) is sixteen times the usage at 20 miles per hour (32 km/hr). (If this is true, how much more fuel is used in traveling one mile at the higher speed than it would be at the lower speed?) To see why these are basically true statements, think about wind blowing at a speed V directly against a flat wall. The wind is nothing more than air molecules that, in addition to their high velocities in random directions, all have an average velocity in a single direction (the velocity of the wind) imposed on them. The individual molecules on hitting the wall deliver to the wall a momentum MV where M is the mass of an individual molecule. Since the wind has been taken as blowing directly onto—that is, perpendicular to—the wall, it is not necessary to distinguish between speed and velocity here.

The collision with the wall halts the forward motion of the molecule that would otherwise carry it through the wall. Therefore, on impact, the change in the molecule's momentum perpendicular to the wall is at least $-MV$. If it bounces straight back, the maximum change occurs, namely $-2MV$, as the molecule's speed changes from $+V$ to $-V$. It has now been shown that the molecule's change in momentum perpendicular to the wall will lie between $-MV$ and $-2MV$. Call it $-qMV$, where q is a positive number between one and two. (The reason for q not always being two—that is, the reason for the change in the molecule's momentum perpendicular to the wall not always being $-2MV$—is that the molecules bounce off the wall in all directions because of the wall's irregularities on a microscopic scale and not just straight back.) For the significance of the molecular momentum change, look back the chapter 3 sidebar on "Newton's Third Law" and the section in that chapter on

(continues)

(continued)

"Conservation of Momentum." Because momentum is always conserved, the molecule's change in momentum ($-qMV$) must be balanced by a change in momentum of the wall that has the same magnitude but the opposite sign ($+qMV$). From the definitions and discussions of chapter 2, this means that the impact of the single molecule against the wall imposes on the wall a force impulse of kMV. From chapter 3, it may be seen why this impulse equals the length of time of the impact Δt multiplied by the average force F imposed on the wall by the molecule during the impact:

$$qMV = F\Delta t$$

So if one knew the duration of the collision, Δt, one could quickly calculate the force delivered by an individual molecule. Then, the thought experiment continues, one could use the number of molecules striking the wall at any one instant to complete the solution of the problem, which is to determine the force of the wind against the wall.

Although the method just described would work, it is what is called a brute-force approach, lacking elegance. Also, it is not that easy to determine the duration time for a single molecular collision. It turns out that there is an approach that has the virtue of never requiring that one know anything as detailed as the duration of a single collision. Instead of dealing with the mass of a single molecule, consider the total mass of all the air hitting the wall during the time T. Let the wall be circular with area A. Making it circular is not necessary but aids with the thought experiment pictures, the most important of which is an imaginary circular cylinder of cross-section A that is lined up with and extends straight out from that wall. (The cylinder is perpendicular to the wall, which is taken to be flat.) If, in one's mind or a sketch one is making while reading this material, the cylinder is made to extend out a distance VT, it will contain all of the molecules that are going to hit the wall during the next T seconds, and it contains only those molecules. For example, if V is 5 meters per second (16 ft/sec) and T is 8 seconds, the pictured cylinder will be 40 meters

(130 feet) long, and it contains all of the molecules heading toward the wall at 5 m/s (16 ft/sec) that are going to strike the wall over the next 8 seconds.

The volume of the cylinder, like any right cylinder, will be equal to its length multiplied by its cross-section, namely VTA. The mass of the air in that cylinder will equal the volume multiplied by the air's mass per unit volume, namely the its density. (*Density* was defined back in chapter 1 in the discussion of Hiero's crown.) Density is traditionally represented by the Greek letter ρ (rho, pronounced "row," the kind associated with small boats or lines of plants in a garden). Therefore, the mass of air M in the cylinder is $VTA\rho$. This is the mass of air that hits the wall of area A during the period T. All of it is traveling at a speed V toward the wall. Recall that the momentum of an object of mass M in a particular direction is M multiplied by the speed of the object in that direction. It makes no difference whether or not the object is a single, hard, and continuous thing or whether or not it consists of a bunch of separate air molecules. The total momentum of the air molecules in that cylinder, therefore, equals the mass of the molecules times their speed, V. Its momentum is, therefore, $VAT\rho V$, which can be written more compactly as $A\rho V^2 T$. (Check the dimensions. The density, ρ, will have dimensions of mass divided by volume, that is, $[\rho]$ equals M/L^3. Dimensional checking is discussed in a number of places in the book, including in the sidebar on "Dimensions and Acceleration" in chapter 2.) This means that the momentum delivered to the wall of area A during the time T is $A\rho V^2 T$.

The same considerations regarding change in momentum apply to the entire mass of molecules hitting the wall during the time T that applied to the single molecule. Therefore, the impulse delivered to the wall by those molecules ranges from $A\rho V^2 T$ to $2A\rho V^2 T$. As before, this can be handled by introducing a positive constant q lying between one and two and stating that the total impulse is $qA\rho V^2 T$.

Unlike the case with the single molecule where it was necessary to determine the duration of the impact, Δt, there is no need to get into

(continues)

(continued)

considerations of microscopic time here. This impulse is equal to the average force of the wind F against the wall times the time interval T over which it is delivered. Therefore,

$$FT = qA\rho V^2 T$$

and one obtains F just by dividing both sides by T.

The following is the force against the wall from wind of speed V blowing against it:

$$F = qA\rho V^2$$

(Equation 9-1)

Since not all walls have an area A, a more useful expression is the force per unit area. The common word for force per unit area is *pressure*. That the pressure against the wall is obtained from Equation 9-1 simply by dividing both sides by A may be seen from the following reasoning. By definition, the force against a wall is the pressure against the wall multiplied by the wall's area. Then, with p representing the wind pressure,

$$F = Ap$$

But, from 9-1, F equals $A q \rho V^2$. Therefore,

$$Ap = Aq\rho V^2$$

so that dividing both sides of the equation by A leads to the expression for p:

$$p = q\rho V^2$$

with $2 \geq q \geq 1$.

All that remains is to look up the value for ρ, the density of air. Under the usual temperature and pressure conditions, ρ is 1.3 kg/m^3 (0.0025 slug/ft^3). Therefore, the pressure from a wind of speed V blowing against a wall, stated in S.I., is

$$p = 1.3qV^2$$

(Equation 9–2)

where V is to be stated in meters per second and p will be given in Newtons per square meter (N/m²). (Show that in U.S. units the expression for p corresponding to Equation 9–2 is $0.0025qV^2$ where V is to be given in feet per second and p will be given in pounds per square foot. Show that both expressions have dimensions of force per unit area.)

Applying the above result to a case where a wind of speed 3.0 m/sec is blowing against a window, show that, for a q of two, the direct wind will exert a pressure of 23.4 N/m². If the window has an area of 2 square meters (22 ft²), this leads to a total force on it of 46.8 N (10.5 pounds).

In summary, the S.I. expression for pressure on a flat surface due to wind blowing directly on that surface with a speed V is $1.3qV^2$ where the speed is to be stated in meters per second. The corresponding expression in U.S. units is $0.0025qV^2$ where V is to be stated in feet per second. Since the speed of wind over land is usually given in miles per hour in the United States, it is convenient to have a hybrid expression in U.S. units, such that the value of speed in miles per hour can be used directly. Show that replacing speed in feet per second, V, with speed in miles per hours, V_{mph}, produces the following expression for p in pounds per square foot:

$$p = 0.0054qV_{mph}^2$$

(Equation 9–3)

For completeness, it must be said that Equation 9–2 and the related Equation 9–3 give not the total pressure on a surface but rather just the increase in pressure due to the wind, an increase that adds but a tiny fraction to the pressure already being exerted by the atmosphere. Near sea level, atmospheric pressure is about 2,000 pounds per square foot (96,200 N/m²). That enormous pressure and associated force does not normally blow windows in or knock walls over is due to the atmosphere

(continues)

(continued)

normally enveloping everything. With equal atmospheric force on the two sides of a window, there is zero net force available to break the pane.

When wind blows along (that is, parallel to) a surface rather than into it, the pressure on the surface is reduced. If the surface is one side of an airplane wing, for example, and the wind on the opposite side of the wing is blowing at a different speed, a pressure difference is set up between the two sides of the wing. This results in a net force on the wing that is perpendicular both to it and to the wind direction. Interestingly, the expression for the pressure difference due to the Bernoulli effect has a form superficially similar to that for the force of wind blowing directly onto a surface as given by Equation 9–2 or Equation 9–3. The difference in pressure Δp across any two-sided object (such as a wall, window, or airplane wing) when the wind blowing parallel to the respective surfaces differs by ΔV from one side to the other is given by the following expression:

$$\Delta p = \tfrac{1}{2}\rho(\Delta V)^2$$

(Equation 9–4)

Repeating, ΔV is the difference in speed between the air flowing parallel to one surface and the air flowing parallel to the other surface. As before, ρ is the density of air. Therefore, the expression in S.I. for the force due to the Bernoulli effect becomes:

$$\Delta P = 0.65(\Delta V)^2$$

(continued from page 254)

Given the area of 50 ft², this pressure leads to a downward force of 5,500 pounds (24,500 N). Added to the weight already there, this would have given the cables a total loading of 7,000 pounds (31,000 N).

LAWYERLY STRATEGY AND ITS DEFLECTION

Given the assumptions she made (solid platform, double the recorded wind speed, and uniform downward direction for the wind), the force calculated by the plaintiffs' engineering expert is still less than 40 percent of the threshold tension force for breaking the cables. It is difficult to see how this model would support the defense assertion. The defense may ask the expert under oath how, since her result was so close to the breaking force, she can be sure that some error did not provide the necessary lowering. Or, the attorney might pose the realistic question as to whether—with all the wildness of the wind that day—it was possible that at some point, instead of the total force being shared equally between the cables, the whole load was placed on one of the cables. Placed on one of the cables, 7,000 pounds would, in fact, bring its tension very close to the rated strength, and once one cable went, the other would be sure to follow (maybe). All the expert has to do is to show how much her simplifications boosted the calculated value, in effect challenging the defense expert to do the calculation without the simplification she used.

LOOKING AT IT FROM THE OTHER END

It has been said that one really has not understood a problem until one has been able to solve it in at least two independent ways. Following the practice suggested by that observation, the engineering expert next did the calculation in reverse. She determined which downward wind speed would have been necessary to increase the loading of the cables by 16,500 pounds (73,400 N). She easily showed that a wind pressure of 330 pounds/ft² (1470 N/m²) would be required. This can be substituted into a modified Equation 9–3, written as a solution for V, namely

$$V_{mph} = 9.52p^{1/2}$$

(Equation 9–5)

where the exponent of ½ on p indicates that the square root of p is to be taken. Substituting p equal to 330 pounds/ft² into Equation 9–5 yields for V_{mph} a value of 172 miles per hour (277 km/hr). Not only is this speed as high as those encountered in F3 tornados on the Fujita Scale (which characterizes F3 destruction as "roofs and some walls torn off well-constructed houses; trains overturned; most trees in forest uprooted"), but it would have been even higher if recognition had been given to the fact that the platform was not a solid plane but an open grillwork.

Thus, the forensic engineering expert showed in two distinct ways that the defense assertion could obtain no support from the potential force that the direct forces of the wind would have imposed on the cables.

But what about the Bernoulli effect? One often hears it vaguely alluded to explain something in a manner benefiting the person citing it. ("Oh, she

Power

Using gravity to impose a force otherwise difficult to apply is a technique as old as sea gulls dropping shellfish on rocks and as current as pile drivers planting footings for the piers to which the gulls will repair to eat their prize. In these examples and thousands of other cases in which a certain effect is achieved, usually the enhancement of force, work input occurs relatively slowly as the gravitational energy of some object is increased. Then, with the help of gravity, a high rate of work output is produced. With glances back to chapter 2, think of a boy carrying a half-slug (7.3-kg) brick up a hill such that when he reaches the top, he and the brick are 200 feet (61 m) higher than they had been at the outset. The brick's gravitational energy was increased by 100-foot-pounds (136 J). The boy did that much work on the brick. If it took him five minutes (300 seconds) to climb the hill, the work done on the brick was occurring at an average rate of 0.33 ft-pounds per second. This would normally be written with more compact units as 0.33 ft-lb/sec, where lb, an abbreviation of the Latin word for *pound, libra,* is widely used in the United States to stand for the full word *pound.* The rate at which work is done or, equivalently, energy is transferred, is called power. In S.I., the compound unit for energy, the m-N, is named the Joule, as mentioned earlier in chapter. The associated compound unit for power in S.I., the Joule per second, is called the Watt, abbreviated W. In the U.S. system, the basic unit for power bears the quaint label *horsepower.* By actual experimentation with horses in the early 19th century, the Englishman James Watt (1736–1819) reported finding the average draft horse was capable of working at the rate of 550 foot-pounds per second, and the horsepower (hp) unit of power was defined

was sucked under the truck by the Bernoulli effect" or "The large truck caused the little car it was passing to be thrown out of control because of the Bernoulli effect.") However, when one examines the claims quantitatively, they rarely—one might even guess never—hold up. In situations similar to the present one, Equation 9–4 is the key. Taking the most extreme case, one completely unrealistic, where the full speed of the wind is passing parallel to the bottom of the platform, taken to be a solid surface,

to be 550 ft-lb/sec. (Show that 1 hp is equal to 746 W.) The S.I. unit for power was named in honor of James Watt.

Return to the boy and the brick to which he has added 100 ft-lb of energy at the very slow average rate of 0.33 ft-lb/sec; this looks even smaller when expressed in hp, namely 0.0006 hp. Picture that he finds a 200-foot drop off at the top of the hill and proceeds to drop the enhanced-energy brick. What happens? A constant gravitational force of $0.5g$ (where g is 32 ft/sec^2) acts on it as it falls. This increases the brick's kinetic energy $\frac{1}{2}MV^2$ at the same rate that its gravitation energy is decreasing. The important point is what happens when the brick hits the pavement. At that point, the entire gravitational energy that the boy added to the brick at the rate of 0.0006 hp is present in the form of kinetic energy, $\frac{1}{2}MV^2$, which is numerically equal to 100 ft-lb. If the brick is brought to a halt in a half-second, that kinetic energy leaves the brick at a rate of 200 ft-lb/sec, that is, 0.36 hp, approximately 600 times the average power expended on the brick by the boy on the way up. During that half-second, the Earth's surface was producing power at the rate of 0.36 hp in bringing the brick to a halt. Looked at another way, the brick would have had a speed of 113 ft/sec (344 m/sec) at impact and a corresponding momentum of 56.5 lb-sec (251 N-sec). The average force required to reduce that momentum to zero in a half-second is 113 lb (502 N). It is unlikely that the boy could have exerted that kind of force on the brick directly with his hand. Hence, the lesson gulls and others learned long ago, and the model by which the defense in the wrongful-death action growing out of the scaffolding collapse would have the court believe that the wind could have indirectly exerted 18,000 pounds (80,000 N) on the cables when by direct action it could apply only a small fraction of this force.

and there is a complete absence of wind on the upper surface, the pressure differential would be but one-fourth the pressure imposed by the wind blowing straight down on the platform, as shown immediately above. (Show this.) Therefore, there was no need to consider further the Bernoulli effect. This left the most interesting of the models described when listing ways above that the wind could increase tension on the cables, that where the wind lifted the platform up and then let it fall. The survivor said that the lift was by two feet and that the cables indeed were broken by the platform as it pulled on them while dropping. The issue: How much force could have been generated by this action. To provide some background for the discussion, the sidebar on Power is presented.

After falling two feet (0.61 m), the 1,500-pound (6,670-N) platform and contents will have acquired a kinetic energy equal to their change in gravitational potential energy in falling the two feet, namely 3,000 ft-pounds (4,100 J). To determine how much force the momentum associated with the platform is capable of exerting on the cables, the investigator applied the condition that they not break and then sought a method of calculating the maximum force which they would have been exerting on the platform while bringing it to a halt. Because of the third law of motion, this would also be the maximum addition to the tensile force exerted on the cables.

From what has been said previously in *Crashes and Collapses*, it may be recalled that when one knows the momentum and the kinetic energy of an object, there are two approaches for determining the force— actually, the average force—involved in halting the object. There is the momentum approach, which requires knowledge of the time interval it took the object to stop; there is also the kinetic energy approach, which requires knowledge of how far the object moved during the stop. In most instances, neither piece of information is readily available. In the present case, the stop commenced the instant the cables became taut and but for the fact that the cables broke would have ended when the platform stopped moving downward. How long would that take? The distance traveled during the stop would have been the amount by which the falling platform stretched the cables while its downward motion was being brought to a halt. Although the platform's momentum and kinetic energy at the instant that the cables became taut were easily calculated for the reported two-foot fall, neither the time nor the travel distance of the halt jumped out at the investigator, nor did any practical way of determining them. That is why she decided to treat the cables as springs, which is what they are, very stiff elastic springs. How this is so will be seen in some detail on the sidebar on "Springs and the Law of Hooke." First, however, the platform's lifting by the wind will be looked at quantitatively.

WHAT LIFTED IT

The lifting up of the platform by the wind corresponds to the low power phase of the boy carrying the brick to the top of the hill, as discussed in the sidebar on "Power." The platform would have been lifted by any updraft sufficient to exert an upward force on it in excess of its weight of 1,500 pounds (6,670 N), a far lesser force-generating requirement than that imposed on a downdraft sufficient to break the cables, 16,500 pounds (73,400 N). The more the upward wind force exceeded the platform weight and the longer it persisted, the higher the platform would have traveled upward.

The minimum updraft speed necessary to cause the platform to lift would be that necessary to exert an upward force of 1,500 pounds (6,670 N), which, with the 50 ft² (4.64 m²) area of the platform, translates to a pressure of 30 lb/ft² (1,400 N/m²). The wind speed in miles per hour that is necessary to exert this pressure can be calculated from Equation 9–5. Substituting 30 lb/ft² (1,400 N/m²) for the value of p in Equation 9–5 leads to the following result for wind speed:

$$V_{mph} = 9.52 \, (30)^{1/2}$$

Evaluating this yields 52 miles per hour (84 km/hr) for the value of V_{mph}, the wind speed. Given the winds reported that day, it is not only possible but very likely that at some point such a wind was directed on the lower surface of the platform.

Reflect on what it means in this context for the platform to be hit by an updraft of this speed. It exactly cancels out the platform's weight, making the platform in effect weightless. However, the platform would not move upward until the wind pressure exceeded the value needed to make the platform weightless. What if the updraft had the speed assumed earlier in the attempt to determine whether a downdraft could have caused the cables to snap under tension, 100 miles per hour (160 km/hr)? Since, from Equation 9–3, the pressure is proportional to the square of the wind speed, it can be seen that the pressure from a 100-miles-per-hour (160-km/hr) wind will exceed 30 lb/ft^2 by a factor of $(100/52)^2$, which is 3.7; that is, a 100-miles-per-hour (160-km/hr) updraft will exert a pressure of 111 lb/ft^2 on the platform, for a total upward force of 5,550 lb (24,700 N).

Subtracting the force of gravity on the platform, the net upward force on the platform when a 100-miles-per-hour (160-km/hr) updraft blows on its lower surface is 1,050 lb (4,670 N). How long would it take this net force to cause the platform to move two feet (0.61 m)? For this, the basic material of chapter 2, showing that an object of mass M acted on by a force F will be accelerated in the direction of the force at a rate a of F/M. Further, that material explained that an object that is accelerating at a rate a after starting from rest will move a distance ½ at^2 during a time interval t. From that fact, it is seen that the time t required for the object to move a distance D will be $(2D/a)^{1/2}$. Putting these two facts together leads to the following equation for t:

$$t = (2DM/F)^{1/2}$$

(Equation 9–6)

Putting the numbers in provides the solution for t, namely, 0.4 seconds. (Check this conclusion.)

Noting that the time required for the travel varies inversely with the square root of the net force F on the platform, it can be seen that, with half the upward force, the time required for the 2-foot (0.61-m) lifting of the platform would increase by a factor of $(2)^{1/2}$, that is, to 0.6 seconds, still very short. However, unlike the example with the boy on the hill described in the sidebar on "Power," the fall time will be even less. Falling 2 feet (0.61 m) under the force of gravity (that is, with the acceleration due to gravity, g) takes 0.35 seconds (Check this.) In summary, if the platform is hit by a sudden four-tenths-second updraft of 100-miles-per-hour (160-km/hr) wind, the platform will rise up two feet, slackening the cables, then drop back, making them taut, within about the same time interval—less than one second for the up-and-down motion.

SEEING THE CABLES AS SPRINGS SOLVES THE PROBLEM

From the sidebar on "Springs and the Law of Hooke," it may be understood that the steel cables that held up the paint platform before the accident can be treated like springs with very high spring constants. This

(continues on page 271)

Springs and the Law of Hooke

The name in physics and engineering that is always associated with springs is that of Robert Hooke (1635–1703). Hooke lived at the same time as Newton, and the two exchanged letters containing the speculations and musings about science and the laws of physics. Although Hooke made contributions in many areas, it is Hooke's law (of springs and all elastic materials) by which he is best known. An elastic stretching or compressing of material is one that is not permanent; that is, it allows the material to return to its original shape once the force causing the distortion is removed. Although rubber bands and springs are what come to mind at first, the fact is that essentially everything in the universe displays elastic behavior to a certain degree. Nitrogen molecules and, for that matter, all molecules display it to a high degree. Steel beams display it to a lesser, though very important, degree. Glass goblets display it to a much lesser degree.

Hooke's law describes one form of elastic behavior where the "stretch" is proportional to the force applied, that is, where the distortion is linear in the applied force. Hooke's law states that the amount by which a spring is stretched is proportional to the stretching force. Because of the importance of springs of various types, Hooke's law is often simply called the spring law or law of springs. The Greek letter Δ (delta) often is used to depict a change in something. Here, it will be used to indicate the amount of stretch in a spring caused by a force F, such as the weight of a fish dangling from the fish scale introduced in chapter 2. Then Hooke's law, the law of springs, becomes

$$F = k\Delta$$

(Equation 9–7)

where the constant of proportionality, k, is called the spring constant. The spring constant will depend on the stiffness of the spring. The bigger k is, the more force is required to cause a particular stretch Δ. This means that if a fish scale is to be used to weigh very heavy fish, such as tuna, the spring constant will have to be much greater than it will be in fish scales used to measure perch and other small fish.

(continues)

(continued)

The fish scale pointer is attached to the end of the spring and moves along the numeric scale in response to the spring being stretched by the fish weight. For a 4-pound fish, it moves twice as far as for a 2-pound fish. Turning around the above equation permits this movement to be described as

$$\Delta = F/k$$

When one "reads" the fish scale, one is observing Δ. The numerical scale on a given instrument is designed with knowledge of what the spring constant was for the scale. Therefore, reading Δ, the amount of stretch is equivalent to reading F, which is the force due to gravity on the object being weighed—that is, the weight of the object. In short, if one knows the spring constant of a spring and can measure how far it is stretched by a force, one knows the force. Also, by knowing the spring constant, one knows how far a given force, such as 1,000 pounds (4,450 N), will stretch the spring. Finally, with an unknown spring, that one can immediately figure out the spring constant, k, by measuring the amount of stretch that a known force causes.

Finally, and this is very important, one can see that the work necessary to stretch a spring by a distance Δ is equal to $\frac{1}{2} k\Delta^2$. (Pause for a moment to note that this looks very much like the form for the kinetic energy of a car, $\frac{1}{2} MV^2$. It is not a mere coincidence!) Recall that work involves a transformation or transfer of energy and that the work in moving an object a distance X by pushing it with a constant force F was FX, that is, the force multiplied by the distance moved. When one is stretching a spring, for example, by moving one end of it parallel to the length of the spring while the other end is held still, the force is not constant. It increases in direct proportion to the distance moved (by the amount the spring is stretched). At any given point, the force needed to stretch the spring further equals the spring constant multiplied by the stretch already introduced. Let X be some amount of stretch less than the final intended stretch, Δ. At that intermediate point, the force that must be applied will be kX. (By Newton's third law, the spring is also applying a force of $-kX$ against the hand or whatever is causing the stretching. This is often referred to as the restoring force since it is the force by which the spring is trying to restore itself to its original length.) The average force applied while stretching the spring by an amount Δ, that is, in moving its free end by this distance, will be equal to the average between the initial applied force, which was zero, and the force applied at the maximum stretch, $k\Delta$. This is $\frac{1}{2}(0 + k\Delta) = \frac{1}{2} k\Delta$. The energy transferred to the spring, E_{SPRING}, from the source of the force will be this average times the total distance the force has moved the end of the spring, Δ.

$$E_{SPRING} = \frac{1}{2} k\Delta^2$$

(Equation 9–8)

Now, it was said that work performed involves energy transformed. In the case of stretching the spring, the energy is transformed into the spring from whatever is producing the force. For the fish scale, the energy put into the spring comes from the lowering of the fish's gravitational energy as it moved to a lower elevation as the spring was being sketched. The reduction in the gravitational potential energy of the fish as it moves lower while the spring stretches by an amount Δ, would be $M_{fish}g\Delta$, where M_{fish} is the mass of the fish. Therefore, one can equate the two expressions. In the case of the fish scale,

$$M_{fish}g\Delta = \frac{1}{2} k\Delta^2$$

Again, note the similarity with the expression for the kinetic energy gained by an object of mass M when it falls a distance h. At any event, the distance Δ by which the fish-scale spring stretches while the fish is being weighed can be seen from dividing both sides of the last equation by Δ, obtaining Δ equal to $2M_{fish}g/k$ which is $2W_{fish}/k$, W_{fish} being the weight of the fish. But this cannot be right since, from Hooke's law, one sees that under a force F (which in this case would be the weight of the fish), the spring stretches a distance F/k, not twice that. The answer to the apparent contradiction is that in attempting to solve the problem by means of conservation of energy, one overlooked what is going on when a fish is

(continues)

(continued)

connected to the hook on the fish scale and allowed to drop. There is overshoot because at the point where the fish has stretched the spring by the distance W_{fish}/k, it (the fish) has picked up kinetic energy and does not stop until it has dumped that kinetic energy by storing it in the spring. In short, the fish placed on the hook of the fish scale bobs down and up and down a number of times until, the energy having been transferred into heat or some other form not involving movement of the fish or spring energy, it settles down where it should as described by Hooke's law.

The spring constant depends on the material of the spring. It also depends on the length of the spring, as one might expect. The longer the spring, the less force is required to stretch it. Very few of the objects obeying Hooke's law look like the spring on a spring door. Much more commonly, they are similar in structure to a solid bar. Picture a metal bar of length L and cross-section A. Now the spring constant, in addition to L and A, will depend on the fundamental stretchiness of the metal. It turns out that this stretchiness factor has been measured for a huge number of materials. The factor goes under the name Young's constant (named for the English physicist Thomas Young [1773–1829]) or stretch modulus. They can be looked up for the metal making up the bar in question. The traditional symbol used to represent the Young's constant is, fittingly enough, Y. It is defined so that if the metal bar just described is found to stretch by a distance ΔL when one end is held fixed and a force F pulls on the other end, one can write

$$Y = (F/A)/(\Delta L/L)$$

But, from Hooke's law,

$$F = k\Delta L$$

and, substituting this expression for F into the definition for Young's constant, that definition can be rearranged to obtain a statement for the bar's spring constant, as follows:

$$k = YA/L$$

(Equation 9–9)

(continued from page 266)

realization led directly to the answer to the question of how much force the cables would need to exert if they did not break while halting the platform from falling after the two-foot drop; that is, it was key to completing the evaluation of the defense response in the wrongful-death action.

The maximum force on the cables would occur at the point where the platform has just come to a halt, the point where all of the gravitational energy lost by the platform in falling has been transformed into spring energy. Let the stretch of each cable at that point be represented by ΔL and the spring constant be k. Then the spring energy stored in each with that stretch will be $\frac{1}{2} k(\Delta L)^2$. The total spring energy then will be twice that, namely, $k(\Delta L)^2$. Representing the drop distance by H, the change in the platform's gravitational energy at that point is WH, where the weight of the platform is represented by W. Therefore,

$$WH = k(\Delta L)^2$$

and

$$\Delta L = (WH/k)^{1/2}$$

(Equation 9–10)

From Hooke's law, the force required to cause this much stretch is:

$$F = k\Delta L$$

Since this will be the tensile force in each cable at its maximum stretch as the cables halt the platform's fall, it will be written as F_{MAX}. Then, introducing the value of ΔL from Equation 9–10, F_{MAX} is obtained in terms of the spring constant, platform weight, and drop distance, as

$$F_{MAX} = (kWH)^{1/2}$$

(Equation 9–11)

Working in U.S. units and substituting $W = 1{,}500$ pounds and $H = 2$ feet, the expression for the maximum tensile force on the cables in terms of the spring constant k of the cables can be stated as follows:

$$F_{MAX} = 55k^{1/2}$$

(Equation 9–12)

From Equation 9–9 at the end of the sidebar on "Springs and the Law of Hooke," the definition of Young's constant allows the spring constant k to be stated as YA/L, where Y is the Young's constant for the material making up the cables, A is the cross-section of each cable, and L is the length of each cable prior to stretching. Earlier in the chapter, the cross section was stated to be 0.077 square inches, which is 0.00054 ft² (0.00005 m²).

Scientific Notation

Given the sizes of the numbers about to be introduced, it is useful to digress at this point to describe what is sometimes called scientific notation. There is nothing new to understand here, just definitions to be noted. In scientific notation, numbers are stated as products of their significant digits multiplied by 10 raised to the appropriate power; for example, 200 can be written as 2×10^2. For another, 5,100,000,000 can be written as 5.1×10^9, and so on. A similar convention allows very small numbers to be written in compact form also. For example, the number 0.001, which is the decimal form for one one-thousandth, can also be written as 1/1,000 or as $1/10^3$. By introducing the notation of negative exponents (powers), $1/10^3$ can be written as 10^{-3}. Although negative exponents may seem very strange on first acquaintance, the important thing to realize is that it is simply a notation, defined for convenience. Thus, by using scientific notation, the cross-sectional area of the cable, 0.00054 ft², can be given the much simpler form 5.4×10^{-4} ft².

The values for Y are usually stated in the United States using units of pounds per square inch (psi). Checking on the Internet or elsewhere, one finds that the value of Y for steel is about 30×10^6 pounds per square inch (psi). However, as can be found from readily available references in the wire rope industry, the 6 × 19 WIRC cables used to support the platform have a Y value of half this, 15×10^6 psi. Show that it can also be stated as 2.16×10^9 lbs/ft² (2.07×10^9 N/m²).

Then, k can be found by substituting the numerical value for Y and the other quantities, including the length of the cable from the center of the tank down to the platform, 125 feet, into Equation 9–9, as follows:

$$k = (2.16 \times 10^9)(5.3 \times 10^{-4})/125 = 0.92 \times 10^4 \text{ pounds/ft}$$

Then, substituting this into Equation 9–12, the expression for maximum force on the cables

$$F_{MAX} = 55 \times (0.92 \times 10^4)^{1/2} = 5{,}280 \text{ pounds (23,500 N)}$$

This is less than 40 percent of the specified tensile strength of the cables. The amount by which it fell short of the force needed to snap the cables in their undamaged condition would have actually been much more than this because of the safety factor that is built into such critical structures as the cables. The argument of the defense was therefore refuted.

As a final point of more than academic interest, the value of ΔL will be evaluated. From Hooke's law,

$$\Delta L = F_{MAX}/k = 5280/(0.92 \times 10^4) = 0.57 \text{ feet (0.17 m)}$$

It was indeed of more than academic interest since it has just been shown that the additional distance that the platform moved down during the cable stretch was not negligible compared to the two-foot drop before the stretch began. However, the problem cannot be corrected by simply setting H to 2.57 feet. It is left as an exercise to figure out how to calculate F_{MAX} when one does not have an explicit value for H at the outset. Even as recalculated, F_{MAX} does not approach the rated breaking strength of the cables.

Recall that the problem of finding F_{MAX} was based on the premise that the cables do not break and that they bring the falling platform to a halt. Since that is not what happened, the conclusion is compelled that they broke under a force less than the calculated F_{MAX}. This supported the plaintiffs' claim that the cables had been weakened by the damage they suffered from the improper installation and that that was what allowed the platform to collapse, killing the painter. It was not the wind. The cables were designed to be strong enough to stand up against all which the wind that day could have done. The testimony of the engineering expert at trial was that the death would not have occurred but for the weakening of the cables. The scaffolding expert testified that the cables had been weakened due to the improper rigging. The jury before whom the case was tried in the early 1990s found in favor of the plaintiffs.

10

Bringing It All Together

The foregoing chapters have given examples of the forensic assignments a person with education and experience in the engineering sciences can expect to receive. As has been mentioned more than once, the wide range of forensic work drawing on the engineering sciences makes it not unusual for persons called on to have difficulty initially identifying the problem that they might attack, let alone how to go about the attack. Occasionally, after reviewing the facts, they may have to confess that they have no idea what they can do to help, that is, to assist in determining the truth of what happened. That is, however, a very rare circumstance. Most persons trained in the engineering sciences and sensitive to the nature of forensic investigations will be able either to begin to work directly on the case or to provide advice as to what type of person the party seeking help needs and where such a person can be found. This chapter differs from those preceding it. Instead of describing how persons specialized in the forensic engineering sciences worked to resolve questions related to legal disputes, it presents several high-profile, injury-causing events and asks how persons in the forensic engineering sciences can respond to requests for technical assistance. In each case, the event was very public and therefore resulted in documentation that is readily accessible. As a result, the elements needed to begin the analysis and to develop a program of investigation can be found on the Internet. For the same reason, many dubious statements can be found on the Internet. In view of this and other considerations, it would seem that one good way to begin in each instance is to start by listing the questions needing to be answered prior to going to the Internet or other resources. Although one's direction might change once the research has gotten underway, that approach will provide an initial focus to one's investigation and provide some help both in avoiding distractions and in developing a means of gauging reliability of the statements one encounters. Reliability is taken up at greater length in the conclusion, following this chapter.

THE WORLD TRADE CENTER COLLAPSE

Probably the most horrible day in the nearly 400-year history of Manhattan was September 11, 2001. With the collapse of the 110-story World Trade Center towers, the murder toll before noon that day exceeded by a significant degree the worst yearly total in New York history. Those who saw those buildings burning—and there were millions who did so without the intervention of television—will carry the images to their graves. Most of them, in spite of the collapse of the first tower coming as a surprise, concluded that the extreme heat from the fires fed by jet fuel from fully fueled planes made the end result inevitable. However, as early as a month later, when the photograph on page 277 was made, the question was raised in some circles as to whether the building collapses had to have happened or whether they were the result of negligent design choices. Older residents of New York and elsewhere turned their thoughts back to a July morning during World War II when another Manhattan tower was struck by a plane. (The photo on page 278 shows the Empire State Building and the remnants of the B-25 bomber that smashed into the 79th-floor level. The photo on page 279 shows another view of the damage that occurred in the collision, which spewed gasoline across office spaces and caused plane parts and other debris to shoot out the opposite side and onto the street and buildings below.) Far from a deliberate act, this collision took place on a foggy morning when the B-25 pilot, seeking the Newark Airport, descended too low over Manhattan.

The World Trade Center towers
before the attacks *(Cecilia Bohan)*

The north tower of the World Trade Center at the moment of attack, as shown
by debris thrust out on the opposite side from the initial impact point *(AP/
Carmen Taylor)*

The World Trade Center as rubble, October 11, 2001   *(Richard Harbus)*

After narrowly avoiding several other tall buildings, he slammed into the Empire State Building, the tallest in New York and the world from its completion in 1934 until the construction of the World Trade Center towers in the 1960s. Although the incident killed and injured office workers, primarily on the 79th floor, firefighters were able to enter the building safely and extinguish the fires caused by the gasoline that fueled the plane. Had the building fallen, it is likely that there would have been even more deaths than on September 11, 2001, because of the number of persons working overtime during the war. The fact that the Empire State Building, built during the depression in the early 1930s, not only did not collapse but did not even suffer structural damage helped generate the

The Empire State Building *(AP)*

The Empire State Building showing effects of the July 1945 crash *(AP)*

Another view of the damage to the
Empire State Building, as it is being
assessed *(AP)*

question as to whether negligence was involved in selecting the 1950s designs for the basic structure of the World Trade Center towers.

Imagine being in a firm of forensic engineering scientists approached by potential plaintiffs in a wrongful-death action alleging architectural malpractice (a form of the negligence tort). They ask the firm to determine whether they have a reasonable claim. Treating this as a serious question requiring proper answers, not those that one might hear from the crowd at the barber shop or any other place known for the presence of people with a ready answer—usually emotion-fueled—for everything, make a list of the preliminary questions that need to be addressed to determine whether the plaintiffs have a case.

Now imagine being in a firm of forensic consultants that is contacted by attorneys for an architectural firm named as defendant in a negligence action as a result of their work on the World Trade Center towers. Whereas would-be plaintiffs have a choice as to whether to proceed with an action after they receive their consultants' report, the defendant has no choice but to go forward. Presumably, many of the questions posed by the forensic engineering scientists hired by the defense will be similar to those raised by the firm hired by the plaintiffs. What additional points might it raise, aimed at defending the architects, and how could it support those points?

COLLAPSE OF TEXAS TOWER NUMBER FOUR

A popular feature at every yearly meeting of the American Academy of Forensic Sciences is the evening program sponsored by an ad hoc group known as The Last Word Society. At that program, one or more famous events from the past, sometimes from the very distant past, are presented as if they were current forensic problems to be solved. The elements of evidence that can be found in the contemporaneous records and elsewhere are brought out and woven together in an attempt either to find an answer to an unsolved murder, fire, or other momentous event or to find a different answer from the one that was accepted at the earlier time. The Texas Tower Number Four collapse might have been selected for Last Word treatment but has not so far.

During that period of the cold war when concern existed that the United States would be attacked by nuclear bombs dropped from planes, great effort was put into detecting approaching enemy planes at a point as far from the national border as possible. The most famous of these efforts, the name of which still lingers in vestigial form in the language, was the Distant Early Warning Line (DEW Line). Less known was the line of radar stations planned and partially installed off the east coast of the country. Originally planned to consist of five structures rising above the ocean about 50 feet with legs buried in the ocean floor in water 100 to 200 feet deep (30–61 m), in a line stretching from Maine to Virginia, only three were installed. The photo on page 281 shows one of them. Nearly obsolete at the time they were erected because of the development of intercontinental missiles, their construction was discontinued, and the existing structures abandoned not long after the tragic end of Texas Tower Number Four.

The structures were referred to as Texas towers because they were modeled after the rigs used in the Gulf of Mexico off the coast of Texas and Louisiana as part of oil extraction operations. They were constructed by private contractors at several U.S. ports and then towed to location

A Texas Tower standing in Atlantic Ocean waters off the East Coast of the United States in the late 1950s *(NOAA)*

and erected with the assistance of the U.S Navy. Once in place and deemed satisfactory, the navy turned them over to the U.S. Air Force, which was then in charge of radar operations. These operations were handled by a crew of 50 to 80 civilians and military personnel.

Texas Tower Four (TT-4), the third to be installed, became operational in 1957. Many details about its design and construction differed from those of the first two towers. It also differed in that, on the completion of the tow of one of its major components starting from the Port of Portland (Maine), it was discovered that several of its braces had been lost somewhere along the way. Most important, however, and most ominous was the fact that from the beginning of occupancy of TT-4, the tower swayed even in moderate seas. In heavy seas, it was truly terrifying according to those who were stationed there. Furthermore, the North Atlantic is notoriously stormy and in the relatively shallow water in which the Texas Towers were placed, waves can rise up very quickly to great heights once storm winds start to blow, and blow they did during the existence of TT-4. It was exposed to at least two hurricanes with winds of more than 100 miles per hour (160 km/hr) and waves to 60 feet (18.3 m). It is said that even when the weather was not wild, visitors to TT-4 were warned against shaving with a straight-edge razor, just as they might be warned on a small oceangoing ship. In addition to the tower's motion that was easily perceived by its occupants, there were the noises that ranged from continuous groaning and scraping to loud clangs. TT-4 became known as Old Shaky and as not a nice place to be.

Efforts were made to find the problems on Old Shaky. In lieu of actually finding the causes of the undesirable instabilities, the military engineers placed more and more steel straps across the underwater support members. Although there were some reports that this helped, the problems ultimately became worse than ever. It reached the point where a major investigation and reconstruction by the U.S. Air Force and its private contractor was scheduled for early 1961. At that time, the TT-4 crew had been reduced from 82 to 28. Unfortunately, before the work could be started, a powerful ocean storm arose, quickly making it impossible to comply with the workers' request that they be evacuated. On the morning of January 15, 1961, TT-4 suddenly vanished from the radar screens of those monitoring it. The occupant compartment had sunk to the bottom taking the 28 men with it. As far as can be determined, there has never been a satisfactory answer as to what went wrong with Texas Tower Four. However, there is a great deal of commentary on the Internet concerning it. There was also a multiday hearing by the Preparedness Investigating Subcommittee of the U.S. Senate's Committee on Armed Services commencing on May 3, 1961, that revealed many of the factors that may be part of the answer. It would be an interesting exercise to determine whether this 1961 tragedy would make a good case study for the Last Word Society.

LESSONS TOO HARD TO LEARN

Near the beginning of this book, it was said that one of the major values of forensic work in the engineering sciences is the improvement in safety that it permits. Every time a serious accident occurs, the analysis that comes after has the potential to produce lessons that will prevent similar accidents in the future. Regrettably, this is less often the case when the lesson is a global one relating to human behavior rather than a specific one relating to mechanical defect. The *Challenger* Commission described in chapter 1, primarily because Richard Feynman was a member of the commission, taught both types of lessons. The specific one was that it was an error to use O-rings that lost their elasticity at temperature below 35°F (2°C) or, more realistically stated, that it was an error to try to launch the *Challenger* at an air temperature below that level. Without a doubt, one or the other of those practices would be corrected in future launches. The bigger and much more important lesson was that engineers with the most detailed knowledge regarding safety must not ignored by higher-ups in an organization in spite of the political pressures to do so. That more important lesson, if it was ever used to implement change, was forgotten, and on February 1, 2003, the nation again was confronted with the tragic loss of seven brave astronauts when the shuttle *Columbia* dramatically broke up on entering to the Earth's atmosphere at the end of an otherwise successful mission. As with the *Challenger* 16 years earlier, the postdisaster investigation turned up a record filled with concern about the repeated loss during flight of the tiles essential for thermally shielding the shuttle's interior during reentry. Had the global lesson taught by the *Challenger* Committee been heeded by NASA, difficult as that might have been, it is very likely that the *Columbia* and its crew would have returned safely to Earth that day in February 2003.

There is an error into which everyone falls to one degree or another at one time or another. It might be called the-risk-goes-down-with-the-passage-of-time fallacy. Officials are warned about the danger of launching the shuttle in cold weather or of ignoring the problems of heat-shield tiles flying off during launch. However, they continue to order launches without correcting the problem even though they realize that there is some risk. The more launches that occur without disaster the smaller in their minds becomes the risk of disaster. (This mistaken reasoning is just the opposite of the error a person flipping a coin makes in believing that 10 heads in a row increases the probability that the next flip will produce tails.) The risk has not been reduced, just the perception of the risk. When, finally, through chance, all of the conditions favorable for the disaster come together and the disaster does occur, those who ignored the risk profess to be surprised. It is all too common for a forensic accident investigator to hear the person who was directly or indirectly responsible for the accident and deaths or injuries that followed, announce that "*That* never happened before!" Who would have thought that fine aluminum dust poured into a chute in a bone-dry atmosphere would have exploded? Who would have thought that terrorists would fly fully fueled planes into the World Trade Center? Who would have thought that the 400th time I dry-labbed my inspections there would have been something unexpected to see?

A head-on view of the rubble and collateral damage from the March 2008 construction-crane collapse in Manhattan *(Chang W. Lee/*New York Times*)*

MARCH 2008 CRANE COLLAPSE

On March 15, 2008, on the east side of Manhattan, a construction crane 21 stories high and growing (along with the building it was being used to access during construction) teetered, then leaned, then fell with a tremendous crash. Much of it landed in the nearest street, crushing vehicles and persons who happened to be there. One segment drove to the ground an entire building. As the result of the collapse, beams shot to the surface, passing through residential buildings on their way down. In spite of all the destruction, only seven people were killed, the same number lost in each of the space-shuttle disasters. However, the event struck fear and foreboding into the millions of New Yorkers who must lead their lives within the collapse zones of numerous similar construction cranes. While it is fairly easy to avoid walking under a ladder (a good idea having nothing to with superstition) or across metal plates in the sidewalk, it is practically impossible for one living or working in Manhattan to avoid being within one or another of those zones. In part for this reason, efforts to find what led the crane to fall in March 2008 were immediate and intense. The initial findings could not have reassured people, since the first investigator reported that the person or persons responsible for inspecting the crane for compliance with safety standards had chosen to dry lab the job. (Dry labs and dry labbing are discussed in chapter 5.) The frightening aspect of this report was the difficulty that people had in believing that the collapsed crane was the only one to which city inspectors had given

An oblique view of the damage, including motor vehicles that had been tossed like proverbial toy cars (Chang W. Lee/New York Times)

the dry lab treatment. This skepticism got a powerful boost when a second Manhattan crane collapsed only three months later.

One of the risks to which dishonest inspectors expose themselves is that even if a disaster at a site that they failed to inspect did not result from that failure, their lapse will be associated with it and their punishment proportional to the size of the disaster and not to the seriousness of the lapse. What can be found out about the March 2008 collapse? Was it due to a defect that would have been revealed had the inspection been done as the records showed? If not, what was it? Did such a defect enable the collapse to occur after the failure of some other part? Often, it is not just one thing, but a combination of two or more failures that causes a disaster. How much can be found about the causes of this accident through research on the Internet? Can this research tell one what the causes were, or is it just announcing what some people think the causes were? How can one have confidence in the reliability of statements by others? What is a global solution to ensuring that safety does not have to rely on the honesty and competence of individuals?

CONCLUSION

Forensic science is, before all else, science. More particularly, it is a particular application of a variety of scientific fields. *Crashes and Collapses* has been concerned with the application for forensic purposes of the collection of disciplines known as the engineering sciences. It was prepared with the understanding that forensic topics attract student interest and that this interest could be used to introduce the science that underlies forensic work. This approach is somewhat the opposite that of traditional textbooks, which seek to introduce the basic concepts and methods of a science in the expectation that the student who has mastered the material will use it eventually in some particular field, such as oil exploration, rocket design, meteorology, construction, or forensic investigation. In contrast to that traditional format, *Crashes and Collapses* started with forensic investigation in various contexts and then brought in the concepts and methods needed to deal with the examples chosen. As has been seen, this allowed a much broader range of basic scientific concepts to be introduced than is usually possible with textbooks directed at one or another scientific or engineering field. This benefit, of course, has been at the expense of breadth in any particular one of the scientific and engineering fields on which it touched. Nonetheless, it has been possible in those segments of the fields dealt with to give an accurate and in most cases an adequate picture of what is involved. For those seeking more information, a list of further reading is included. In some cases, the suggested books contain the conventional approach to the presentation of a specific scientific field, such as Newtonian mechanics. Others elaborate further on very specific topics, such as eyewitness testimony.

It is hoped that this book has provided at least the start of the knowledge needed to test for reliability the statements made by others, whether they be friends, scholars, or commentators regarding the public scene and whether they be in written or spoken words. Taking the measure of statements intended to convey information lies at the heart of the forensic enterprise, for which skepticism is the necessary first response. It is necessary but not sufficient since it is impossible to investigate everything personally. One must therefore develop reliability-gauging rules enabling one to make use of information appearing in witness statements, in official reports, in public documents, and in Internet sources. The preceding chapters have been aimed in part at showing why no statement, no conclusion standing alone, should be accepted as true. It is important at an early age to learn not to parrot what one has heard from others as if it were true (that is, factual). It is important to learn at an early age that most of the supposed facts one is told by others have no more significance as indicators than that the person doing the telling has heard or read the statement previously. This lesson can be learned quickly by regularly asking people who relate statements that are supposedly true how it is that they acquired the information they are relating. Alternatively, to repeat advice given earlier, one should inquire of a person who has just announced some action or some event whether he or she knows for a fact that it has happened. This can be done without being rude.

More often than not, the person who expresses reluctance to believe everything he or she hears or reads is asked how one can operate in the world without believing in something. Often, people in the heat of argument or simply in the course of a good-natured discussion will resort to either/or reasoning: Either one believes the announcement by officials and the news read on television or one is limited to accepting only that information one can personally verify. The response to this type of argument is to break loose from the limitation on choices that it presents. The proper first response is to tell the person that that is a false dichotomy [die COT a mee]. In this sense, a dichotomy is the division of a whole into two and only two parts. To say that an apple consists only of skin and seeds would be a dichotomy and a false one (at the very least, it leaves out the fruit and the stem). The most common false dichotomies are of the all-or-nothing variety. Either one should believe everything one is told by strangers or one should believe nothing. The middle ground is the one to occupy. The following are some rules for evaluating statements by those unknown to one personally and, in many cases, by those one does know:

1. Is the person making the statement in a position to have personal knowledge of what he or she is describing? In most cases, the answer is no, and the person is simply repeating something said by someone else who may or may not have had personal knowledge of the subject. The lack of reliability of this type of statement is the basis for the rule against hearsay testimony in court. Witness Jim can be cross-examined and scrutinized regarding his statement that he saw an explosion just before the fire broke out, as the finder of fact tries to determine whether such an explosion occurred. In contrast, if Witness Sally is to testify that Jim told her that he saw an explosion, the most that one can do with Sally on the witness stand is to try to determine whether it is true that Jim told her that. It contributes nothing toward learning the truth of the statement that an explosion occurred, the hearsay statement.

2. If so, does the person have personal knowledge of it? This of course was the ultimate thrust of the first rule. However, it is often possible from one's own knowledge to determine that the speaker could not possibly have had personal knowledge of the event spoken of and therefore to discount what the person says. It is not uncommon in investigating motor vehicle crashes to learn that a person whose house is near the crash site and who is eagerly describing what happened was in fact at work all day in another state, a serious limitation to the reliability of his statements about a noontime crash. Even if the person could have personal knowledge, it often happens that he or she does not; for example, was the person who was on the front porch of the house directly across from where an assault took place actually looking in the right direction when the event happened, or did he look up when he heard a noise and believe in retrospect that he had seen the entire sequence that his mind tells him must have happened?

3. If the person describing an event did not have personal knowledge of it, what is that person's basis for believing the truth of what he or she is saying? Failure to observe an event

personally does not mean that the person does not have a good reason for believing it, but the investigator needs to be able to evaluate that reason in assessing the reliability of the informant's belief. For example, it may be very reasonable to believe that one's new puppy has chewed up one's new slippers without seeing the act, if the puppy and new slippers were alone together, and afterward the slippers were in pieces.

4. Is there reason to believe that the person recounting the event is biased? This goes back to the comments about prejudice in forensic investigations and tests. The sources of information may have their own biases, either personal or philosophical. For example, the automobile mechanic who is convinced that excessive litigation is ruining the country may tend not to find a defective part on the car that was in an accident and to do this without necessarily being dishonest.

But what does one do when the statements are such that their direct evaluation for reliability requires advanced technical training in a specialized field? Trial judges in federal courts and in most state courts in the United States are regularly required to rule on the reliability of such statements offered as forensic evidence. The techniques that they use, some of which were suggested by the Supreme Court of the United States, have broader applicability than just the courtroom. When a scientific conclusion is presented with the hope that it can be introduced as evidence, the first task is to determine the type of theory or method used to arrive at that conclusion. Is the theory or method widely accepted as valid by a broad range of scientists? How frequently does this theory or technique lead to the wrong answer? If the person offering the conclusions cannot answer that question, the conclusions should not be accepted as reliable. Does the person scoff at the idea that double-blind experiments are desirable whenever possible to test a theory or to ensure lack of bias in a measurement?

In summary, there are many abilities and characteristics necessary in a person who is to be a successful forensic investigator. Some involve specific skills and knowledge. This book has laid out some of the skills possessed by persons working in one branch or another of that broad undertaking that goes under the name of engineering sciences. These skills are developed over the extended period that engineers and scientists spend on the their formal education in college and university and, later, from the informal training that they absorb during their continuing forensic work. *Crashes and Collapses* has attempted, by indirect example and by very direct exhortation, to show the attitudes that all investigators should adopt at the outset of their careers—which, for many people in the field, occurs as early as their high school years and before—and nourish throughout their professional lives. Education, objectivity, and skepticism, tempered and stimulated by curiosity and joy in figuring things out, are the combination that drives a satisfying scientific life including one devoted to forensic work.

GLOSSARY

accelerant a term that arson investigators use to refer to gasoline or other flammable liquid used to start an incendiary fire

acceleration a change in velocity with time; used also to refer to change in speed

acceleration due to gravity, g the rate at which all objects independent of weight are accelerated downward due to gravity when allowed to fall freely near the surface of the Earth

accident a general term used to refer to any event causing injury or property damage where at least one party affected did not intend for the event to take place

accident reconstruction the term that has come to be used to refer to accident analysis whenever the accident involves motor vehicles

articulated boom a boom with more than one semi-independent segment

artifact the physical aspect of a scene or object or depiction of a scene or object that is introduced by the measurement or observation process

black box a term used to refer to event-data recorders in surface vehicles and flight-data recorders, a misnomer since neither type of recorder is housed in a black box

blind testing experimentation or study where one or more of those carrying out the testing or experimentation is not aware of some key factor leading to the work being needed

burden of going forward a term used to characterize the responsibility of one party or the other in a legal action

but-for question refers to the existence of a but-for factor, which is a factor that is necessary to have existed for a particular event, especially an accident, to take place

case law   the law created by judges, usually in appellate cases, through interpretation of statutory or common law

catalytic converter   a device in modern motor-vehicle-exhaust systems, intended to improve the degree of fuel combustion and to reduce harmful emissions

cataracts   a fogging of the lens in the eye, usually as the result of aging

Challenger **commission**   a group appointed by President Reagan to investigate the disaster that lead to the destruction of the space shuttle *Challenger* in 1986, noteworthy because of the forensic role played by physicist Richard B. Feynman, one of its members

clockwise   the direction the hands of a clock rotate, a convenient reference for describing the rotation of other objects, such as motor vehicles in the course of an accident

coefficient of friction   a variable characterizing two surfaces in such a way as to enable one to know the tangential force required to slide one of the surfaces across the other one if one knows the weight or other force pressing the two surfaces together

cold shock   the brittle fracture that can occur to the filament of an unlit incandescent light on a motor vehicle because of the inertial forces arising from the vehicle being involved in a crash

common law   a broader name for case law, referring to the body of law developed in common-law countries, especially those influenced by the British legal system, through legal decisions handed down by judges, in contrast to statutory law, and most important in modern times in civil litigation

compression force   a force, also referred to as a stress, tending to squeeze—that is, to compress—a material

confirmation bias   the bias that leads one to restrict one's investigation to a search for evidence that will confirm a theory for an event, instead of looking for any and all evidence that will explain the event

counterclockwise   opposite to the direction of rotation of the hands on an analogue clock and of the shadow on a sundial in the Northern Hemisphere, a convenient way to refer to the rotation of any physical object, such as a motor vehicle in the course of an accident sequence

critical speed   the fastest speed at which a vehicle can follow a particular curved path without laying down a critical-speed scuffmark

critical-speed scuffmark   the tire tracks left by a vehicle as its tires slide sideways while continuing to roll as the vehicle follows a curved path at the critical speed for the curvature of that path and the coefficient of friction between the road and the vehicle's tires, a mark that can be used to learn the speed of the vehicle that made it

cross-examination   the examination of a witness during a trial following up on the direct examination of the witness, usually carried out by the attorney for the party adverse to the one who called the witness to the witness stand and conducted the direct examination

cubit   a unit of length approximately 1.5 feet (0.45 m) long, used for thousands of years and based on the cubitum

cubitum   the length of the human forearm

deadman switch   a device that automatically interrupts power to machinery whenever it ceases to be affirmatively engaged by the person responsible for operating the machinery, such as a railroad engineer or a mower of lawns

density   the mass or weight of a material per unit volume

dimension   a property characterizing the nature of an entity, including length, time, mass, and temperature

directed verdict   the verdict that a judge may issue, taking the decision away from the jury, at the end of the introduction of evidence by one party or the other to a dispute

direct examination   the questioning under oath of a witness called to testify, carried out by the party offering the witness in court to introduce evidence

directly proportional to   chracterization of the relation between two variables when the first variable changes linearly in response to the change of the second variable, such as the gravitational energy of an object changing linearly with the elevation of the object above the ground

dry lab   a noun or a verb phrase with emphasis on the first word and referring to the running of a sham test or experiment, where, instead of actually doing the test or measurement, a person writes the results as if he or she had done so

electrical induction the generation of electric voltage in a wire by passing the wire through a magnetic field, or by moving a magnetic field past the wire

exemplar an object that is similar or identical in key aspects to another object, a label given to a physical object that has been examined or tested to gain information about how a similar object performed or behaved in an event of forensic interest

expert witness a person who by virtue of his or her special expertise is permitted to give opinion evidence in litigation, as opposed to factual evidence directly concerning the event underlying the litigation

fact something that is true, as opposed to a legal fact, which is a finding by the court and may or may not be true

fact witness a person who testifies under oath in the course of litigation as to personal knowledge regarding one or another of the events underlying the litigation

feedback mechanism the process by which the output of some operation has the capacity to affect the input to the operation and consequently the subsequent output of the operation

field of vision that part of the external world that is focused on a person's retina at any particular time

force a push or a pull

force moment an aspect of force tending to rotate the object against which it is exerted, stated with respect to a particular center of potential rotation, and having a rotational effect directly proportional to the moment arm linking the force to the center

fovea that small area of the retina that has the greatest sensitivity to light and the highest resolution

foveal vision vision involving images focused on the fovea

fulcrum a pivot point, such as the point about which a teeter-totter board rotates

fundamental laws as used here, those laws of nature governing the way the universe operates

furlong a specialized unit for the length dimension, equal to 660 feet (200 m)

gouges as used here, the divots in pavement caused by forceful impacts against the pavement of motor vehicles resulting from collisions

horsepower a unit for power in the U.S. system of units, equal to 550 ft-pounds per second (746 watts)

hot shock the distortion that occurs in the filaments of incandescent lights, such as headlights, brake lights, and turn-signal lights in cars, when the car is involved in a crash while the filaments are lit (hot)

hydraulic controls a valving system by which force is deliverable through hydraulic fluid pressure to effect movement within machinery

if and only if refers to a condition that is both necessary and sufficient for something to take place, as for example saying that a piece of ice (frozen water) will melt if and only if the temperature of its surroundings rises above the freezing temperature of water

imperial system of units earlier name for U.S. system of units, dating from the time that it was the system of units for the British Empire

incendiary deliberately ignited

increment an amount of increase, usually relatively small compared to the total

inertial mass that aspect of an object by which the object resists having its velocity changed

instrument-tapping fallacy the tendency to examine an answer more closely if it does not conform with expectations

interface the intersection between two surfaces; the region where two surfaces are in contact with one another

intuitively said of knowledge that is difficult to articulate or explain, but knowledge nonetheless, such as the way in which humans recognize the faces of people they know

jerk as used here, the change of acceleration with respect to time

kinetic energy energy that is strictly associated with motion, such that an object of mass M moving at a speed V has a kinetic energy of $\frac{1}{2}MV^2$

law of buoyancy law of nature attributed to Archimedes, consisting of the statement that an object in liquid has its weight reduced from its value in air by an amount equal to the weight of the liquid the object displaces

laws of motion the fundamental laws first assembled by Newton describing how objects behave in response to forces

lee an area shielded from the wind partially or completely

libra (lb) Latin for *pound*, lb being the abbreviation for *libra* and often used instead of the word *pound* in describing force, especially that of weight, or pressure in U.S. units

line of sight an unobstructed view

longitudinal striations stripes running parallel to the long dimension of something, usually with respect to marks made by motor-vehicle tires on pavement, usually when the tires are skidding without rotating

man-under event subway accident involving a person on the tracks being struck or run over by a train

mass the essence of an object, determining the inertia of the object and also the degree to which the object is affected by gravity

metering a measured change, as in the gradual movement of a boom effected by a carefully controlled flow of hydraulic fluid in the system controlling the boom

moment arm refers to the line drawn from a reference point perpendicular to the extension of the line representing the force to which the moment arm refers, and in particular to the length of that line

Newton's third law the most important of Newton's laws of motion and the most misunderstood, it states that if object A imposes a force on object B, then simultaneously and as a consequence, object B is imposing on object A a force of equal magnitude but in the opposite direction

perception-reaction time the total time interval from the instant that an object, especially one representing a danger, enters a person's field of vision until the instant at which the person's reaction to that object is complete, as for example the time between when a child running in front of a woman's car enters her field of vision and when she fully applies her brakes

perception time the time interval a person requires to perceive an object once the object has entered the person's field of vision

peripheral vision vision associated with an image being focused on any part of the retina other than the fovea

physical evidence the best type of evidence, referring as it does to physical objects and physical marks created by an event under investigation, objects and marks that can be examined directly by looking at and/or handling them or through examining documentation of them, as opposed to evidence consisting of oral or written statements by witnesses to the event or to occurrences associated with the event, including the least reliable evidence of all, eyewitness testimony

plaintiff's verdict   a trial verdict by a judge or jury that is in favor of the plaintiff in the lawsuit that was the subject of the trial

pneumatic controls   machinery controls relying on air pressure

potential energy   refers to certain types of energy that are easily converted into kinetic energy, such as gravitational energy given to an object by lifting it to a higher elevation or spring energy created by compressing or stretching a spring

precedents   rulings that govern what lower courts can do, such as rulings by the Supreme Court of the United States on scientific evidence that govern all courts in the federal system (though not state courts, though they often are influenced by rulings of the federal courts). Rulings by highest courts in states govern lower courts in that state

proportionality constant   the number that establishes how rapidly a variable that is directly proportional to a second variable changes as the second variable changes, such as the force F needed to stretch a spring is directly proportional to the distance X by which the spring has been stretched, such that $F = kX$ and k is the proportionality constant

PRT   abbreviation for perception-reaction time

reaction time   the interval of time that passes from the instant that a person has perceived an object until the instant that the person has taken an action in reaction to the presence of the object

retina   the light sensitive part of the eye, at the back of the eyeball, and positioned to receive images of the outside world focused on it by the lens of the eye

retroreflectors   objects or surfaces that reflect light incident on them back in essentially the direction from which the light came

rhodopsin   a chemical in the retina that plays a vital role in the mechanism converting incident light into electric signals to the brain, a chemical that changes in concentration in response to changes in the level of light incident on the retina

right angles, at   also perpendicular, the circumstance by which a line intersects a line or a surface so that the angle made by the intersection is 90° or, in radians, $\pi/2$

round off, rounding off   the elimination of superfluous digits on the right side of a number consisting of a string of digits, usually done so as not to overspecify the precision by which the number is known, such as converting 2,312,511 to 2,300,000 when it is not possible to know the number to a precision of better than two digits

scientific notation   the use of powers of 10 to represent very large or very small numbers, such as representing 2,300,000 by 2.3×10^6 and 0.00000123 as 1.23×10^{-6}

scuff marks, scuffs   in accident reconstruction, marks left by tires sliding partially or completely sideways, with or without rotating

signature marks   in accident reconstruction, telltale marks, usually in or on a motor vehicle, showing that a specific event had occurred, such as lipstick on a deployed air bag or a bent steering wheel

significant digits   the only nonzero digits that can be legitimately used in a number in view of the precision with which the number is known, so that if there are only two significant digits in the number that works out to be 2,312,511, one must round off the number to 2,300,000

significant figures   another name for significant digits

skid marks   as used in accident reconstruction, generally limited to the marks left by nonrotating tires on a vehicle that skidded to a stop

speed   the rate at which the position of an object changes with time

square of the speed   the number obtained by multiplying the magnitude of an object's speed by itself

square root   the number that when multiplied by itself yields the original number

static electricity   the voltage that results from an accumulation or deficit of electrons in an object or localized portion of an object, observable when one walks across a carpet in dry atmosphere, so that the deficit or accumulation produced by the rubbing of shoe bottoms on the carpet is not dissipated quickly through the flow of compensating charge, or the effect one can obtain by rubbing a plastic pen, which has a low ability to conduct the flow of charge but which is not attainable with a metal pen, which has a high ability to redistribute any localized inequality of charge concentration

statutory law   also called black-letter law, the type of law that is enacted by legislative bodies, as opposed to courts, the type of law that govern criminal prosecutions but not, generally, civil litigation

striations   a synonym for stripes that is used to refer to the lines in tire marks, especially the lateral lines in critical-speed scuff marks, which more often than not are referred to as lateral striations, and occasionally for the longitudinal lines in skid marks, when they are called longitudinal striations

Système International   the system of units (weights and measures) used throughout the world except by laypersons and some professional workers in the United States

tensile force   a pulling force, usually used to refer to a pulling force in a cable or a beam, the opposite of compressional force

tension   tensile force

theory of universal gravitation   Newton's theory that the force that causes objects to fall to the ground is the same type of force that keeps the Moon in its orbit about the Earth, the Earth in its orbit about the Sun, and so forth, and that the gravitational attraction between two objects is inversely proportional to the square of the distance between the objects

thermocouple   two different types of metal joined together so that their junction produces a voltage that varies with the temperature and can therefore be used as a means of measuring temperature remotely from the point of interest

time-distance calculation   phrase commonly used in accident reconstruction to label the determination of where a vehicle was during the time leading up to an accident, often for the purpose of comparing that determination with that of where the vehicle would have been had it been traveling at a specific speed, usually lower than the one it was estimated to have been traveling at the time of the accident

torts   private wrongs dealt with through civil litigation, as opposed to public wrongs dealt with through criminal prosecution

track width   the distance between the tires on the left side of a vehicle and those on the right side

truncating   a draconian reduction of the number of digits in a decimal number, wherein numbers to the right of a certain point are simply chopped off without attention paid to rounding off, usually the result of machine calculations

ullage   in the context of tanks containing liquids, the distance from the top of the tank to the top of the liquid

units   the way in which dimensions are stated, such as the foot being the basic unit for the length dimension in the U.S. units system, and the meter being the counterpart in the S.I.

varies inversely   the description of how a variable changes as a result of the change in a second variable when an increase in the second variable results in a decrease in the first variable and vice versa, such that for example a doubling of the second variable causes the first variable to be cut in half and a halving of the second variable causes a doubling of the first variable

velocity   when used in connection with an object, it is a statement of the speed of the object and the instantaneous direction of movement of the object, such that, for example, an object moving to the west at a constant speed V has both a constant speed and a constant velocity but that an object moving in a circle at a constant speed has a constant speed but a continuously changing velocity, since its direction of motion is continuously changing

visual acuity   the degree to which one can resolve detail in an object being viewed

watt   the unit of power in S.I., where it is one joule per second; also the surname of the man, James Watt, for whom the unit is named

weight   as commonly used, the force with which an object is pulled down toward the surface of the Earth

work   the transformation of energy from one form to another

Young's modulus   a measure of the elasticity of material, for example, of the stiffness of a spring made from the material

FURTHER READING

Print and Internet

Adair, Robert K. *The Physics of Baseball.* New York: Harper and Row, 1990. With text aimed at the interested layperson, it explains many of the common events in baseball and in doing so provides further illustration of basic physics ideas.

American Academy of Forensic Sciences (AAFS). Available online. URL: http://www.aafs.org. Accessed on April 17, 2008. Being the home page for the AAFS, the leading forensic science organization in North America, this Web site contains a wide range of information concerning forensic activities worldwide and also a list of colleges and universities with educational programs in forensic work.

Archimedes online: URL: http://en.wikipedia.org/wiki/Archimedes. Accessed on April 17, 2008. This Wikipedia entry includes the "Eureka!" story recounted in chapter 1 of *Crashes and Collapses* as well as much more about the remarkable Archimedes.

Bohan, Thomas L., and Arthur C. Damask, eds. *Forensic Accident Investigation: Motor Vehicles.* San Francisco: Lexis-Nexis, 1995, 1997. This two-volume set with pocket supplements through 2006 was aimed at a mixed audience of accident reconstructionists and attorneys trying accident cases. It was presumed that the attorneys would have no technical background. Therefore, while the level of the material varies, much of it is accessible to secondary school students and some to middle school students.

Brancazio, Peter J. *Sport Science: Physical Laws and Optimum Performance.* New York: Simon & Schuster, 1983. Another joyful treatment of sports using the basic rules of science, and especially Newton's laws of motion.

Bryson, Bill. *A Short History of Nearly Everything.* New York: Broadway Books, 2004. In spite of the generality implied by its title, the publication is directed at the development of a discussion of the history of scientific thought and its significance, expressed in the always humorous Bryson style and definitely aimed at the reader with no prior mathematical or scientific knowledge.

Feynman, Richard P., Robert B. Leighton, and Matthew Sands. *The Feynman Lectures on Physics, Volumes I and II.* Reading, Mass.: Addison-Wesley Publishing Co., 1963. Richard Feynman's introductory physics lectures on motion and electricity, given but once, as an experiment in Caltech pedagogy, much of the material is nevertheless accessible to senior high school students with an interest in science.

"Feynman's Appendix to the Rogers Commission Report on the Space Shuttle *Challenger* Accident: Personal Observations on the Reliability of the Shuttle." Available online: URL: http://www.uky.edu/~holler/msc/roles/feynrept.html. Accessed on April 17, 2008. This provides a good introduction to further study for those interested in the *Challenger* disaster and the commission that investigated it.

Gonick, Larry, and Art Huffman. *The Cartoon Guide to Physics.* New York: Collins Reference, 1990. An introduction to the basics of physics that, though superficially whimsical, appears to be capable of transferring a great deal of information even to those with no prior background in science or mathematics.

Gordon, J. E. *The New Science of Strong Materials, or Why You Don't Fall Through the Floor,* 2d edition. Princeton, N.J.: Princeton University Press, 1976. A highly readable introduction to the information one needs in order to commence thinking about any type of structural collapse, be it that of cranes, scaffolding, or buildings.

Jargodzki, Christopher P., and Franklin Potter. *Mad About Physics: Braintwisters, Paradoxes and Curiosities.* New York: John Wiley & Sons, Inc., 2001. Contains hundreds of mental puzzles that draw upon the basics of physics.

Loftus, Elizabeth F. *Eyewitness Testimony.* Cambridge, Mass.: Harvard University Press. By the scientist who practically singlehandedly exposed the "recovered memories" phenomenon as bogus, this volume examines more generally the psychology of memory and its often deleterious effect in the courtroom.

Macaulay, David. *The Way Things Work*. Boston, Mass.: Houghton Mifflin Co., 1988. Illustrated explanations of technology from basic mechanics to electronics.

National Academy of Science (NAS) homepage. Available online. URL: http://www.nationalacademies.org. Accessed on April 17, 2008. Established during the presidential administration of Abraham Lincoln, the NAS is the quasi-private authority to which the U.S. government turns for answers to disputed scientific questions, including those relating to forensic science techniques. As of Summer 2008, the NAS is on the verge of issuing a much-anticipated report on the state of forensic sciences in the United States.

National Highway Traffic Safety Administration (NHTSA) homepage. Available online. URL: http://www.nhtsa.gov. Accessed on April 10, 2008. NHTSA maintains standards for vehicle and roadway safety; the site includes descriptions of vehicle crash tests.

National Transportation Safety Board (NTSB) homepage. Available online. URL: http://www.ntsb.gov. Accessed on April 10, 2008. The home page of the NTSB, the U.S. government agency responsible for investigating crashes of aircraft and other vehicles engaged in public transportation.

Paulo, John Allen. *Innumeracy: Mathematical Illiteracy and Its Consequences*. New York: Hill & Wang, 1988. One of the first, and still the best, modern refutation of the wrongheaded idea that one is not harmed by being unable to reason quantitatively.

Robins, Patrick J. *Eyewitness Reliability in Motor Vehicle Accident Reconstruction and Litigation*. Tucson, Ariz.: Lawyers and Judges Publishing Company, Inc., 2001. Expands on the cautions provided in *Crashes and Collapses* concerning the pitfalls of eyewitness accounts in accident reconstruction.

Rosenberg, Jennifer. "The Plane That Crashed into the Empire State Building." Available online. URL: http://history1900s.about.com/od/1940s/a/empirecrash.htm. Accessed on April 17, 2008. One of many Web sites discussing the plane crash described in chapter 10 of *Crashes and Collapses*.

Texas Tower Organization homepage. Available online. URL: http://www.texastower.com. Accessed on April 17, 2008. This is a lead-in to innumerable Web sites and other source material discussing the collapse of Texas Tower 4, as described in *Crashes and Collapses.*

Walker, Jearl. *The Flying Circus of Physics, with Answers.* New York: John Wiley & Sons, 1977. The very best of the thought-provoking questions about universally observed events, prepared with thoughtful answers by the longtime author of the Scientific American feature on mathematics.

Weinberg, Steven. *Facing Up: Science and Its Cultural Adversaries,* Cambridge, Harvard University Press, 2001. A further discussion of a topic repeatedly touched on in *Crashes and Collapses,* the egregiously mistaken belief that, because of social and political pressures, physical science is no more dependable than social science.

INDEX

Note: *Italic* page numbers indicate illustrations; page numbers followed by *t* indicate tables.